William Hazlitt, Evariste Régis Huc

Travels in Tartary, Thibet and China during the Years 1844-5-6

Vol. I

William Hazlitt, Evariste Régis Huc

Travels in Tartary, Thibet and China during the Years 1844-5-6
Vol. I

ISBN/EAN: 9783337216566

Printed in Europe, USA, Canada, Australia, Japan

Cover: Foto ©Andreas Hilbeck / pixelio.de

More available books at **www.hansebooks.com**

Travels in Tartary, Thibet and China

DURING THE YEARS 1844-5-6

BY M. HUC

TRANSLATED FROM THE FRENCH BY W. HAZLITT
REPRINT EDITION

VOL. I

ILLUSTRATED WITH FIFTY ENGRAVINGS ON WOOD

CHICAGO
THE OPEN COURT PUBLISHING COMPANY
LONDON AGENTS
KEGAN PAUL, TRENCH, TRUEBNER & CO.
1898

PUBLISHERS' PREFACE.

CONSIDERING the many myths that are now rife about Thibetan Mahatmas and the sensational reports of recent would-be travelers, whose fictitious discoveries are seriously accepted by many readers, it seems appropriate to remind the reading public of a famous but now almost forgotten book, "The Travels in Tartary, Thibet, and China" of the two Jesuit missionaries Huc and Gabet. These gentlemen did not find in Thibet lost manuscripts of the life of Jesus, nor do they describe the Thibetans as savages. Their half-dead servants did not take kodak pictures of them while being tortured on the rack. Nor did they use the powers of hypnotism in their dealings with the Lamas and while being subjected to outrageous tortures. There is, in fact, nothing incredible in M. Huc's story, and yet, perhaps because of this reason, the book is far more interesting than any report that has since appeared.

The sensation which M. Huc's book created on its first appearance has subsided, and it is now only known to scholars and historians. Indeed the book is out of print and can, both in its original French and in its German and English translations, only be had through second-hand book dealers, where the copies are at a high premium. Under these circumstances it seems desirable that the book should be reprinted and once more placed before the reading public. What a storehouse it is for the ethnologist, geographer, the scholar interested in religious customs, the reader of travels, and the student of human nature!

The book undoubtedly deserves a revision, and many things which were puzzling to our Jesuit travelers may, in the light of the better knowledge of to-day, have found their explanation. For instance, some botanist may be able to tell us what the tree of the ten thousand images is; ethnologists may now know much about the barbarous ceremony mentioned in Vol. I., Chap. IX., which is probably a mere trick played on a credulous audience for the purpose of extracting their money. Further, the reasons for the similarities which Huc and Gabet observed between Buddhist ceremonies and the rituals of the Roman Church are also better understood to-day. But what will be of keenest interest to us is the description of the personal character of the Thibetans and their Lamas. There is a certain family likeness between them and the Western nations. They also are kind-hearted and inspired with good intentions. It is true they fear invasions and are constantly on their guard against the English, on whom they look with extraordinary suspicion. The greatest crime for a traveler is to draw maps, which is taken as a sure sign of being a spy in the English service. In fact, the sole trouble which Messrs. Huc and Gabet encountered was on account of the maps which were discovered in their baggage, but they were at once released from captivity and protected against maltreatment when the court arrived at the conclusion that these maps were printed and could not have been drawn by the travelers for the purpose of betraying the country.

A careful reader will also notice that our French travelers are sometimes quick in their judgment.*

Being unable to give trustworthy information about all these and similar complications contained in M. Huc's reports, we prefer to leave the book as it stands and republish it without comments of our own, leaving this task to critics and readers who are better equipped for the purpose.

---

* Sandara, a young Lama of unusual talents and broad experience, who is suspected by his brethren in the Lamasery of being a freethinker, is engaged as a teacher in Thibetan by the Jesuit missionaries. At first he is praised for the extraordinary interest he takes in Christianity by M. Huc, who sees him in a hopeful vision develop into a Thibetan Apostle. Later on, however, Sandara becomes impatient with his French pupils and addresses them with such words as these: "What! you learned fellows want to have the same thing told you three times over? Why, if I were to tell a donkey the same thing three times over he'd remember it." It is on this occasion that Messrs. Huc and Gabet change their opinion of their Thibetan teacher, declaring that, "All the fine things that they had imagined of Sandara vanished like a dream." He is now suspected of being "a dissipated knave" whose only aim was to ease the French missionaries of their money; yet they deemed it wise to submit, "For," says M. Huc, "his very rudeness we considered, would aid our progress in acquiring the Thibetan language." And "this system, though somewhat tedious and decidedly displeasing to our self-love was incomparably superior to the method practised by the (over-polite) Chinese Christians toward the European missionaries in giving them Chinese lessons." In spite of M. Huc's accusation, Sandara proves a faithful and honest friend in times of emergency. Not only does he see through the malicious lies of Samdadchiemba, when he claims to have been robbed of things which he stole himself, but also succeeds in recovering the tent of the missionaries which had been pawned by the rascally inn-keeper on New Year's day, for the sake of paying some debts. (See Vol. II., Chap. II.) In this instance, as on other occasions, M. Huc always depicts the situation from the point of view which he takes at the moment.

For similar reasons, the transcriptions of foreign names have been left as they stood in the original translation.

The Thibetans are a warlike race, but their military tendencies are subdued by an extreme religious devotion, which, far from being exclusively Buddhistic, seems among their educated men to be as broad as it is among the most scholarly philosophers of Europe and of America. Think only of the Thibetan custom, strongly reminding us of the Christian Angelus, of the whole people praying in common at certain hours! Think of the interest which the Regent of Lhassa took in the Christian religion! How he trembled when the maps were found, and how he triumphed when the innocence of our travelers was brought out! How eagerly he studied the Christian doctrines! With what humor he treated the ignorant Lamas and their superstition, typical of the popular Buddhism of the masses! Even when the Chinese Plenipotentiary urged to him the danger of Christianity's replacing Buddhism in Thibet, the attitude of the Regent of Lhassa towards the Jesuits remained unaltered. He said to them: "Religious persons, men of prayer, belonging to all countries, are strangers nowhere. Such is the doctrine taught by our holy books. Lhassa being the peculiar assembling place and abode of men of prayer, that title of itself should always secure for you liberty and protection." His answer to the Chinese Plenipotentiary is also characteristic: "If the doctrine which these men hold is a false doctrine, the Thibetans will not embrace it: if on the contrary it is true, what have we to fear? How can the truth be prejudicial to men."

And so this book, apart from its interest to the general reader, will also be welcome to all persons interested in Christian missions and to all students of Buddhism and its institutions.

THE OPEN COURT PUBLISHING CO.

PREFACE.

THE Pope having, about the year 1844, been pleased to establish an Apostolic Vicariat of Mongolia, it was considered expedient, with a view to further operations, to ascertain the nature and extent of the diocese thus created, and MM. Gabet and Huc, two Lazarists attached to the petty mission of Si-Wang, were accordingly deputed to collect the necessary information. They made their way through difficulties which nothing but religious enthusiasm in combination with French elasticity could have overcome, to Lha-Ssa, the capital of Thibet, and in this seat of Lamanism were becoming comfortably settled, with lively hopes and expectations of converting the Talé-Lama into a branch-Pope, when the Chinese Minister, the noted Ke-Shen, interposed on political grounds, and had them deported to China. M. Gabet was directed by his superiors to proceed to France, and lay a complaint before his Government, of the arbitrary treatment which he and his fellow Missionary had experienced. In the steamer which conveyed him from Hong Kong to Ceylon, he found Mr. Alexander Johnstone, secretary to Her Majesty's Plenipotentiary in China; and this gentleman perceived so much, not merely of entertainment, but of important information in the conversations he had with M. Gabet, that he committed to paper the leading features of the Reverend Missionary's statements, and on his return to his official post, gave his manuscripts to Sir John Davis, who, in his turn, considered their contents so interesting, that he embodied a copy of them in a despatch to Lord Palmerston. Subsequently the two volumes, here translated, were prepared by M. Huc, and published in Paris. Thus it is, that to Papal aggression in the East, the Western World is indebted for a work exhibiting, for the first time, a complete representation of countries previously almost unknown to Europeans, and indeed considered practically inaccessible; and of a religion, which, followed by no fewer than 170,000,000 persons, presents the most singular analogies in its leading features with the Catholicism of Rome.

CONTENTS OF VOLUME I.

	PAGE
PREFACE	v
CONTENTS	vii
LIST OF ILLUSTRATIONS	xi

CHAPTER I.

French Mission of Peking—Glance at the Kingdom of Ouniot — Preparations for Departure—Tartar-Chinese Inn—Change of Costume—Portrait and Character of Samdadchiemba—Sain-Oula (the Good Mountain)—The Frosts on Sain-Oula, and its Robbers—First Encampment in the Desert—Great Imperial Forest—Buddhist Monuments on the Summit of the Mountains—Topography of the Kingdom of Gechekten—Character of its Inhabitants—Tragical Working of a Mine—Two Mongols Desire to have their Horoscope Taken—Adventure of Samdadchiemba—Environs of the Town of Tolon-Noor...................... 1

CHAPTER II.

Inn at Tolon-Noor—Aspect of the City—Great Foundries of Bells and Idols—Conversation with the Lamas of Tolon-Noor—Encampment—Tea-Bricks—Meeting with Queen Mourguevan—Taste of the Mongols for Pilgrimages—Violent Storm—Account from a Mongol Chief of the War of the English against China—Topography of the Eight Banners of the Tchakar—The Imperial Herds—Form and Interior of the Tents—Tartar Manners and Customs—Encampment at the Three Lakes—Nocturnal Apparitions—Samdadchiemba Relates the Adventures of his Youth—Gray Squirrels of Tartary—Arrival at Chaborté......... 28

CHAPTER III.

Festival of the Loaves of the Moon—Entertainment in a Mongol Tent—Toolholos, or Rhapsodists of Tartary—Invocation to Timour—Tartar Education—Industry of the Women—Mongols in Quest of Missing Animals—Remains of an Abandoned City—Road from Pekin to Kiaktha—Commerce between China and Russia—Russian Convent at Pekin—A Tartar Solicits us to Cure his Mother from a Dangerous Illness—Tartar Physicians—The Intermittent Fever Devil—Various Forms of Sepulture in Use Among the Mongols—Lamasery of the Five Towers—Obsequies of the Tartar Kings—Origin of the Kingdom of Efe—Gymnastic Exercises of the Tartars—Encounter with three Wolves—Mongol Carts.. 61

CONTENTS.

CHAPTER IV.

PAGE

Young Lama Converted to Christianity—Lamasery of Tchortchi—Alms for the Construction of Religious Houses—Aspect of the Buddhist Temples—Recitation of Lama Prayers—Decorations, Paintings, and Sculptures of the Buddhist Temples—Topography of the Great Kouran in the Country of the Kalkhas—Journey of the Guison-Tamba to Peking—The Kouren of the Thousand Lamas—Suit Between the Lama-King and His Ministers—Purchase of a Kid—Eagles of Tartary—Western Toumet—Agricultural Tartars—Arrival at the Blue Town—Glance at the Mantchou Nation—Mantchou Literature—State of Christianity in Mantchouria—Topography and Productions of Eastern Tartary—Skill of the Mantchous with the Bow.. 89

CHAPTER V.

The Old Blue Town—Quarter of the Tanners—Knavery of the Chinese Traders—Hotel of the Three Perfections—Spoliation of the Tartars by the Chinese—Money Changer's Office—Tartar Coiner—Purchase of Two Sheep-skin Robes—Camel Market—Customs of the Cameleers—Assassination of a Grand Lama of the Blue Town—Insurrection of the Lamaseries—Negotiation Between the Court of Peking and that of Lha-Ssa—Domestic Lamas—Wandering Lamas—Lamas in Community—Policy of the Mantchou Dynasty with Reference to the Lamaseries—Interview with a Thibetian Lama—Departure from the Blue Town.. 116

CHAPTER VI.

A Tartar-eater—Loss of Arsalan—Great Caravan of Camels—Night Arrival at Tchagan-Kouren—We Are Refused Admission Into the Inns—We Take up Our Abode with a Shepherd—Overflow of the Yellow River—Aspect of Tchagan-Kouren—Departure Across the Marshes—Hiring a Bark—Arrival on the Banks of the Yellow River—Encampment Under the Portico of a Pagoda—Embarkation of the Camels—Passage of the Yellow River—Laborious Journey Across the Inundated Country—Encampment on the Banks of the River........ 138

CHAPTER VII.

Mercurial Preparation for the Destruction of Lice—Dirtiness of the Mongols—Lama Notions About the Metempsychosis—Washing—Regulations of Nomadic Life—Aquatic and Passage Birds—The Yuen-Yang—The Dragon's Foot—Fishermen of the Paga-Gol—Fishing Party—Fisherman Bit by a Dog—Kou-Kouo, or, St. Ignatius's Bean—Preparations for Departure—Passage of the Paga-Gol—Dangers of the Voyage—Devotion of Samdadchiemba—The Prime Minister of the King of the Ortous—Encampment............................. 159

CHAPTER VIII.

Glance at the Country of the Ortous—Cultivated Lands—Sterile, Sandy Steppes of the Ortous—Form of the Tartar-Mongol Government—Nobility—Slavery—A small Lamasery—Election and Enthronization of a Living Buddha—Discipline of the Lamaseries—Lama Studies—Violent Storm—Shelter in some Artificial Grottoes—Tartar Concealed in a Cavern—Tartaro-Chinese Ancedote—Ceremonies of Tartar Marriages—Polygamy—Divorce—Character and Costume of the Mongol Women.. 179

CHAPTER IX.

Departure of the Caravan—Encampment in a Fertile Valley—Intensity of the Cold—Meeting with numerous Pilgrims—Barbarous and Diabolical Ceremonies of Lamanism—Project for the Lamasery of Rache-Tchurin—Dispersion and Rallying of the Little Caravan—Anger of Samdadchiemba—Aspect of the Lamasery of Rache-Tchurin—Different Kinds of Pilgrimages Around the Lamaseries—Turning Prayers—Quarrel Between Two Lamas—Similarity of the Soil—Description of the Tabsoun-Noor or Salt Sea—Remarks on the Camels of Tartary 206

CHAPTER X.

Purchase of a Sheep—A Mongol Butcher—Great Feast *à la Tartare*—Tartar Veterinary Surgeons—Strange Cure of a Cow—Depth of the Wells of the Ortous—Manner of Watering the Animals—Encampment at the Hundred Wells—Meeting with the King of the Alechan—Annual Embassies of the Tartar Sovereigns to Peking—Grand Ceremony in the Temple of the Ancestors—The Emperor Gives Counterfeit Money to the Mongol Kings—Inspection of Our Geographical Map—The Devil's Cistern—Purification of the Water—A Lame Dog—Curious Aspect of the Mountains—Passage of the Yellow River 231

CHAPTER XI.

Sketch of the Tartar Nations 262

CHAPTER XII.

Hotel of Justice and Mercy—Province of Kan-Sou—Agriculture—Great Works for the Irrigation of the Fields—Manner of Living in Inns—Great Confusion in a Town Caused by our Camels—Chinese Life-guard—Mandarin Inspector of the Public Works—Ning-Hia—Historical and Topographical Details—Inn of the Five Felicities—Contest with a Mandarin, Tchong-Wei—Immense Mountains of Sand—Road to Ili—Unfavorable Aspect of Kao-Tan-Dze—Glance at the Great Wall—Inquiry after the Passports—Tartars Traveling in China—Dreadful Hurricane—Origin and Manners of the Inhabitants of Kan-Sou—The Dchiahours—Interview with a Living Buddha—Hotel of the Temperate Climates—Family of Samdadchiemba—Mountain of Ping-Keou—Fight Between an Innkeeper and his Wife—Water-mills—Knitting—Si-Ning-Fou—House of Rest—Arrival at Tang-Keou-Eul 290

We have ourselves seen some that weighed twelve pounds. One moment sometimes suffices to exterminate whole flocks. In 1843, during one of these storms, there was heard in the air a sound as of a rushing wind, and therewith fell, in a field near a house, a mass of ice larger than an ordinary millstone. It was broken to pieces with hatchets, yet, though the sun burned fiercely, three days elapsed before these pieces entirely melted.

The droughts and the inundations together, sometimes occasion famines which well-nigh exterminate the inhabitants. That of 1832, in the twelfth year of the reign of *Tao-Kouang*,[1] is the most terrible of these on record. The Chinese report that it was everywhere announced by a general presentiment, the exact nature of which no one could explain or comprehend. During the winter of 1831, a dark rumor grew into circulation. *Next year*, it was said, *there will be neither rich nor poor; blood will cover the mountains; bones will fill the valleys* (Ou fou, ou kioung; hue man chan, kou man tchouan.) These words were in every one's mouth; the children repeated them in their sports; all were under the domination of these sinister apprehensions when the year 1832 commenced. Spring and summer passed away without rain, and the frosts of autumn set in while the crops were yet green; these crops of course perished, and there was absolutely no harvest. The population was soon reduced to the most entire destitution. Houses, fields, cattle, everything was exchanged for grain, the price of which attained its weight in gold. When the grass on the mountain sides was devoured by the starving creatures, the depths of the earth were dug into for roots. The fearful prognostic, that had been so often repeated, became accomplished. Thousands died upon the hills, whither they had crawled in search of grass; dead bodies filled the roads and houses; whole villages were depopulated to the last man. There was, indeed, *neither rich nor poor;* pitiless famine had leveled all alike.

It was in this dismal region that we awaited with impatience the courier, whom, for a second time, we had despatched into the kingdom of Naiman. The day fixed for his return came and passed, and several others followed, but brought no camels, nor Lama, nor courier, which seemed

---

[1] Sixth Emperor of the Tartar-Mantchou dynasty. He died in the year 1849.

to us most astonishing of all. We became desperate; we could not longer endure this painful and futile suspense. We devised other means of proceeding, since those we had arranged appeared to be frustrated. The day of our departure was fixed; it was settled, further, that one of our Christians should convey us in his car to *Tolon-Noor*, distant from the Contiguous Defiles about fifty leagues. At *Tolon-Noor* we were to dismiss our temporary conveyance, proceed alone into the desert, and thus start on our pilgrimage as well as we could. This project absolutely stupefied our Christian friends; they could not comprehend how two Europeans should undertake by themselves a long journey through an unknown and inimical country: but we had reasons for abiding by our resolution. We did not desire that any Chinese should accompany us. It appeared to us absolutely necessary to throw aside the fetters with which the authorities had hitherto contrived to shackle missionaries in China. The excessive caution, or rather the imbecile pusillanimity of a Chinese catechist, was calculated rather to impede than to facilitate our progress in Tartary.

On the Sunday, the day preceding our arranged departure, everything was ready; our small trunks were packed and padlocked, and the Christians had assembled to bid us adieu. On this very evening, to the infinite surprise of all of us, our courier arrived. As he advanced, his mournful countenance told us before he spoke, that his intelligence was unfavorable. "My spiritual fathers," said he, "all is lost; you have nothing to hope; in the kingdom of Naiman there no longer exist any camels of the Holy Church. The Lama doubtless has been killed; and I have no doubt the devil has had a direct hand in the matter."

Doubts and fears are often harder to bear than the certainty of evil. The intelligence thus received, though lamentable in itself, relieved us from our perplexity as to the past, without in any way altering our plan for the future. After having received the condolences of our Christians, we retired to rest, convinced that this night would certainly be that preceding our nomadic life.

The night was far advanced, when suddenly numerous voices were heard outside our abode, and the door was shaken with loud and repeated knocks. We rose at once; the Lama, the camels, all had arrived; there was quite a little revolution. The order of the day was instantly changed. We resolved to depart, not on the Monday, but on the Tuesday; not in a car, but on camels, in true Tartar fashion. We returned to our beds perfectly delighted; but we could not sleep, each of us occupying the remainder of the night with plans for effecting the equipment of the caravan in the most expeditious manner possible.

Next day, while we were making our preparations for departure, our Lama explained his extraordinary delay. First, he had undergone a long illness; then he had been occupied a considerable time in pursuing a camel which had escaped into the desert; and finally, he had to go before some tribunal, in order to procure the restitution of a mule which had been stolen from him. A lawsuit, an illness, and a camel hunt were amply sufficient reasons for excusing the delay which had occurred. Our courier was the only person who did not participate in the general joy; he saw it must be evident to every one that he had not fulfilled his mission with any sort of skill.

All Monday was occupied in the equipment of our caravan. Every person gave his assistance to this object. Some repaired our traveling-house, that is to say, mended or patched a great blue linen tent; others cut for us a supply of wooden tent pins; others mended the holes in our copper kettle, and renovated the broken leg of a joint stool; others prepared cords, and put together the thousand and one pieces of a camel's pack. Tailors, carpenters, braziers, rope-makers, saddle-makers, people of all trades assembled in active co-operation in the courtyard of our humble abode. For all, great and small, among our Christians, were resolved that their spiritual fathers should proceed on their journey as comfortably as possible.

On Tuesday morning, there remained nothing to be done but to perforate the nostrils of the camels, and to insert in the aperture a wooden peg, to use as a sort of a bit. The arrangement of this was left to our Lama. The wild piercing cries of the poor animals pending the painful operation, soon collected together all the Christians of the village. At this moment, our Lama became exclusively the hero of the expedition. The crowd ranged themselves in a circle around him; every one was curious to see how, by gently pulling the cord attached to the peg in its nose, our Lama could make the animal obey him, and kneel at his pleasure. Then, again, it was an interesting thing for the Chinese to watch our Lama packing on the camels' backs the baggage of the two missionary travelers. When the arrangements were completed, we drank a cup of tea, and proceeded to the chapel; the Christians recited prayers for our safe journey; we received their farewell, interrupted with tears, and proceeded on our way. Samdadchiemba, our Lama cameleer,

The Travelers setting out on their Journey.

gravely mounted on a black, stunted, meager mule, opened the march, leading two camels laden with our baggage; then came the two missionaries, MM. Gabet and Huc, the former mounted on a tall camel, the latter on a white horse.

Upon our departure we were resolved to lay aside our accustomed usages, and to become regular Tartars. Yet we did not at the outset, and all at once, become exempt from the Chinese system. Besides that, for the first mile or two of our journey, we were escorted by our Chinese Christians, some on foot, and some on horseback, our first stage was to be an inn kept by the Grand Catechist of the Contiguous Defiles.

The progress of our little caravan was not at first wholly successful. We were quite novices in the art of saddling and girthing camels, so that every five minutes we had to

halt, either to rearrange some cord or piece of wood that
hurt and irritated the camels, or to consolidate upon their
backs, as well as we could, the ill-packed baggage that
threatened, ever and anon, to fall to the ground. We advanced, indeed, despite all these delays, but still very slowly.
After journeying about thirty-five lis,[1] we quitted the cultivated district and entered upon the Land of Grass. There
we got on much better; the camels were more at their ease
in the desert, and their pace became more rapid.

We ascended a high mountain, where the camels evinced
a decided tendency to compensate themselves for their
trouble, by browsing, on either side, upon the tender stems
of the elder tree or the green leaves of the wild rose. The
shouts we were obliged to keep up, in order to urge forward
the indolent beasts, alarmed infinite foxes, who issued from
their holes and rushed off in all directions. On attaining
the summit of the rugged hill we saw in the hollow beneath
the Christian inn of *Yan-Pa-Eul*. We proceeded towards
it, our road constantly crossed by fresh and limpid streams,
which, issuing from the sides of the mountain, reunite at
its foot and form a rivulet which encircles the inn. We
were received by the landlord, or, as the Chinese call him,
the Comptroller of the Chest.

Inns of this description occur at intervals in the deserts
of Tartary, along the confines of China. They consist almost universally of a large square enclosure, formed by high
poles interlaced with brushwood. In the center of this enclosure is a mud house, never more than ten feet high.
With the exception of a few wretched rooms at each extremity, the entire structure consists of one large apartment,
serving at once for cooking, eating, and sleeping; thoroughly
dirty, and full of smoke and intolerable stench. Into this
pleasant place all travelers, without distinction, are ushered,
the portion of space applied to their accommodation being
a long, wide *Kang*, as it is called, a sort of furnace, occupying more than three-fourths of the apartment, about four
feet high, and the flat, smooth surface of which is covered
with a reed mat, which the richer guests cover again with a
traveling carpet of felt, or with furs. In front of it, three
immense coppers, set in glazed earth, serve for the preparation of the traveler's milk-broth. The apertures by which

---

[1] The Chinese *Li* is about equivalent to the quarter of an English mile.

Kang of a Tartar-Chinese Inn

these monster boilers are heated communicate with the interior of the *Kang*, so that its temperature is constantly maintained at a high elevation, even in the terrible cold of winter. Upon the arrival of guests, the Comptroller of the Chest invites them to ascend the *Kang*, where they seat themselves, their legs crossed tailor-fashion, round a large table, not more than six inches high. The lower part of the room is reserved for the people of the inn, who there busy themselves in keeping up the fire under the caldrons, boiling tea, and pounding oats and buckwheat into flour for the repast of the travelers. The *Kang* of these Tartar-Chinese inns is, till evening, a stage full of animation, where the guests eat, drink, smoke, gamble, dispute, and fight: with nightfall, the refectory, tavern, and gambling house of the day is suddenly converted into a dormitory. The travelers who have any bed-clothes unroll and arrange them; those who have none, settle themselves as best they may in their personal attire, and lie down, side by side, round the table.

When the guests are very numerous they arrange themselves in two circles, feet to feet. Thus reclined, those so disposed, sleep; others, awaiting sleep, smoke, drink tea, and gossip. The effect of the scene, dimly exhibited by an imperfect wick floating amid thick, dirty, stinking oil, whose receptacle is ordinarily a broken tea-cup, is fantastic, and to the stranger, fearful.

The Comptroller of the Chest had prepared his own room for our accommodation. We washed, but would not sleep there; being now Tartar travelers, and in possession of a good tent, we determined to try our apprentice hand at setting it up. This resolution offended no one, it was quite understood we adopted this course, not out of contempt towards the inn, but out of love for a patriarchal life. When we had set up our tent, and unrolled on the ground our goatskin beds, we lighted a pile of brushwood, for the nights were already growing cold. Just as we were closing our eyes, the Inspector of Darkness startled us with beating the official night alarm, upon his brazen *tam-tam*, the sonorous sound of which, reverberating through the adjacent valleys struck with terror the tigers and wolves frequenting them, and drove them off.

We were on foot before daylight. Previous to our departure we had to perform an operation of considerable importance—no other than an entire change of costume, a complete metamorphosis. The missionaries who reside in China, all, without exception, wear the secular dress of the people, and are in no way distinguishable from them; they bear no outward sign of their religious character. It is a great pity that they should be thus obliged to wear the secular costume, for it is an obstacle in the way of their preaching the gospel. Among the Tartars, a *black man*—so they discriminate the laity, as wearing their hair, from the clergy, who have their heads close shaved—who should talk about religion would be laughed at, as impertinently meddling with things, the special province of the Lamas, and in no way concerning him. The reasons which appear to have introduced and maintained the custom of wearing the secular habit on the part of the missionaries in China, no longer applying to us, we resolved at length to appear in an ecclesiastical exterior becoming our sacred mission. The views of our vicar apostolic on the subject, as explained in his written instructions, being conformable with our wish, we did not hesitate. We resolved to adopt the secular dress of the Thibetian Lamas; that is to say, the dress which they wear when not actually performing their idolatrous ministry in the Pagodas. The costume of the Thibetian Lamas suggested itself to our preference as being in unison with that worn by our young neophyte, Samdadchiemba.

We announced to the Christians of the inn that we were resolved no longer to look like Chinese merchants; that we were about to cut off our long tails, and to shave our heads. This intimation created great agitation: some of our disciples even wept; all sought by their eloquence to divert us from a resolution which seemed to them fraught with danger; but their pathetic remonstrances were of no avail; one touch of a razor, in the hands of Samdadchiemba, sufficed to sever the long tail of hair, which, to accommodate Chinese fashions, we had so carefully cultivated ever since our departure from France. We put on a long yellow robe, fastened at the right side with five gilt buttons, and round the waist by a long red sash; over this was a red jacket, with a collar of purple velvet; a yellow cap, surmounted by a red tuft, completed our new costume. Breakfast followed this decisive operation, but it was silent and sad. When the Comptroller of the Chest brought in some glasses and an urn, wherein smoked the hot wine drunk by the Chinese, we told him

The Missionaries in their Lamanesque Costume.

that having changed our habit of dress, we should change also our habit of living. "Take away," said we, "that wine and that chafing dish; henceforth we renounce drinking and smoking. You know," added we, laughing, "that good Lamas abstain from wine and tobacco." The Chinese Christians who surrounded us did not join in the laugh; they looked at us without speaking and with deep commiseration, fully persuaded that we should inevitably perish of privation and misery in the deserts of Tartary. Breakfast finished, while the people of the inn were packing up our tent, saddling the camels, and preparing for our departure, we took a couple of rolls, baked in the steam of the furnace, and walked out to complete our meal with some wild currants growing on the bank of the adjacent rivulet. It was soon announced to us that everything was ready—so, mounting our respective animals, we proceeded on the road to Tolon-Noor, accompanied by Samdadchiemba.

We were now launched, alone and without a guide, amid a new world. We had no longer before us paths traced out by the old missionaries, for we were in a country where none before us had preached Gospel truth. We should no longer have by our side those earnest Christian converts, so zealous to serve us; so anxious, by their friendly care, to create around us as it were an atmosphere of home. We were abandoned to ourselves, in a hostile land, without a friend to advise or to aid us, save Him by whose strength we were supported, and whose name we were seeking to make known to all the nations of the earth.

As we have just observed, Samdadchiemba was our only traveling companion. This young man was neither Chinese, nor Tartar, nor Thibetian. Yet, at the first glance, it was easy to recognize in him the features characterizing that which naturalists call the Mongol race. A great flat nose, insolently turned up; a large mouth, slit in a perfectly straight line, thick, projecting lips, a deep bronze complexion, every feature contributed to give to his physiognomy a wild and scornful aspect. When his little eyes seemed starting out of his head from under their lids, wholly destitute of eyelash, and he looked at you wrinkling his brow, he inspired you at once with feelings of dread and yet of confidence. The face was without any decisive character: it exhibited neither the mischievous knavery of the Chinese, nor the frank good-nature of the Tartar, nor the courageous energy of the Thibetian; but was made up of a mixture of all three. Samdadchiemba was a *Dchiahour*. We shall hereafter have occasion to speak more in detail of the native country of our young cameleer.

At the age of eleven, Samdadchiemba had escaped from his Lamasery, in order to avoid the too frequent and too severe corrections of the master under whom he was more immediately placed. He afterwards passed the greater portion of his vagabond youth, sometimes in the Chinese towns, sometimes in the deserts of Tartary. It is easy to comprehend that this independent course of life had not tended to modify the natural asperity of his character; his intellect was entirely uncultivated; but, on the other hand, his muscular power was enormous, and he was not a little vain of this quality, which he took great pleasure in parading. After having been instructed and baptized by M.-Gabet, he had attached himself to the service of the missionaries. The journey we were now undertaking was perfectly in harmony with his erratic and adventurous taste. He was, however, of no mortal service to us as a guide across the deserts of Tartary, for he knew no more of the country than we knew ourselves. Our only informants were a compass, and the excellent map of the Chinese empire by Andriveau-Goujon.

Samdadchiemba.

The first portion of our journey, after leaving Yan-Pa-Eul, was accomplished without interruption, sundry anathemas excepted, which were hurled against us as we ascended a mountain, by a party of Chinese merchants, whose mules, upon sight of our camels and our own yellow attire, became frightened, and took to their heels at full speed, dragging after them, and in one or two instances, overturning the wagons to which they were harnessed.

The mountain in question is called *Sain-Oula* (Good-Mountain), doubtless *ut lucus a non lucendo*, since it is notorious for the dismal accidents and tragical adventures of which it is the theater. The ascent is by a rough, steep path, half-choked up with fallen rocks. Midway up is a small temple, dedicated to the divinity of the mountain,

Mountain of Sain-Oula.

Sain-Nai, (the Good Old Woman;) the occupant is a priest, whose business it is, from time to time, to fill up the cavities in the road, occasioned by the previous rains, in consideration of which service he receives from each passenger a small gratuity, constituting his revenue. After a toilsome journey of nearly three hours we found ourselves at the summit of the mountain, upon an immense plateau, extending from east to west a long day's journey, and from north to south still more widely. From this summit you discern, afar off in the plains of Tartary, the tents of the Mongols, ranged semi-circularly on the slopes of the hills, and looking in the distance like so many beehives. Several rivers derive their source from the sides of this mountain. Chief among these is the *Chara-Mouren* (Yellow River—distinct, of course, from the great Yellow River of China, the *Hoang-Ho*)—the capricious course of which the eye can follow on through the kingdom of *Gechekten*, after traversing which, and then the district of *Naiman*, it passes the stake-boundary into Mantchouria, and flowing from north to south, falls into the sea, approaching which it assumes the name *Léao-Ho*.

The *Good Mountain* is noted for its intense frosts. There is not a winter passes in which the cold there does not kill many travelers. Frequently whole caravans, not arriving at their destination on the other side of the mountain, are sought and found on its bleak road, man and beast frozen to death. Nor is the danger less from the robbers and the wild beasts with whom the mountain is a favorite haunt, or rather a permanent station. Assailed by the brigands, the unlucky traveler is stripped, not merely of horse and money, and baggage, but absolutely of the clothes he wears, and then left to perish from cold and hunger.

Not but that the brigands of these parts are extremely polite all the while; they do not rudely clap a pistol to your ear, and bawl at you: "Your money or your life!" No; they mildly advance with a courteous salutation: "Venerable elder brother, I am on foot; pray lend me your horse—I've got no money, be good enough to lend me your purse—It's quite cold to-day, oblige me with the loan of your coat." If the venerable elder brother charitably complies, the matter ends with, "Thanks, brother;" but otherwise, the request is forthwith emphasized with the arguments of a cudgel; and if these do not convince, recourse is had to the saber.

The sun declining ere we had traversed this platform, we resolved to encamp for the night. Our first business was to seek a position combining the three essentials of fuel, water, and pasturage; and, having due regard to the ill reputation of the *Good Mountain*, privacy from observation as complete as could be effected. Being novices in traveling, the idea of robbers haunted us incessantly, and we took everybody we saw to be a suspicious character,

First Encampment.

against whom we must be on our guard. A grassy nook, surrounded by tall trees, appertaining to the Imperial Forest, fulfilled our requisites. Unlading our dromedaries, we raised, with no slight labor, our tent beneath the foliage, and at its entrance installed our faithful porter, Arsalan, a dog whose size, strength, and courage well entitled him to his appellation, which, in the Tartar-Mongol dialect, means, "Lion." Collecting some *argols*[1] and dry branches of trees, our kettle was soon in agitation, and we threw into the boiling water some Kouamien, prepared paste, something like Vermicelli, which, seasoned with some parings of bacon, given us by our friends at Yan-Pa-Eul, we hoped would furnish satisfaction for the hunger that began to gnaw us. No sooner was the repast ready, than each of us, drawing forth from his girdle his wooden cup, filled it with Kouamien, and raised it to his lips. The preparation was detestable—uneatable. The manufacturers of Kouamien always salt it for its longer preservation; but this paste of ours had been salted beyond all endurance. Even Arsalan would not eat the composition. Soaking it for a while in

[1] Dried dung, which constitutes the chief, and indeed in many places the sole fuel in Tartary.

cold water, we once more boiled it up, but in vain; the dish remained nearly as salt as ever; so, abandoning it to Arsalan and to Samdadchiemba, whose stomach by long use was capable of anything, we were fain to content ourselves with the *dry-cold*, as the Chinese say; and taking with us a couple of small loaves, walked into the Imperial Forest, in order at least to season our repast with an agreeable walk. Our first nomade supper, however, turned out better than we had expected, Providence placing in our path numerous *Ngao-la-Eul* and *Chan-ly-Houng* trees, the former, a shrub about five inches high, which bears a pleasant wild cherry; the other, also a low but very bushy shrub, producing a small scarlet apple, of a sharp agreeable flavor, of which a very succulent jelly is made.

The Imperial Forest extends more than a hundred leagues from north to south, and nearly eighty from east to west. The Emperor Khang-Hi, in one of his expeditions into Mongolia, adopted it as a hunting ground. He repaired thither every year, and his successors regularly followed his example, down to *Kia-King*, who, upon a hunting excursion, was killed by lightning at *Ge-ho-Eul*. There has been no imperial hunting there since that time—now twenty-seven years ago. *Tao-Kouang*, son and successor of *Kia-King*, being persuaded that a fatality impends over the exercise of the chase, since his accession to the throne has never set foot in *Ge-ho-Eul*, which may be regarded as the Versailles of the Chinese potentates. The forest, however, and the animals which inhabit it, have been no gainers by the circumstance. Despite the penalty of perpetual exile decreed against all who shall be found, with arms in their hands, in the forest, it is always half full of poachers and wood-cutters. Gamekeepers, indeed, are stationed at intervals throughout the forest; but they seem there merely for the purpose of enjoying a monopoly of the sale of game and wood. They let any one steal either, provided they themselves get the larger share of the booty. The poachers are in especial force from the fourth to the seventh moon. At this period, the antlers of the stags send forth new shoots, which contain a sort of half-coagulated blood, called *Lou-joung*, which plays a distinguished part in the Chinese *Materia Medica*, for its supposed chemical qualities, and fetches accordingly an exorbitant price. A *Lou-joung* sometimes sells for as much as a hundred and fifty ounces of silver.

Deer of all kinds abound in the forest; and tigers, bears, wild boars, panthers, and wolves are scarcely less numerous. Woe to the hunters and wood-cutters who venture otherwise than in large parties into the recesses of the forest; they disappear, leaving no vestige behind.

The fear of encountering one of these wild beasts kept us from prolonging our walk. Besides, night was setting in, and we hastened back to our tent. Our first slumber in the desert was peaceful, and next morning early, after a breakfast of oatmeal steeped in tea, we resumed our march along the great *Plateau*. We soon reached the great *Obo*, whither the Tartars resort to worship the Spirit of the Mountain.

Buddhist Monuments.

The monument is simply an enormous pile of stones, heaped up without any order, and surmounted with dried branches of trees, from which hang bones and strips of cloth, on which are inscribed verses in the Thibet and Mongol languages. At its base is a large granite urn in which the devotees burn incense. They offer, besides, pieces of money, which the next Chinese passenger, after sundry ceremonious genuflexions before the Obo, carefully collects and pockets for his own particular benefit.

These Obos, which occur so frequently throughout Tartary, and which are the objects of constant pilgrimages on the part of the Mongols, remind one of the *loca excelsa* denounced by the Jewish prophets.

It was near noon before the ground, beginning to slope, intimated that we approached the termination of the plateau. We then descended rapidly into a deep valley, where we found a small Mongolian encampment, which we passed without pausing, and set up our tent for the night on the margin of a pool further on. We were now in the kingdom of Gechekten, an undulating country, well watered, with abundance of fuel and pasturage, but desolated by bands of robbers. The Chinese, who have long since taken possession of it, have rendered it a sort of general refuge for malefactors; so that " man of Gechekten " has become a synonym for a person without fear of God or man, who will commit any murder, and shrink from no crime. It would seem as though, in this country, nature resented the encroachments of man upon her rights. Wherever the plough has passed, the soil has become poor, arid, and sandy, producing nothing but oats, which constitute the food of the people. In the whole district there is but one trading town, which the Mongols call *Altan-Somé*, (Temple of Gold). This was at first a great Lamasery, containing nearly 2000 Lamas. By degrees Chinese have settled there, in order to traffic with the Tartars. In 1843, when we had occasion to visit this place, it had already acquired the importance of a town. A highway, commencing at Altan-Somé, proceeds towards the north, and after traversing the country of the *Khalkhas*, the river *Keroulan*, and the *Khinggan* mountains, reaches Nertechink, a town of Siberia.

The sun had just set, and we were occupied inside the tent boiling our tea, when Arsalan warned us, by his barking, of the approach of some stranger. We soon heard the trot of a horse, and presently a mounted Tartar appeared at the door. "*Mendou*," he exclaimed, by way of respectful salutation to the supposed Lamas, raising his joined hands at the same time to his forehead. When we invited him to drink a cup of tea with us, he fastened his horse to one of the tent-pegs, and seated himself by the hearth. " Sirs Lamas," said he, " under what quarter of the heavens were you born ? " " We are from the western heaven; and you, whence come you ? " " My poor abode is towards the north, at the end of the valley you see there on our right." " Your country is a fine country." The Mongol shook his head sadly, and made no reply. " Brother," we proceeded, after a moment's silence, " the Land of Grass is still very extensive in the kingdom of Gechekten. Would it not be better to cultivate your plains ? What good are these bare lands to you ? Would not fine crops of corn be preferable to mere grass ? " He replied, with a tone of deep and settled conviction, " We Mongols are formed for living in tents, and pasturing cattle. So long as we kept to that in the kingdom of Gechekten, we were rich and happy. Now, ever since the Mongols have set themselves to cultivating the land, and building houses, they have become poor. The *Kitats* (Chinese) have taken possession of the country; flocks, herds, lands, houses, all have passed into their hands. There remain to us only a few prairies, on which still live, under their tents, such of the Mongols as have not been forced by utter destitution to emigrate to other lands." " But if the Chinese are so baneful to you, why did you let them penetrate into your country ? " " Your words are the words of truth, Sirs Lamas; but you are aware that the Mongols are men of simple hearts. We took pity on these wicked Kitats, who came to us weeping, to solicit our charity. We allowed them, through pure compassion, to cultivate a few patches of land. The Mongols insensibly followed their example, and abandoned the nomadic life. They drank the wine of the Kitats, and smoked their tobacco, on credit; they bought their manufactures on credit at double the real value. When the day of payment came, there was no money ready, and the Mongols had to yield, to the violence of their creditors, houses, lands, flocks, everything." " But could you not seek justice from the tribunals ? " " Justice from the tribunals ! Oh, that is out of the question. The Kitats are skilful to talk and to lie. It is impossible for a Mongol to gain a suit against a Kitat. Sirs Lamas, the kingdom of Gechekten is undone ! " So saying, the poor Mongol rose, bowed, mounted his horse, and rapidly disappeared in the desert.

We travelled two more days through this kingdom, and

everywhere witnessed the poverty and wretchedness of its scattered inhabitants. Yet the country is naturally endowed with astonishing wealth, especially in gold and silver mines, which of themselves have occasioned many of its worst calamities. Notwithstanding the rigorous prohibition to work these mines, it sometimes happens that large bands of Chinese outlaws assemble together, and march, sword in hand, to dig into them. These are men professing to be endowed with a peculiar capacity for discovering the precious metals, guided, according to their own account, by the conformation of mountains, and the sorts of plants they produce. One single man, possessed of this fatal gift, will suffice to spread desolation over a whole district. He speedily finds himself at the head of thousands and thousands of outcasts, who overspread the country, and render it the theater of every crime. While some are occupied in working the mines others pillage the surrounding districts, sparing neither persons nor property, and committing excesses which the imagination could not conceive, and which continue until some mandarin, powerful and courageous enough to suppress them, is brought within their operation, and takes measures against them accordingly.

Calamities of this nature have frequently desolated the kingdom of Gechekten; but none of them are comparable with what happened in the kingdom of Ouniot, in 1841. A Chinese *mine discoverer*, having ascertained the presence of gold in a particular mountain, announced the discovery, and robbers and vagabonds at once congregated around him, from far and near, to the number of 12,000. This hideous mob put the whole country under subjection, and exercised for two years its fearful sway. Almost the entire mountain passed through the crucible, and such enormous quantities of metal were produced, that the price of gold fell in China fifty per cent. The inhabitants complained incessantly to the Chinese mandarins, but in vain; for these worthies only interfere where they can do so with some benefit to themselves. The King of Ouniot himself feared to measure his strength with such an army of desperadoes.

One day, however, the Queen of Ouniot, repairing on a pilgrimage to the tomb of her ancestors, had to pass the valley in which the army of miners was assembled. Her car was surrounded; she was rudely compelled to alight, and it was only upon the sacrifice of her jewels that she was permitted to proceed. Upon her return home, she reproached the King bitterly for his cowardice. At length,

Military Mandarin.

stung by her words, he assembled the troops of his two banners, and marched against the miners. The engagement which ensued was for a while doubtful; but at length the miners were driven in by the Tartar cavalry, who massacred them without mercy. The bulk of the survivors took refuge in the mine. The Mongols blocked up the apertures with huge stones. The cries of the despairing wretches within were heard for a few days, and then ceased forever. Those of the miners who were taken alive had their eyes put out, and were then dismissed.

We had just quitted the kingdom of Gechekten, and entered that of Thakar, when we came to a military encampment, where were stationed a party of Chinese soldiers charged with the preservation of the public safety. The hour of repose had arrived; but these soldiers, instead of giving us confidence by their presence, increased, on the contrary, our fears; for we knew that they were themselves the most daring robbers in the whole district. We turned aside, therefore, and ensconced ourselves between two rocks, where we found just space enough for our tent. We had scarcely set up our temporary abode, when we observed, in the distance, on the slope of the mountains, a numerous body of horsemen at full gallop. Their rapid but irregular evolutions seemed to indicate that they were pursuing something which constantly evaded them. By and by, two of the horsemen, perceiving us, dashed up to our tent, dismounted, and threw themselves on the ground at the door. They were Tartar-Mongols. "Men of prayer," said they, with voices full of emotion, "we come to ask you to draw our horoscope. We have this day had two horses stolen from us. We have fruitlessly sought traces of the robbers, and we therefore come to you, men whose power and learning is beyond all limit, to tell us where we shall find our property." "Brothers," said we, "we are not Lamas of Buddha; we do not believe in horoscopes. For a man to say that he can, by any such means, discover that which is stolen, is for them to put forth the words of falsehood and deception." The poor Tartars redoubled their solicitations; but when they found that we were inflexible in our resolution, they remounted their horses, in order to return to the mountains.

Samdadchiemba, meanwhile, had been silent, apparently paying no attention to the incident, but fixed at the fireplace, with his bowl of tea to his lips. All of a sudden he knitted his brows, rose, and came to the door. The horsemen were at some distance; but the Dchiahour, by an exertion of his strong lungs, induced them to turn round in their saddles. He motioned to them, and they, supposing we had relented, and were willing to draw the desired horoscope, galloped once more towards us. When they had come within speaking distance :—"My Mongol brothers," cried Samdadchiemba, "in future be more careful; watch your herds well, and you won't be robbed. Retain these words of mine on your memory: they are worth all the horoscopes in the world." After this friendly address, he gravely re-entered the tent, and seating himself at the hearth, resumed his tea.

We were at first somewhat disconcerted by this singular proceeding; but as the horsemen themselves did not take the matter in ill part, but quietly rode off, we burst into a laugh. "Stupid Mongols!" grumbled Samdadchiemba; "they don't give themselves the trouble to watch their animals, and then, when they are stolen from them, they run about wanting people to draw horoscopes for them. After all, perhaps, it's no wonder, for nobody but ourselves tells them the truth. The Lamas encourage them in their credulity; for they turn it into a source of income. It is difficult to deal with such people. If you tell them you can't draw a horoscope, they don't believe you, and merely suppose you don't choose to oblige them. To get rid of them, the best way is to give them an answer haphazard." And here Samdadchiemba laughed with such expansion, that his little eyes were completely buried. "Did you ever draw a horoscope?" asked we. "Yes," replied he, still laughing. "I was very young at the time, not more than fifteen. I was traveling through the Red Banner of Thakar, when I was addressed by some Mongols who led me into their tent. There they entreated me to tell them, by means of divination, where a bull had strayed, which had been missing three days. It was to no purpose that I protested to them I could not perform divination, that I could not even read. 'You deceive us,' said they; 'you are a *Dchiahour* and we know that the Western Lamas can all divine more or less.' As the only way of extricating myself from the dilemma, I resolved to imitate what I had seen the Lamas do in their divinations. I directed one person to collect eleven sheep's droppings, the dryest he could find. They were immediately brought. I then seated myself very gravely; I counted the droppings over and over; I arranged them in rows, and then counted them again; I rolled them up and down in threes; and then appeared to meditate. At last I said to the Mongols, who were impatiently awaiting the result of the horoscope: 'If you would find your bull, go seek him towards the north.' Before the words were well out of my mouth, four men were on horseback, galloping off towards the north. By the most curious chance in the world, they had not proceeded far, before the missing animal made its appearance, quietly browsing. I at once got the character of a diviner of the first class, was entertained in the most liberal manner for a week, and when I departed had a stock of butter and tea given me enough for another week. Now that I belong to Holy Church, I know that these things are wicked and prohibited; otherwise I would have given these horsemen a word or two of horoscope, which perhaps would have procured for us, in return, a good cup of tea with butter."

The stolen horses confirmed in our minds the ill reputation of the country in which we were now encamped; and we felt ourselves necessitated to take additional precaution. Before night-fall we brought in the horse and the mule, and fastened them by cords to pins at the door of our tent, and made the camels kneel by their side, so as to close up the entrance. By this arrangement no one could get near us without our having full warning given us by the camels, which, at the least noise, always make an outcry loud enough to awaken the deepest sleeper. Finally, having suspended from one of the tent-poles our traveling lantern, which we kept burning all the night, we endeavored to obtain a little repose, but in vain; the night passed away, without our getting a wink of sleep. As to the *Dchiahour*, whom nothing ever troubled, we heard him snoring with all the might of his lungs until daybreak.

We made our preparations for departure very early, for we were eager to quit this ill-famed place, and to reach *Tolon-Noor*, which was now distant only a few leagues.

On our way thither, a horseman stopped his galloping steed, and, after looking at us for a moment, addressed us: "You are the chiefs of the Christians of the Contiguous Defiles?" Upon our replying in the affirmative, he dashed off again; but turned his head once or twice, to have another look at us. He was a Mongol, who had charge of some herds at the Contiguous Defiles. He had often seen us there; but the novelty of our present costume at first prevented his recognizing us. We met also the Tartars who, the day before, had asked us to draw a horoscope for them. They had repaired by daybreak, to the horse-fair at *Tolon-Noor*, in the hope of finding their stolen animals; but their search had been unsuccessful.

The increasing number of travelers, Tartars and Chinese, whom we now met, indicated the approach to the great town of Tolon-Noor. We already saw in the distance, glittering under the sun's rays, the gilt roofs of two magnificent Lamaseries that stand in the northern suburbs of the town. We journeyed for some time through a succession of cemeteries; for here, as elsewhere, the present generation is surrounded by the ornamental sepulchers of past generations. As we observed the numerous population of that large town, environed as it were by a vast circle of bones and monumental stones, it seemed as though death was continuously engaged in the blockade of life. Here and there, in the vast cemetery which completely encircles the city, we remarked little gardens, where, by dint of extreme labor, a few miserable vegetables were extracted from the earth: leeks, spinach, hard bitter lettuces, and cabbages, which, introduced some years since from Russia, have adapted themselves exceedingly well to the climate of Northern China.

With the exception of these few esculents, the environs of Tolon-Noor produced absolutely nothing whatever. The soil is dry and sandy, and water terribly scarce. It is only here and there that a few limited springs are found, and these are dried up in the hot season.

City of Tolon-Noor.

CHAPTER II.

Inn at Tolon-Noor—Aspect of the City—Great Foundries of Bells and Idols—Conversation with the Lamas of *Tolon-Noor*—Encampment—Tea-Bricks—Meeting with Queen *Mourguevan*—Taste of the Mongols for Pilgrimages—Violent Storm—Account from a Mongol Chief of the War of the English against China—Topography of the Eight Banners of the *Tchakar*—The Imperial herds—Form and Interior of the Tents—Tartar Manners and Customs—Encampment at the Three Lakes—Nocturnal Apparitions—Samdadchiemba relates the Adventures of his Youth—Gray Squirrels of Tartary—Arrival at *Chaborté*.

OUR entrance into the city of Tolon-Noor was fatiguing and full of perplexity; for we knew not where to take up our abode. We wandered about for a long time in a labyrinth of narrow, tortuous streets, encumbered with men and animals and goods. At last we found an inn. We unloaded our dromedaries, deposited the baggage in a small room, foddered the animals, and then, having affixed to the door of our room the padlock which, as is the custom, our landlord gave us for that purpose, we sallied forth in quest of dinner. A triangular flag floating before a house in the next street indicated to our joyful hearts an eating-house.

A long passage led us into a spacious apartment, in which were symmetrically set forth a number of little tables. Seating ourselves at one of these, a tea-pot, the inevitable prelude in these countries to every meal, was set before each of us. You must swallow infinite tea, and that boiling hot, before they will consent to bring you anything else. At last, when they see you thus occupied, the Comptroller of the Table pays you his official visit, a personage of immensely elegant manners, and ceaseless volubility of tongue, who, after entertaining you with his views upon the affairs of the world in general, and each country in particular, concludes by announcing what there is to eat, and requesting your judgment thereupon. As you mention the dishes you desire, he repeats their names in a measured chant, for the information of the Governor of the Pot. Your dinner is served up with admirable promptitude; but before you commence the meal, etiquette requires that you rise from your seat, and invite all the other company present to partake. "Come," you say, with an engaging gesture, "come my friends, come and drink a glass of wine with me; come and eat a plate of rice;" and so on. "No, thank you," replies everybody; "do you rather come and seat yourself at my table. It is I who invite you;" and so the matter ends. By this ceremony you have "manifested your honor," as the phrase runs, and you may now sit down and eat it in comfort, your character as a gentleman perfectly established.

When you rise to depart, the Comptroller of the Table again appears. As you cross the apartment with him, he chants over again the names of the dishes you have had, this time appending the prices, and terminating with the sum total, announced with especial emphasis, which, proceeding to the counter, you then deposit in the money-box. In general, the Chinese restaurateurs are quite as skilful as those of France in exciting the vanity of the guests, and promoting the consumption of their commodities.

Two motives had induced us to direct our steps, in the first instance, to Tolon-Noor: we desired to make more purchases there to complete our traveling equipment, and, secondly, it appeared to us necessary to place ourselves in communication with the Lamas of the country, in order to obtain information from them as to the more important localities of Tartary. The purchases we needed to make gave us occasion to visit the different quarters of the town. Tolon-Noor (Seven Lakes) is called by the Chinese *Lama-Miao* (Convent of Lamas). The Mantchous designate it the *Nadan-Omo*, and the Thibetians, the *Tsot-Dun*, both translations of Tolon-Noor, and, equally with it, meaning "Seven Lakes." On the map published by M. Andriveau-Goujon,[1] this town is called *Djo-Naiman-Soumé*, which in Mongol means, "The Hundred and Eight Convents." This name is perfectly unknown in the country itself.

Tolon-Noor is not a walled city, but a vast agglomeration of hideous houses, which seem to have been thrown together with a pitchfork. The carriage portion of the streets is a marsh of mud and putrid filth, deep enough to stifle and bury the smaller beasts of burden that not unfrequently fall within it, and whose carcases remain to aggravate the general stench; while their loads become the prey of the innumerable thieves who are ever on the alert. The foot-path is a narrow, rugged, slippery line on either side, just wide enough to admit the passage of one person.

Yet, despite the nastiness of the town itself, the sterility of the environs, the excessive cold of its winter, and the intolerable heat of its summur, its population is immense, and its commerce enormous. Russian merchandise is brought hither in large quantities by the way of Kiakta. The Tartars bring incessant herds of camels, oxen, and horses, and carry back in exchange tobacco, linen, and tea. This constant arrival and departure of strangers communicates to the city an animated and varied aspect. All sorts of hawkers are at every corner offering their petty wares; the regular traders, from behind their counters, invite with honeyed words and tempting offers, the passers-by to come in and buy. The Lamas, in their red and yellow robes, gallop up and down, seeking admiration for their equestrianism, and the skilful management of their fiery steeds.

The trade of Tolon-Noor is mostly in the hands of men from the province of *Chan-Si*, who seldom establish themselves permanently in the town; but after a few years, when their money-chest is filled, return to their own country. In this vast emporium, the Chinese invariably make fortunes,

---

[1] With the exception of a very few inaccuracies, this map of the Chinese empire is a most excellent one. We found it of the most valuable aid throughout our journey.—HUC.
An English version of the map is prefixed to this volume.—ED.

and the Tartars invariably are ruined. Tolon-Noor, in fact, is a sort of great pneumatic pump, constantly at work in emptying the pockets of the unlucky Mongols.

The magnificent statues, in bronze and brass, which issue from the great foundries of Tolon-Noor, are celebrated not only throughout Tartary, but in the remotest districts of Thibet. Its immense workshops supply all the countries subject to the worship of Buddha with idols, bells, and vases employed in that idolatry. While we were in the town, a monster statue of Buddha, a present from a friend of Oudchou-Mourdchin to the Talè-Lama, was packed for Thibet, on the backs of six camels. The larger statues are cast in detail, the component parts being afterward soldered together.

Bell and Idol Foundry.

We availed ourselves of our stay at Tolon-Noor to have a figure of Christ constructed on the model of a bronze original which we had brought with us from France. The workmen so marvelously excelled, that it was difficult to distinguish the copy from the original. The Chinese work more rapidly and cheaply, and their complaisance contrasts most favorably with the tenacious self-opinion of their brethren in Europe.

During our stay at Tolon-Noor, we had frequent occasion to visit the Lamaseries, or Lama monasteries, and to converse with the idolatrous priests of Buddhism. The Lamas appeared to us persons of very limited information ; and as to their symbolism, in general, it is little more refined or purer than the creed of the vulgar. Their doctrine is still undecided, fluctuating amidst a vast fanaticism of which they can give no intelligible account. When we asked them for some distinct, clear, positive idea what they meant, they were always thrown into utter embarrassment, and stared at one another. The disciples told us that their masters knew all about it; the masters referred us to the omniscience of the Grand Lamas; the Grand Lamas confessed themselves ignorant, but talked of some wonderful saint, in some Lamasery at the other end of the country: *he* could explain the whole affair. However, all of them, disciples and masters, great Lamas and small, agree in this that their doctrine came from the West : " The nearer you approach the West," said they unanimously, " the purer and more luminous will the doctrine manifest itself. When we expounded to them the truths of Christianity, they never discussed the matter; they contented themselves with calmly saying, " Well, we don't suppose that our prayers are the only prayers in the world. The Lamas of the West will explain everything to you. We believe in the traditions that have come from the West."

In point of fact there is no Lamasery of any importance in Tartary, the Grand Lama or superior of which is not a man from Thibet. Any Tartar Lama who has visited *Lha-Ssa* [Land of Spirits], or *Monhe-Dhot* [Eternal Sanctuary], as it is called in the Mongol dialect, is received, on his return, as a man to whom the mysteries of the past and of the future have been unveiled.

After maturely weighing the information we had obtained from the Lamas, it was decided that we should direct our steps towards the West. On October 1st we quitted Tolon-Noor; and it was not without infinite trouble that we managed to traverse the filthy town with our camels. The poor animals could only get through the quagmire streets by fits and starts; it was first a stumble, then a convulsive jump, then another stumble and another jump, and so on. Their loads shook on their backs, and at every step we expected to see the camel and camel-load prostrate in the mud. We considered ourselves lucky when, at distant intervals, we came to a comparatively dry spot, where the camels could travel, and we were thus enabled to readjust and tighten the baggage. Samdadchiemba got into a desperate ill temper; he went on, and slipped, and went on again, without uttering a single word, restricting the visible manifestation of his wrath to a continuous biting of the lips.

Upon attaining at length the western extremity of the town, we got clear of the filth indeed, but found ourselves involved in another evil. Before us there was no road marked out, not the slightest trace of even a path. There was nothing but an apparently interminable chain of small hills, composed of fine, moving sand, over which it was impossible to advance at more than a snail's pace, and this only with extreme labor. Among these sand-hills, moreover, we were oppressed with an absolutely stifling heat. Our animals were covered with perspiration, ourselves devoured with a burning thirst; but it was in vain that we looked round in all directions, as we proceeded, for water; not a spring, not a pool, not a drop presented itself.

It was already late, and we began to fear we should find no spot favorable for the erection of our tent. The ground, however, grew by degrees firmer, and we at last discerned some signs of vegetation. By and by, the sand almost disappeared, and our eyes were rejoiced with the sight of continuous verdure. On our left, at no great distance, we saw the opening of a defile. M. Gabet urged on his camel, and went to examine the spot. He soon made his appearance at the summit of a hill, and with voice and hand directed us to follow him. We hastened on, and found that Providence had led us to a favorable position. A small pool, the waters of which were half concealed by thick reeds and other marshy vegetation, some brushwood, a plot of grass: what could we under the circumstances desire more? Hungry, thirsty, weary as we were, the place seemed a perfect Eden.

The camels were no sooner squatted, than we all three, with one accord, and without a word said, seized, each man his wooden cup, and rushed to the pond to satisfy his thirst. The water was fresh enough; but it affected the nose violently with its strong muriatic odor. I remembered to have drunk water just like it in the Pyrenees, at the good town of Ax, and to have seen it for sale in the chemists' shops elsewhere in France: and I remembered, further, that by reason of its being particularly stinking and particularly nasty, it was sold there at fifteen sous per bottle.

After having quenched our thirst, our strength by degrees returned, and we were then able to fix our tent, and each man to set about his especial task. M. Gabet proceeded to cut some bundles of horn-beam wood; Samdadchiemba collected argols in the flap of his jacket; and M. Huc, seated at the entrance of the tent, tried his hand at drawing a fowl, a process which Arsalan, stretched at his side, watched with greedy eye, having immediate reference to the entrails in course of removal. We were resolved, for once and away, to have a little festival in the desert; and to take the opportunity to indulge our patriotism by initiating our *Dchiahour* in the luxury of a dish prepared according to the rules of the *cuisinier Français*. The fowl, artistically dismembered, was placed at the bottom of our great pot. A few roots of synapia, prepared in salt water, some onions, a clove of garlic, and some allspice, constituted the seasoning. The preparation was soon boiling, for we were that day rich in fuel. Samdadchiemba, by and by, plunged his hand into the pot, drew out a limb of the fowl, and, after carefully inspecting it, pronounced supper to be ready. The pot was taken from the trivet, and placed upon the grass. We all three seated ourselves around it, so that our knees almost touched it, and each, armed with two chopsticks, fished out the pieces he desired from the abundant broth before him.

When the meal was completed, and we had thanked God for the repast he had thus provided us with in the desert, Samdadchiemba went and washed the caldron in the pond. That done, he brewed us some tea. The tea used by the Tartars is not prepared in the same way as that consumed by the Chinese. The latter, it is known, merely employ the smaller and tenderer leaves of the plant, which they simply infuse in boiling water, so as to give it a golden tint; the coarser leaves, with which are mixed up the smaller tendrils, are pressed together in a mold, in the form and of the size of the ordinary house brick. Thus prepared, it becomes an article of considerable commerce, under the designation of Tartar tea, the Tartars being its exclusive consumers, with the exception of the Russians, who drink great quantities of it. When required for use, a piece of the brick is broken off, pulverized, and boiled in the kettle, until the water assumes a reddish hue. Some salt is then thrown in, and effervescence commences. When the liquid has become almost black, milk is added, and the beverage, the grand luxury of the Tartars, is then transferred to the teapot. Samdadchiemba was a perfect enthusiast of this tea. For our parts, we drank it in default of something better.

Next morning, after rolling up our tent, we quitted this asylum without regret indeed, for we had selected and occupied it altogether without preference. However, before departing, we set up, as an *ex-voto* of our gratitude for its reception of us for a night, a small wooden cross, on the site of our fireplace, and this precedent we afterwards followed, at all our encamping places. Could missionaries leave a more appropriate memorial of their journey through the desert!

We had not advanced an hour's journey on our way, when we heard behind us the trampling of many horses, and the confused sound of many voices. We looked back, and saw hastening in our direction a numerous caravan. Three horsemen soon overtook us, one of whom, whose costume bespoke him a Tartar mandarin, addressed us with a loud voice, "Sirs, where is your country?" "We come from the west." "Through what districts has your beneficial shadow passed?" "We have last come from Tolon-Noor." "Has peace accompanied your progress?" "Hitherto we have journeyed in all tranquillity. And you: are you at peace? And what is your country?" "We are Khalkhas, of the kingdom of Mourguevan." "Have the rains been abundant? Are your flocks and herds flourishing!" "All goes well in our pasture-grounds." "Whither proceeds your caravan?" "We go to incline our foreheads before the *Five Towers.*" The rest of the caravan had joined us in the course of this abrupt and hurried conversation. We were on the banks of a small stream, bordered with brushwood. The chief of the caravan ordered a halt, and the camels formed, as each came up, a circle, in the center of which was drawn up a close carriage upon four wheels. " Sok ! sok ! " cried the camel drivers, and at the word, and as with one motion, the entire circle of intelligent animals knelt. While numerous tents, taken from their backs, were set up, as it were, by enchantment, two mandarins, decorated with the blue button, approached the carriage, opened the door, and handed out a Tartar lady, covered with a long silk robe. She was the Queen of the Khalkhas repairing in pilgrimage to the famous Lamasery of the Five Towers, in the province of *Chan-Si.* When she saw us, she saluted us with the ordinary form of raising both her hands : " Sirs Lamas," she said, " is this place auspicious for an encampment? " " Royal Pilgrim of Mourguevan," we replied, " you may light your fires here in all security. For ourselves, we must proceed on our way, for the sun was already high when we folded our tent." And so saying, we took our leave of the Tartars of Mourguevan.

Our minds were deeply excited upon beholding this queen

Queen of Mourguevan.

and her numerous suite performing this long pilgrimage through the desert: no danger, no distance, no expense, no privation deters the Mongols from their prosecution. The Mongols are, indeed, an essentially religious people; with them the future life is everything, the things of this world nothing. They live in the world as though they were not of it; they cultivate no lands, they build no houses, they regard themselves as foreigners traveling through life; and this feeling, deep and universal, develops itself in the practical form of incessant journeys.

The taste for pilgrimages which, at all periods of the world's history, has manifested itself in religious people, is a thing worthy of earnest attention. The worship of the true God led the Jews, several times a year, to Jerusalem. In profane antiquity, those who took any heed to religious belief at all repaired to Egypt, in order to be initiated in the mysteries of Osiris, and to seek lessons of wisdom from his priests. It was to travelers that the mysterious sphynx of Mount Phicæus proposed the profound enigma of which Œidpus discovered the solution. In the middle ages, the spirit of pilgrimage held predominant sway in Europe, and the Christians of that epoch were full of fervor for this species of devotion. The Turks, while they were yet believers, repaired to Mecca in great caravans; and in our travels in Central Asia, we constantly met numerous pilgrims going to or fro, all of them profoundly filled with and earnestly impelled by a sincere sentiment of religion. It is to be remarked that pilgrimages have diminished in Europe, in proportion as faith has become rationalist, and as people have taken to discuss the truths of religion. Wherever faith remains earnest, simple, unquestioning, in the breasts of men, these pilgrimages are in vigor. The reason is, that the intensity of simple faith creates a peculiarly profound and energetic feeling of the condition of man, as a wayfarer upon the earth; and it is natural that this feeling should manifest itself in pious wayfarings. Indeed the Catholic Church, which is the depository of all truth, has introduced processions into the liturgy, as a memorial of pilgrimages, and to remind men that this earth is a desert, wherein we commence, with our birth, the awful journey of eternity.

We had left far behind us the pilgrims of Mourguevan,

and began to regret that we had not encamped in their company upon the banks of the pleasant stream, and amid the fat pastures which it fed. Sensations of fear grew upon us, as we saw great clouds arise in the horizon, spread, and gradually obscure the sky. We looked anxiously around, in all directions, for a place in which we could commodiously halt for the night, but we saw no indication whatever of water. While we were deep in this perplexity, some large drops of rain told us that we had no time to lose. "Let us make haste, and set up the tent," cried Samdadchiemba vehemently. "You need not trouble yourselves any more in looking for water; you will have water enough presently. Let us get under shelter before the sky falls on our heads." "That is all very well," said we, "but we must have some water for the animals and ourselves to drink. You alone require a bucket of water for your tea every evening. Where shall we find some water?" "My fathers, you will very speedily have more water than you like. Let us encamp, that's the first thing to be done. As to thirst, no one will need to die of that this evening: dig but a few holes about the tent, and they'll soon overflow with rain-water. But we need not even dig holes," added Samdadchiemba, extending his right hand; "do you see that shepherd there and his flock? You may be sure water is not far off." Following with our eyes the direction of his finger, we perceived in a lateral valley a man driving a large flock of sheep. We immediately turned aside, and hastened after the man. The rain which now began to fall in torrents redoubled our celerity. To aggravate our distress, the lading of one of the camels just at this moment became loose, and slipped right round towards the ground, and we had to wait while the camel knelt, and Samdadchiemba readjusted the baggage on its back. We were, consequently, thoroughly wet through before we reached a small lake, now agitated and swollen by the falling torrent. There was no occasion for deliberating that evening as to the particular site on which we should set up our tent; selection was out of the question, when the ground all about was deeply saturated with the rain.

The violence of the rain itself mitigated; but the wind absolutely raged. We had infinite trouble to unroll our miserable tent heavy and impracticable with wet, like a large sheet just taken from the washing-tub. The difficulty seemed insuperable when we attempted to stretch it upon its poles, and we should never have succeeded at all, but for the extraordinary muscular power with which Samdadchiemba was endowed. At length we effected a shelter from the wind, and from a small cold rain with which it was accompanied. When our lodging was established, Samdadchiemba addressed us in these consolatory words: —" My spiritual fathers, I told you we should not die to-day of thirst; but I am not at all sure that we don't run some risk of dying of hunger." In point of fact, there seemed no possibility of making a fire. There was not a tree, not a shrub, not a root to be seen. As to argols, they were out of the question; the rain had long since reduced that combustible of the desert to a liquid pulp.

We had formed our resolution, and were on the point of making a supper of meal steeped in a little cold water, when we saw approaching us two Tartars, leading a small camel. After the usual salutations, one of them said: " Sirs Lamas, this day the heavens have fallen; you, doubtless, have been unable to make a fire." " Alas! how should we make a fire, when we have no argols?" " Men are all brothers, and belong each to the other. But laymen should honor and serve the holy ones; therefore it is that we have come to make a fire for you." The worthy Tartars had seen us setting up our tent, and conceiving our embarrassment, had hastened to relieve it by a present of two bundles of argols. We thanked Providence for this unexpected succor, and the Dchiahour immediately made a fire, and set about the preparation of an oatmeal supper. The quantity was on this occasion augmented in favor of the two friends who had so opportunely presented themselves.

During our modest repast, we noticed that one of these Tartars was the object of especial attention on the part of his comrade. We asked him what military grade he occupied in the Blue Banner. " When the banners of Tchakar marched two years ago against the Rebels of the South,[1] I held the rank of Tchouanda." " What! were you in that famous war of the South? But how is it that you, shepherds of the plains, have also the courage of soldiers? Ac-

[1] The English, then at war with the Chinese, were designated by the Tartars the *Rebels of the South.*

customed to a life of peace, one would imagine that you would never be reconciled to the terrible trade of a soldier which consists in killing others or being killed yourselves." " Yes, yes, we are shepherds, it is true; but we never forget that we are soldiers also, and that the Eight Banners compose the army of reserve of the Grand Master (the Emperor). You know the rule of the Empire; when the enemy appears, they send against them, first—the *Kitat* soldiers; next, the banners of the *Solon* country are set in motion. If the war is not finished then, all they have to do is to give the signal to the banners of the *Tchakar*, the mere sound of whose march always suffices to reduce the rebels to subjection."

The Emperor Tao-Kouang.

"Were all the banners of Tchakar called together for this southern war?" " Yes, all; at first it was thought a small matter, and every one said that it would never affect the Tchakar. The troops of Kitat went first, but they did nothing; the banners of Solon also marched; but they could not bear the heat of the South;—then the Emperor sent us his sacred order. Each man selected his best horse, removed the dust from his bow and quiver, and scraped the rust from his lance. In every tent a sheep was killed for the feast of departure. Women and children wept, but we addressed to them the words of reason. 'Here,' said we, 'for six generations have we received the benefits of the Sacred Master, and he has asked from us nothing in return. Now that he has need of us can we hold back? He has given to us the fine region of Tchakar to be a pasture-land for our cattle, and at the same time a barrier for him against the Khalkhas. But now, since it is from the South the rebels came, we must march to the South. Was not reason in our mouths, Sirs Lamas? Yes, we resolved to march. The Sacred Ordinance reached us at sunrise, and already by noon the *Bochchous* at the head of their men, stood by the *Tchouanda;* next to these were the *Nourou-Tchayn*, and then the *Ougourda*. The same day we marched to Peking; from Peking they led us to Tien-Tsin-Veï, where we remained for three months." "Did you fight," asked Samdadchiemba; "did you see the enemy?" "No, they did not dare to appear. The Kitat told us everywhere that we were marching upon certain and unavailing death. 'What can you do,' asked they, 'against sea-monsters? They live in the water like fish. When you least expect them, they appear on the surface, and hurl their fire-bombs at you; while, the instant your bow is bent to shoot them, down they dive like frogs.' Then they essayed to frighten us; but we soldiers of the Eight Banners know not fear. Before our departure the great Lamas had opened the Book of Celestial Secrets, and had thence learned that the matter would end well for us. The Emperor had attached to each Tchouanda a Lama learned in medicine, and skilled in all the sacred auguries, who was to cure all the soldiers under him of the diseases of the climate, and to protect us from the magic of the sea-monsters. What then had we to fear? The rebels, hearing that the invincible troops of Tchakar were approaching, were seized with fear, and sought peace. The Sacred Master, of his immense mercy, granted it, and we returned to the care of our flocks."

The narrative of this *Illustrious Sword* was to us full of intense interest. We forgot for a moment the misery of our position amid the desert. We were eager to collect further details of the expedition of the English against China ; but night falling, the two Tartars took their way homeward.

Thus left once more alone, our thoughts became exceedingly sad and somber. We shuddered at the idea so recalled to us of the long night just commencing. How were we to get any sleep ? The interior of the tent was little better than a mud heap ; the great fire we had been keeping up had not half dried our clothes ; it had merely resolved a portion of the water into a thick vapor that steamed about us. The furs, which we used at night by way of mattress, were in a deplorable condition, not a whit better for the purpose than the skin of a drowned cat. In this doleful condition of things, a reflection, full of gentle melancholy, came into our minds, and consoled us ; we remembered that we were the disciples of Him who said, "The foxes have holes, and the birds of the air have nests ; but the Son of Man hath not where to lay his head."

We became so fatigued, after remaining awake the greater part of the night, that sleep conquering us, we fell into a restless doze, seated over the embers of the fire, our arms crossed, and our heads bent forward, in the most uncomfortable position possible.

It was with extreme delight that we hailed the termination of that long and dreary night. At daybreak, the blue, cloudless sky, presaged compensation for the wretchedness of the preceding evening. By and by, the sun rising clear and brilliant, inspired us with hope that our still wet clothes would soon get dry as we proceeded on our way. We speedily made all preparations for departure, and the caravan set forth. The weather was magnificent. By degrees, the large grass of the prairie raised its broad head, which had been depressed by the heavy rain ; the ground became firmer, and we experienced, with delight, the gentle heat of the sun's ascending rays. At last, to complete our satisfaction, we entered upon the plains of the Red Banner, the most picturesque of the whole Tchakar.

Tchakar signifies, in the Mongol tongue, *Border Land*. This country is limited, on the east by the kingdom of *Gechekten*, on the west by *Western Toumet*, on the north by the *Souniot*, on the south by the Great Wall. Its extent is 150 leagues long, by 100 broad. The inhabitants of the *Tchakar* are all paid soldiers of the Emperor. The foot soldiers receive twelve ounces of silver per annum, and the cavalry twenty-four.

The *Tchakar* is divided into eight banners—in Chinese *Pa-Ki*—distinguished by the name of eight colors : white, blue, red, yellow, French white, light blue, pink, and light yellow. Each banner has its separate territory, and a tribunal, named *Nourou-Tchayn*, having jurisdiction over all the matters that may occur in the Banner. Besides this tribunal, there is, in each of the Eight Banners, a chief called *Ou-Gourdha*. Of the eight *Ou-Gourdhas* one is selected to fill at the same time, the post of governor-general of the Eight Banners. All these dignitaries are nominated and paid by the Emperor of China. In fact, the Tchakar is nothing more or less than a vast camp, occupied by an army of reserve. In order, no doubt, that this army may be at all times ready to march at the first signal, the Tartars are severely prohibited to cultivate the land. They must live upon their pay, and upon the produce of their flocks and herds. The entire soil of the Eight Banners is inalienable. It sometimes happens that an individual sells his portion to some Chinese ; but the sale is always declared null and void if it comes in any shape before the tribunals.

It is in these pasturages of the Tchakar that are found the numerous and magnificent herds and flocks of the Emperor, consisting of camels, horses, cattle, and sheep. There are 360 herds of horses alone, each numbering 1200 horses. It is easy from this one detail, to imagine the enormous extent of animals possessed here by the Emperor. A Tartar, decorated with the white button, has charge of each herd. At certain intervals, inspectors-general visit the herds, and if any deficiency in the number is discovered, the chief herdsman has to make it good at his own cost. Notwithstanding this impending penalty, the Tartars do not fail to convert to their own use the wealth of the Sacred Master, by means of a fraudulent exchange. Whenever a Chinese has a broken-winded horse, or a lame ox, he takes it to the imperial herdsman, who, for a trifling consideration, allows him to select what animal he pleases in exchange, from among the imperial herds. Being thus always provided with the actual number of animals, they can benefit by their fraud in perfect security.

Never in more splendid weather had we traversed a more splendid country. The desert is at times horrible, hideous; but it has also its charms—charms all the more intensely appreciated, because they are rare in themselves, and because they would in vain be sought in populated countries. Tartary has an aspect altogether peculiar to itself : there is nothing in the world that at all resembles a Tartar landscape. In civilized countries you find, at every step, populous towns, a rich and varied cultivation, the thousand and one productions of arts and industry, the incessant movements of commerce. You are constantly impelled onwards, carried away, as it were, by some vast whirlwind. On the other hand, in countries where civilization has not as yet made its way into the light, you ordinarily find nothing but primeval forests in all the pomp of their exuberant and gigantic vegetation. The soul seems crushed beneath a nature all powerful and majestic. There is nothing of the kind in Tartary. There are no towns, no edifices, no arts, no indusrty, no cultivation, no forests ; everywhere it is prairie, sometimes interrupted by immense lakes, by majestic rivers, by rugged and imposing mountains ; sometimes spreading out into vast limitless plains. There, in these verdant solitudes, the bounds of which seem lost in the remote horizon, you might imagine yourself gently rocking on the calm waves of some broad ocean. The aspect of the prairies of Mongolia excites neither joy nor sorrow, but rather a mixture of the two, a sentiment of gentle, religious melancholy, which gradually elevates the soul, without wholly excluding from its contemplation the things of this world ; a sentiment which belongs rather to Heaven than to earth, and which seems in admirable conformity with the nature of intellect served by organs.

You sometimes in Tartary come upon plains more animated than those you have just traversed ; they are those, whither the greater supply of water and the choicest pastures have attracted for a time a number of nomadic families. There you see rising in all directions tents of various dimensions, looking like balloons newly inflated, and just about to take their flight into the air. Children, with a sort of hod at their backs, run about collecting argols, which they pile up in heaps round their respective tents. The matrons look after the calves, make tea in the open air, or prepare milk in various ways ; the men, mounted on fiery horses, and armed with a long pole, gallop about, guiding to the best pastures the great herds of cattle which undulate, in the distance all around, like waves of the sea.

All of a sudden these pictures, so full of animation, disappear, and you see nothing of that which of late was so full of life. Men, tents, herds, all have vanished in the twinkling of an eye. You merely see in the desert heaps of embers, half-extinguished fires, and a few bones, of which birds of prey are disputing the possession. Such are the sole vestiges which announce that a Mongol tribe has just passed that way. If you ask the reason of these abrupt migrations, it is simply this :—the animals having devoured all the grass that grew in the vicinity, the chief had given the signal for departure ; and all the shepherds, folding their tents, had driven their herds before them, and proceeded, no matter whither, in search of fresh fields and pastures new.

Tartar Encampment.

After having journeyed the entire day through the delicious prairies of the Red Banner, we halted to encamp for the night in a valley that seemed full of people. We had scarcely alighted, when a number of Tartars approached, and offered their services. After having assisted us to unload our camels, and set up our house of blue linen, they invited us to come and take tea in their tents. As it was late, however, we stayed at home, promising to pay them a visit next morning ; for the hospitable invitation of our new neighbors determined us to remain for a day amongst them. We were, moreover, very well pleased to profit by the beauty of the weather, and of the locality, to recover from the fatigues we had undergone the day before.

Next morning, the time not appropriated to our little household cares, and the recitation of our Breviary, was devoted to visiting the Mongol tents, Samdadchiemba being left at home in charge of the tent.

We had to take especial care to the safety of our legs, menaced by a whole host of watchdogs. A small stick sufficed for the purpose; but Tartar etiquette required us to leave these weapons at the threshold of our host's abode. To enter a man's tent with a whip or a stick in your hand is as great an insult as you can offer to the family; and quite tantamount to saying, "You are all dogs."

Visiting amongst the Tartars is a frank, simple affair, altogether exempt from the endless formalities of Chinese gentility. On entering, you give the word of peace *amor* or *mendou*, to the company generally. You then seat yourself on the right of the head of the family, whom you find squatting on the floor, opposite the entrance. Next, everybody takes from a purse suspended at his girdle a little snuff-bottle, and mutual pinches accompany such phrases as these : "Is the pasturage with you rich and abundant?" "Are your herds in fine condition?" "Are your mares productive?" "Did you travel in peace?" "Does tranquillity prevail?" and so on. These questions and their answers being interchanged always with intense gravity on both sides, the mistress of the tent, without saying a word, holds out her hand to the visitor. He as silently takes from his breast-pocket the small wooden bowl, the indispensable *vade mecum* of all Tartars, and presents it to his hostess, who fills it with tea and milk, and returns it. In the richer, more easily circumstanced families, visitors have a small table placed before them, on which is butter, oatmeal, grated millet, and bits of cheese, separately contained in little boxes of polished wood. These Tartar delicacies the visitors take mixed with their tea. Such as propose to treat their guests in a style of perfect magnificence make them partakers of a bottle of Mongol wine, warmed in the ashes. This wine is nothing more than skimmed milk, subjected for awhile to vinous fermentation, and distilled through a rude apparatus that does the office of an alembic. One must be a thorough Tartar to relish or even endure this beverage, the flavor and odor of which are alike insipid.

The Mongol tent, for about three feet from the ground, is cylindrical in form. It then becomes conical, like a pointed hat. The woodwork of the tent is composed below of a trellis-work of crossed bars, which fold up and expand at pleasure. Above these, a circle of poles, fixed in the trellis-work, meets at the top, like the sticks of an umbrella. Over the woodwork is stretched, once or twice, a thick covering of coarse linen, and thus the tent is composed. The door, which is always a folding door, is low and narrow. A beam crosses it at the bottom by way of threshold, so that on entering you have at once to raise your feet and lower your head. Besides the door there is another opening at the top of the tent to let out the smoke. This opening can at any time be closed with a piece of felt fastened above it in the tent, and which can be pulled over it by means of a string, the end of which hangs by the door.

The interior is divided into two compartments; that on the left, as you enter, is reserved for the men, and thither the visitors proceed. Any man who should enter on the right side would be considered excessively rude. The right compartment is occupied by the women, and there you find the culinary utensils: large earthen vessels of glazed earth, wherein to keep the store of water; trunks of trees, of different sizes, hollowed into the shape of pails, and destined to contain the preparations of milk, in the various forms which they make it undergo. In the center of the tent is a large trivet, planted in the earth, and always ready to receive the large iron bell-shaped caldron that stands by, ready for use.

Behind the hearth, and facing the door, is a kind of sofa, the most singular piece of furniture that we met with among the Tartars. At the two ends are two pillows, having at their extremity plates of copper, gilt, and skilfully engraved. There is probably not a single tent where you do not find this little couch, which seems to be an essential article of

Interior of a Tartar Tent.

furniture; but strange to say, during our long journey we never saw one of them which seemed to have been recently made. We had occasion to visit Mongol families, where everything bore the mark of easy circumstances, even of affluence, but everywhere alike this singular couch was shabby, and of ancient fabric. But yet it seems made to last forever, and is regularly transmitted from generation to generation.

In the towns where Tartar commerce is carried on, you may hunt through every furniture shop, every broker's, every pawnbroker's, but you meet with not one of these pieces of furniture, new or old.

At the side of the couch, towards the men's quarter, there is ordinarily a small square press, which contains the various odds and ends that serve to set off the custom of this simple people. This chest serves likewise as an altar for a small image of Buddha. The divinity, in wood or copper, is usually in a sitting posture, the legs crossed, and enveloped up to the neck in a scarf of old yellow silk. Nine copper vases, of the size and form of our liquor glasses, are symmetrically arranged before Buddha. It is in these small chalices that the Tartars daily make to their idol offerings of water, milk, butter and meal. A few Thibetian books, wrapped in yellow silk, perfect the decoration of the little pagoda. Those whose heads are shaved, and who observe celibacy, have alone the privilege of touching these prayer-books. A layman, who should venture to take them into his impure and profane hands, would commit a sacrilege.

A number of goats' horns, fixed in the woodwork of the tent, complete the furniture of the Mongol habitation. On these hang the joints of beef or mutton destined for the family's use, vessels filled with butter, bows, arrows, and matchlocks; for there is scarcely a Tartar family which does not possess at least one fire-arm. We were, therefore, surprised to find M. Timkouski, in his Journey to Peking,[1] making this strange statement: "The sound of our fire-arms attracted the attention of the Mongols, who are acquainted only with bows and arrows." The Russian writer should have known that fire-arms are not so foreign to the Tartars as he imagined; since it is proved that already, as early as the commencement of the 13th century, *Tcheng-Kis-Khan* had artillery in his armies.

The odor pervading the interior of the Mongol tents, is, to those not accustomed to it, disgusting and almost insupportable. This smell, so potent sometimes that it seems to make one's heart rise to one's throat, is occasioned by the mutton grease and butter with which everything on or about a Tartar is impregnated. It is on account of this habitual filth, that they are called *Tsao-Ta-Dze* (Stinking Tartars), by the Chinese, themselves not altogether inodorous, or by any means particular about cleanliness.

Among the Tartars, household and family cares rest entirely upon the woman; it is she who milks the cows, and prepares the butter, cheese, etc.; who goes, no matter how far, to draw water; who collects the argol fuel, dries it, and piles it around the tent. The making of clothes, the tanning of skins, the fulling of cloth, all appertains to her; the sole assistance she obtains, in these various labors, being that of her sons, and then only while they are quite young.

The occupations of the men are of very limited range; they consist wholly in conducting the flocks and herds to

---

[1] "Voyage à Peking, à travers la Mongolie, par M. G. Timkouski," chap. ii., p. 57.

pasture. This for men accustomed from their infancy to horseback is rather an amusement than a labor. In point of fact, the nearest approach to fatigue they ever incur, is when some of their cattle escape; they then dash off at full gallop, in pursuit, up hill and down dale, until they have found the missing animals, and brought them back to the herd. The Tartars sometimes hunt; but it is rather with a view to what they can catch than from any amusement they derive from the exercise; the only occasions on which they go out with their bows and matchlocks are when they desire to shoot roebucks, deer, or pheasants, as presents for their chiefs. Foxes they always course. To shoot them, or take them in traps, would, they consider, injure the skin, which is held in high estimation among them. They ridicule the Chinese immensely on account of their trapping these animals at night. "We," said a famous hunter of the Red Banner to us, "set about the thing in an honest straightforward way. When we see a fox, we jump on horseback, and gallop after him till we have run him down."

With the exception of their equestrian exercises, the Mongol Tartars pass their time in an absolute *far niente*, sleeping all night, and squatting all day in their tents, dozing, drinking tea, or smoking. At intervals, however, the Tartar conceives a fancy to take a lounge abroad; and his lounge is somewhat different from that of the Parisian idler; he needs neither cane nor quizzing glass; but when the fancy occurs, he takes down his whip from its place above the door, mounts his horse, always ready saddled outside the door, and dashes off into the desert, no matter whither. When he sees another horseman in the distance, he rides up to him; when he sees the smoke of a tent, he rides up to that; the only object in either case being to have a chat with some new person.

The two days we passed in these fine plains of the *Tchakar*, were not without good use. We were able at leisure to dry and repair our clothes and our baggage; but, above all, it gave us an opportunity to study the Tartars close at hand, and to initiate ourselves in the habits of the nomad peoples. As we were making preparations for departure, these temporary neighbors aided us to fold our tent and to load our camels. "Sirs Lamas," said they, "you had better encamp to night at the Three Lakes; the pasturage there is good and abundant. If you make haste you will reach the place before sunset. On this side, and on the other side of the Three Lakes, there is no water for a considerable distance. Sirs Lamas, a good journey to you!" "Peace be with you, and farewell!" responded we, and with that proceeded once more on our way, Samdadchiemba heading the caravan, mounted on his little black mule. We quitted this encampment without regret, just as we had quitted preceding encampments; except indeed, that here we left, on the spot where our tent had stood, a greater heap of ashes, and that the grass around it was more trodden than was usual with us.

During the morning the weather was magnificent, though somewhat cold. But in the afternoon the north wind rose, and began to blow with extreme violence. It soon became so cutting, that we regretted we had not with us our great fur caps, to operate as a protector for the face. We hurried on, in order the sooner to reach the Three Lakes, and to have the shelter there of our dear tent. In the hope of discovering these lakes, that had been promised us by our late friends, we were constantly looking right and left, but in vain. It grew late, and, according to the information of the Tartars, we began to fear we must have passed the only encampment we were likely to find that day. By dint of straining our eyes, we at length got sight of a horseman, slowly riding along the bottom of a lateral valley. He was at some distance from us; but it was essential that we should obtain information from him. M. Gabet accordingly hastened after him, at the utmost speed of his tall camel's long legs. The horseman heard the cries of the camel, looked back, and seeing that some one was approaching him, turned his horse round, and galloped towards M. Gabet. As soon as he got within earshot: "Holy personage," cried he, "has your eye perceived the yellow goats? I have lost all traces of them." "I have not seen the yellow goats; I seek water, and cannot find it. Is it far hence?" "Whence came you? Whither go you?" "I belong to the little caravan you see yonder. We have been told that we should this evening on our way, find lakes, upon the banks of which we could commodiously encamp; but hitherto we have seen nothing of the kind." "How could that be? 'Tis but a few minutes ago you passed within a few yards of the water. Sir Lama, permit me to attend your shadow; I will guide you to the Three Lakes." And so saying, he gave his horse three swinging lashes with his whip, in order to put it into a pace commensurate with that of the camel. In a minute he had joined us. "Men of prayer," said the hunter, "you have come somewhat too far; you must turn back. Look" (pointing with his bow) "yonder; you see those storks hovering over some reeds: there you will find the Three Lakes." "Thanks, brother," said we; "we regret that we cannot show you your yellow goats as clearly as you have shown us the Three Lakes." The Mongol hunter saluted us, with his clasped hands raised to his forehead, and we proceeded with entire confidence towards the spot he had pointed out. We had advanced but a few paces before we found indications of the near presence of some peculiar waters. The grass was less continuous and less green, and cracked under our animals' hoofs like dried leaves; the white efflorescence of saltpetre manifested itself more and more thickly. At last we found ourselves on the bank of one lake, near which were two others. We immediately alighted, and set about erecting our tent; but the wind was so violent that it was only after long labor and much patience that we completed the task.

While Samdadchiemba was boiling our tea, we amused ourselves with watching the camels as they luxuriously licked up the saltpetre with which the ground was powdered. Next they bent over the edge of the lake, and inhaled long, insatiable draughts of the brackish water, which we could see ascending their long necks as up some flexible pump.

We had been for some time occupied in this not unpicturesque recreation, when, all of a sudden, we heard behind us a confused, tumultuous noise, resembling the vehement flapping of sails, beaten about by contrary and violent winds. Soon we distinguished, amid the uproar, loud cries proceeding from Samdadchiemba. We hastened towards him, and were just in time to prevent, by our cooperation, the typhoon from uprooting and carrying off our linen *louvre*. Since our arrival, the wind, augmenting in violence, had also changed its direction; so that it now blew exactly from the quarter facing which we had placed the opening of our tent. We had especial occasion to fear that the tent would be set on fire by the lighted argols that were driven about by the wind. Our first business therefore was to tack about; and after a while we succeeded in making our tent secure, and so got off with our fear and a little fatigue. The misadventure, however, put Samdadchiemba into a desperately bad humor throughout the evening; for the wind, by extinguishing the fire, delayed the preparation of his darling tea.

The wind fell as the night advanced, and by degrees the weather became magnificent; the sky was clear, the moon full and bright, and the stars glittered like diamonds. Alone, in this vast solitude, we distinguished in the distance only the fantastic and indistinct outline of the mountains which loomed in the horizon like gigantic phantoms, while the only sound we heard was the cries of the thousand aquatic birds, as, on the surface of the lakes, they contended for the ends of the reeds and the broad leaves of the water-lily. Samdadchiemba was by no means a person to appreciate the charms of this tranquil scene. He had succeeded in again lighting the fire, and was absorbed in the preparation of his tea. We accordingly left him squatted before the kettle, and went to recite the service, walking round the larger lake, which was nearly half a league in circuit. We had proceeded about half round it, praying alternately, when insensibly our voices fell, and our steps were stayed. We both stopped spontaneously, and listened intently, without venturing to interchange a word, and even endeavoring to suppress our respiration. At last we expressed to each other the cause of our mutual terror, but it was in tones low and full of emotion: "Did you not hear, just now, and quite close to us, what seemed the voices of men?" "Yes, a number of voices, speaking as though in secret consultation." "Yet we are alone here: —'tis very surprising. Hist! let us listen again." "I hear nothing; doubtless we were under some illusion." We resumed our walk, and the recitation of our prayers. But we had not advanced ten steps, before we again stopped; for we heard, and very distinctly, the noise which had before alarmed us, and which seemed the confused vague murmur of several voices discussing some point in under tones. Yet nothing was visible. We got upon a hillock, and thence, by the moon's light, saw, at a short distance, some human forms moving in the long grass. We could hear their voices too, but not distinctly enough to know whether they spoke Chinese or Tartar. We retraced our steps to our tent, as rapidly as was consistent with the maintenance of silence; for we took these people to be robbers, who, having perceived our tent, were deliberating as to the best means of pillaging us.

"We are not in safety here," said we to Samdadchiemba; "we have discovered, quite close to us, a number of men, and we have heard their voices. Go and collect the animals, and bring them to the tent." "But," asked Samdadchiemba, knitting his brows, "if the robbers come, what shall we do? May we fight them? May we kill them? Will Holy Church permit that?" "First go and collect the animals; afterwards we will tell you what we must do." The animals being brought together, and fastened outside the tent, we directed our intrepid Samdadchiemba to finish his tea, and we returned on tiptoe to the spot where we had seen and heard our mysterious visitors. We looked around in every direction, with eye and ear intent; but we could neither see nor hear any one. A well-trodden pathway, however, which we discovered among the reeds of tall grass on the margin of the greater lake, indicated to us that those whom we had taken to be robbers were inoffensive passengers, whose route lay in that direction. We returned joyfully to our tent, where we found our valorous Samdadchiemba actively employed in sharpening, upon the top of his leather boots, a great Russian cutlass, which he had purchased at *Tolon-Noor.* "Well," exclaimed he, fiercely, trying with his thumb the edge of his sword, "where are the robbers?" "There are no robbers; unroll the goatskins, that we may go to sleep." "'Tis a pity there are no robbers; for here is something that would have cut into them famously!" "Ay, ay, Samdadchiemba, you are wonderfully brave now, because you know there are no robbers." "Oh, my spiritual fathers, it is not so; one should always speak the words of candor. I admit that my memory is very bad, and that I have never been able to learn many prayers; but as to courage, I may boast of having as much of it as another." We laughed at this singularly expressed sally. "You laugh, my spiritual fathers," said Samdadchiemba. "Oh, you do not know the Dchiahours. In the west, the land of *San-Tchouan* (Three Valleys) enjoys much renown. My countrymen hold life in little value; they have always a saber by their side, and a long matchlock on their shoulder. For a word, for a look, they fight and kill one another. A Dchiahour, who has never killed any one, is considered to have no right to hold his head up among his countrymen. He cannot pretend to the character of a brave man." "Very fine! Well, you are a brave man, you say: tell us how many men did you kill when you were in the Three Valleys?" Samdadchiemba seemed somewhat disconcerted by this question; he looked away, and broke out into a forced laugh. At last, by way of diverting the subject, he plunged his cup into the kettle, and drew it out full of tea. "Come," said we, "drink your tea, and then tell us about your exploits."

Samdadchiemba wiped his cup with the skirt of his jacket, and having replaced it in his bosom, addressed us gravely, thus: "My spiritual fathers, since you desire I should speak to you about myself, I will do so; it was a great sin I committed, but I think Jehovah pardoned me when I entered the holy Church.

"I was quite a child, not more, at the utmost, than seven years old. I was in the fields about my father's house, tending an old she-donkey, the only animal we possessed. One of my companions, a boy about my own age, came to play with me. We began quarreling, and from words fell to blows. I struck him on the head with a great root of a tree that I had in my hand, and the blow was so heavy that he fell motionless at my feet. When I saw my companion stretched on the earth, I stood for a moment as it were paralyzed, not knowing what to think or to do. Then an awful fear came over me, that I should be seized and killed. I looked all about me in search of a hole wherein I might conceal my companion, but I saw nothing of the kind. I then thought of hiding myself. At a short distance from our house there was a great pile of brushwood, collected for fuel. I directed my steps thither, and with great labor made a hole, into which, after desperately scratching myself, I managed to creep up to my neck, resolved never to come out of it.

"When night fell, I found they were seeking me. My mother was calling me in all directions; but I took good care not to answer. I was even anxious not to move the brushwood, lest the sound should lead to my discovery, and, as I anticipated, to my being killed. I was terribly frightened when I heard a number of people crying out and disputing, I concluded, about me. The night passed away; in the morning I felt devouringly hungry. I began to cry; but I could not even cry at my ease, for I feared to be discovered by the people whom I heard moving about, and I was resolved never to quit the brushwood."—"But were you not afraid you should die of hunger?"—"The idea never occurred to me; I felt hungry indeed, but that was all. The reason I had for concealing myself was that I might not die; for I thought that if they did not find me, of course they could not kill me."—"Well, and how long did you remain in the brushwood?"—"Well, I have often heard people say that you can't remain long without eating; but those who say so, never tried the experiment. I can answer for it, that a boy of seven years old can live, at all events, three days and four nights without eating anything whatever.

"After the fourth night, early in the morning, they found me in my hole. When I felt they were taking me out, I struggled as well as I could and endeavored to get away. My father took me by the arm. I cried and sobbed, 'Do not kill me, do not kill me,' cried I; 'it was not I who killed *Nasamboyan*.' They carried me to the house, for I would not walk. While I wept, in utter despair, the people about me laughed. At last they told me not to be afraid, for that Nasamboyan was not dead, and soon afterwards Nasamboyan came into the room as well as ever, only that he had a great bruise on his face. The blow I had struck him had merely knocked him down, and stunned him."

When the Dchiahour had finished this narrative, he looked at us in turns, laughing and repeating, again and again, "Who will say people cannot live without eating?" "Well," said we, "this is a very good beginning, Samdadchiemba; but you have not told us yet how many men you have killed." "I never killed any one; but that was merely because I did not stay long enough in my native Three Valleys; for at the age of ten they put me into a great Lamasery. I had for my especial master a very rough cross man, who gave me the strap every day, because I could not repeat the prayers he taught me. But it was to no purpose he beat me; I could learn nothing: so he left off teaching me, and sent me out to fetch water and collect fuel. But he continued to thrash me as hard as ever, until the life I led became quite insupportable, and at last I ran off with some provisions, and made my way towards Tartary. After walking several days, haphazard, and perfectly ignorant where I was, I encountered the train of a Grand Lama who was repairing to Peking. I joined the caravan, and was employed to take charge of a flock of sheep that accompanied the party, and served for its food. There was no room for me in any of the tents, so I had to sleep in the open air. One evening I took up my quarters behind a rock, which sheltered me from the wind. In the morning, waking somewhat later than usual, I found the encampment struck, and the people all gone. I was left alone in the desert. At this time I knew nothing about east, west, north, or south; I had consequently no resource but to wander on at random, until I should find some Tartar station. I lived in this way for three years—now here, now there, exchanging such slight services as I could render for my food and tent-room. At last I reached Peking and presented myself at the gate of the Great Lamasery of *Hoang-Sse*, which is entirely composed of Dchiahour and Thibetian Lamas. I was at once admitted, and my countrymen having clubbed together to buy me a red scarf and a yellow cap, I was enabled to join the chorus in the recitation of prayers, and, of consequence, to claim my share in the distribution of alms."—We interrupted Samdadchiemba at this point, in order to learn from him how he could take part in the recitation of prayers, without having learned either to read or pray.—"Oh," said he, "the thing was easy enough. They gave me an old book; I held it on my knees, and mumbling out some gibberish between my lips, endeavored to catch the tone of my neighbours. When they turned over a leaf, I turned over a leaf; so that, altogether, there was no reason why the leader of the chorus should take any notice of my maneuver.

"One day, however, a circumstance occurred that very

nearly occasioned my expulsion from the Lamasery. An ill-natured Lama, who had remarked my method of reciting the prayers, used to amuse himself with mocking me, and creating a laugh at my expense. When the Emperor's mother died, we were all invited to the *Yellow Palace* to recite prayers. Before the ceremony commenced, I was sitting quietly in my place, with my book on my knees, when this roguish fellow came gently behind me, and looking over my shoulder mumbled out something or other in imitation of my manner. Losing all self-possession, I gave him so hard a blow upon the face, that he fell on his back. The incident excited great confusion in the *Yellow Palace*. The superiors were informed of the matter, and by the severe rules of Thibetian discipline, I was liable to be flogged for three days with the black whip, and then my hands and feet in irons, to be imprisoned for a year in the tower of the Lamasery. One of the principals, however, who had taken notice of me before, interposed in my favor. He went to the Lamas who constituted the council of discipline, and represented to them the fact that the disciple who had been struck was a person notorious for annoying his companions, and that I had received extreme provocation from him. He spoke so warmly in my favor that I was pardoned on the mere condition of making an apology. I accordingly placed myself in the way of the Lama whom I had offended : 'Brother,' said I, 'shall we go and drink a cup of tea together?' 'Certainly,' replied he; 'there is no reason why I should not drink a cup of tea with you.' We went out, and entered the first tea-house that presented itself. Seating ourselves at one of the tables in the tea-room, I offered my snuff-bottle to my companion, saying : 'Elder brother, the other day we had a little disagreement; that was not well. You must confess that you were not altogether free from blame. I, on my part, admit that I dealt too heavy a blow. But the matter has grown old; we will think no more about it.' We then drank our tea, interchanged various civilities, and so the thing ended."

These and similar anecdotes of our Dchiahour had carried us far into the night. The camels, indeed, were already up and browsing their breakfast on the banks of the lake. We had but brief time before us for repose. "For my part," said Samdadchiemba, "I will not lie down at all, but look after the camels. Day will soon break. Meantime I'll make a good fire, and prepare the *pan-tan*."

It was not long before Samdadchiemba roused us with the intimation that the sun was up, and the *pan-tan* ready. We at once rose, and after eating a cup of *pan-tan*, or, in other words, of oatmeal diluted with boiling water, we planted our little cross upon a hillock, and proceeded upon our pilgrimage.

It was past noon when we came to a place where three wells had been dug, at short distances, the one from the other. Although it was early in the day, we still thought we had better encamp here. A vast plain, on which we could discern no sort of habitation, stretched out before us to the distant horizon; and we might fairly conclude it destitute of water, since the Tartars had taken the trouble to dig these wells. We therefore set up our tent. We soon found, however, that we had selected a detestable encampment. With excessive nastiness of very brackish and very fetid water was combined extreme scarcity of fuel. We looked about for argols, but in vain. At last Samdadchiemba, whose eyes were better than ours, discerned in the distance a sort of enclosure, in which he concluded that cattle had been folded. He took a camel with him to the place in the hope of finding plenty of argols there, and he certainly returned with an ample supply of the article; but unfortunately the precious manure-fuel was not quite dry; it absolutely refused to burn. The Dchiahour essayed an experiment. He hollowed out a sort of furnace in the ground, surmounting it with a turf chimney. The structure was extremely picturesque, but it labored under the enormous disadvantage of being wholly useless. Samdadchiemba arranged and rearranged his fuel, and puffed, and puffed, with the full force of his potent lungs. It was all lost labor. There was smoke enough, and to spare; we were enveloped in smoke, but not a spark of fire: and the water in the kettle remained relentlessly passive. It was obvious that to boil our tea or heat oatmeal was out of the question. Yet we were anxious, at all events, to take the chill off the water, so as to disguise, by the warmth, its brackish flavor and its disagreeable smell. We adopted this expedient.

You meet in the plains of Mongolia with a sort of gray squirrel, living in holes like rats. These animals construct, over the opening of their little dens, a sort of miniature dome, composed of grass, artistically twisted, and designed as a shelter from wind and rain. These little heaps of dry grass are of the form and size of mole-hills. The place where we had now set up our tent abounded with these gray squirrels. Thirst made us cruel, and we proceeded to level the house-domes of these poor little animals, which retreated into their holes below as we approached them. By means of this vandalism we managed to collect a sackful of efficient fuel, and so warmed the water of the well, which was our only aliment during the day.

Our provisions had materially diminished, notwithstanding the economy to which the want of fire on this and other occasions had reduced us. There remained very little meal or millet in our store bags, when we learned, from a Tartar whom we met on the way, that we were at no great distance from a trading station called *Chaborté* (Slough). It lay, indeed, somewhat out of the route we were pursuing; but there was no other place at which we could supply ourselves with provisions, until we came to Blue-Town, from which we were distant a hundred leagues. We turned therefore obliquely to the left, and soon reached Chaborté.

Russian Convent at Peking.

CHAPTER III.

Festival of the Loaves of the Moon—Entertainment in a Mongol tent—*Toolholos*, or Rhapsodists of Tartary—Invocation to Timour—Tartar Education—Industry of the Women.—Mongols in quest of missing animals—Remains of an abandoned City—Road from Peking to Kiaktha—Commerce between China and Russia—Russian Convent at Peking—A Tartar solicits us to cure his mother from a dangerous Illness—Tartar Physicians—The intermittent Fever Devil—Various forms of Sepulture in use among the Mongols—Lamasery of the Five Towers—Obsequies of the Tartar Kings—Origin of the kingdom of Efe—Gymnastic Exercises of the Tartars—Encounter with three Wolves—Mongol Carts.

We arrived at Chaborté on the fifteenth day of the eighth moon, the anniversary of great rejoicings among the Chinese. This festival, known as the *Yué Ping* (Loaves of the Moon), dates from the remotest antiquity. Its original purpose was to honor the moon with superstitious rites. On this solemn day, all labor is suspended; the workmen receive from their employers a present of money; every person puts on his best clothes; and there is merrymaking in every family. Relations and friends interchange cakes of varous sizes, on which is stamped the image of the moon; that is to say, a hare crouching amid a small group of trees.

Since the fourteenth century, this festival has borne a

political character, little understood, apparently, by the Mongols; but the tradition of which is carefully preserved by the Chinese. About the year 1368, the Chinese were desirous of shaking off the yoke of the Tartar dynasty, founded by Tcheng-Kis-Khan, and which had then swayed the empire for nearly a hundred years. A vast conspiracy was formed throughout all the provinces, which was simultaneously to develop itself, on the 15th day of the eighth moon, by the massacre of the Mongol soldiers, who were billeted upon each Chinese family, for the double purpose of maintaining themselves and their conquest. The signal was given by a letter concealed in the cakes which, as we have stated, are on that day, mutually interchanged throughout the country. The massacre was effected, and the Tartar army dispersed in the houses of the Chinese, utterly annihilated. This catastrophe put an end to the Mongol domination; and ever since, the Chinese, in celebrating the festival of *Yué-Ping*, have been less intent upon the superstitious worship of the moon, than upon the tragic event to to which they owed the recovery of their national independence.

The Mongols seem to have entirely lost all memory of the sanguinary revolution; for every year they take their full part in the festival of the Loaves of the Moon, and thus celebrate, without apparently knowing it, the triumph which their enemies heretofore gained over their ancestors.

At a gunshot from the place where we were encamped, we perceived several Mongol tents, the size and character of which indicated easiness of circumstances in the proprietors. This indication was confirmed by the large herds of cattle, sheep, and horses, which were pasturing around. While we were reciting the Breviary in our tent, Samdadchiemba went to pay a visit to these Mongols. Soon afterwards, we saw approaching an old man with a long white beard, and whose features bespoke him a personage of disstinction. He was accompanied by a young Lama, and by a little boy who held his hand. "Sirs Lamas," said the old man, "all men are brothers: but they who dwell in tents are united one with another as flesh with bone. Sirs Lamas, will you come and seat yourselves, for a while, in my poor abode? The fifteenth of this moon is a solemn epoch; you are strangers and travelers, and therefore cannot this evening occupy your places at the hearth of your own noble family. Come and repose for a few days with us; your presence will bring us peace and happiness." We told the good old man that we could not wholly accept his offer, but that, in the evening, after prayers, we would come and take tea with him, and converse for a while about the Mongol nation. The venerable Tartar hereupon took his leave; but he had not been gone long, before the young Lama who had accompanied him returned, and told us that his people were awaiting our presence. We felt that we could not refuse at once to comply with an invitation so full of frank cordiality, and accordingly, having directed our Dchiahour to take good care of the tent, we followed the young Lama who had come in quest of us.

Upon entering the Mongol tent, we were struck and astonished at finding a cleanliness one is little accustomed to see in Tartary. There was not the ordinary coarse fireplace in the center, and the eye was not offended with the rude dirty kitchen utensils which generally encumber Tartar habitations. It was obvious, besides, that everything had been prepared for a festival. We seated ourselves upon a large red carpet; and there was almost immediately brought to us, from the adjacent tent, which served as a kitchen, some tea with milk, some small loaves fried in butter; cheese, raisins, and jujubs.

After having been introduced to the numerous Mongols by whom we found ourselves surrounded, the conversation insensibly turned upon the festival of the Loaves of the Moon. "In our Western Land," said we, "this festival is unknown; men there adore only Jehovah, the Creator of the heavens, and of the earth, of the sun, of the moon, and of all that exists." "Oh, what a holy doctrine!" exclaimed the old man, raising his clasped hands to his forehead; "the Tartars themselves, for that matter, do not worship the moon; but seeing that the Chinese celebrate this festival, they follow the custom without very well knowing why." —"You say truly; you do not, indeed, know why you celebrate this festival. That is what we heard in the land of the *Kitat* (Chinese). But do you know why the Kitat celebrate it?" and thereupon we related to these Mongols what we knew of the terrible massacre of their ancestors. Upon the completion of our narrative, we saw the faces of all our audience full of astonishment. The young men whispered to one another; the old man preserved a mournful silence; his head bent down, and big tears flowing from his eyes. "Brother rich in years," said we, "this story does not seem to surprise you as it does your young men, but it fills your heart with emotion."—" Holy personages," replied the elder, raising his head, and wiping away the tears with the back of his hand, "the terrible event which occasions such consternation in the minds of my young men was not unknown to me, but I would I had never heard of it, and I always struggle against its recollection, for it brings the hot blood into the forehead of every Tartar, whose heart is not sold to the Kitat. A day known to our great Lamas will come, when the blood of our fathers, so shamefully assassinated, will at length be avenged. When the holy man who is to lead us to vengeance shall appear, every one of us will rise and follow in his train; then we shall march, in the face of day, and require from the Kitat an account of the Tartar blood which they shed in the silence and dark secrecy of their houses. The Mongols celebrate every year this festival, most of them seeing in it merely an indifferent ceremony; but the Loaves of the Moon-day ever recalls, in the hearts of a few amongst us, the memory of the treachery to which our fathers fell victims, and the hope of just vengeance."

After a brief silence, the old man went on: "Holy personages, whatever may be the associations of this day, in other respects it is truly a festival for us, since you have deigned to enter our poor habitation. Let us not further occupy our breasts with sad thoughts. Child," said he to a young man seated on the threshold of the tent, "if the mutton is boiled enough, clear away these things." This command having been executed, the eldest son of the family entered, bearing in both hands a small oblong table, on which was a boiled sheep, cut into four quarters, heaped one on the other. The family being assembled round the table, the chief drew a knife from his girdle, severed the sheep's tail, and divided it into two equal pieces, which he placed before us.

With the Tartars, the tail is considered the most delicious portion of their sheep, and accordingly the most honorable. These tails of the Tartarian sheep are of immense size and weight, the fat upon them alone weighing from six to eight pounds.

The fat and juicy tail having thus been offered a homage to the two stranger guests, the rest of the company, knife in hand, attacked the four quarters of the animal, and had speedily, each man, a huge piece before him. Plate or fork there was none, the knees supplied the absence of the one, the hands of the other, the flowing grease being wiped off, from time to time, upon the front of the jacket. Our own embarrassment was extreme. That great white mass of fat had been given to us with the best intentions, but, not quite clear of European prejudices, we could not make up our stomachs to venture, without bread or salt, upon the lumps of tallow that quivered in our hands. We briefly consulted, in our native tongue, as to what on earth was to be done under these distressing circumstances. Furtively, to replace the horrible masses upon the table would be imprudent; openly to express to our Amphytrion our repugnance to this *par excellence* Tartarian delicacy, was impossible, as wholly opposed to Tartar etiquette. We devised this plan: we cut the villainous tail into numerous pieces, and insisted, in that day of general rejoicing, upon the company's partaking with us of this precious dish. There was infinite reluctance to deprive us of the treat; but we persisted, and by degrees got entirely clear of the abominable mess, ourselves rejoicing, instead, in a cut from the leg, the savor of which was more agreeable to our early training. The Homeric repast completed, a heap of polished bones alone remaining to recall it, a boy, taking from the goat's-horn on which it hung a rude three-stringed violin, presented it to the chief, who, in his turn, handed it to a young man of modest mien, whose eyes lighted up as he received the instrument. "Noble and holy travelers," said the chief, " I have invited a Toolholos to embellish this entertainment with some recitations." The minstrel was already preluding with his fingers upon the strings of his instrument. Presently he began to sing, in a strong, emphatic voice, at times interweaving with his verses recitations full of fire and animation. It was interesting to see all those Tartar faces bent towards the minstrel, and accompanying the meaning of his words with the movements of their features. The *Toolholos* selected, for his subjects, national traditions, which warmly excited the feelings of his audience. As to ourselves, very slightly acquainted with the history of Tartary, we took small interest in all those illustrious unknown, whom the Mongol rhapsodist marshaled over the scene.

When he had sung for some time, the old man presented to him a large cup of milk-wine. The minstrel placed his instrument upon his knees, and with evident relish proceeded to moisten his throat, parched with the infinitude of marvels he had been relating. While, having finished his draught, he was licking the brim of his cup: "*Toolholos*," said we, "the songs you have sung were all excellent. But you have as yet said nothing about the Immortal Tamerlane: the 'Invocation to Timour,' we have heard, is a famous song, dear to the Mongols." "Yes, yes," exclaimed several voices at once, "sing us the 'Invocation to Timour.'" There was a moment's silence, and then the Toolholos, having refreshed his memory, sang, in a vigorous and warlike tone, the following strophes:—

"When the divine Timour dwelt within our tents, the Mongol nation was redoubtable and warlike; its least movements made the earth bend; its mere look froze with fear the ten thousand peoples upon whom the sun shines.

"O divine Timour, will thy great soul soon revive?
Return! return! we await thee, O Timour!

"We live in our vast plains, tranquil and peaceful as sheep; yet our hearts are fervent and full of life. The memory of the glorious age of Timour is ever present to our minds. Where is the chief who is to place himself at our head, and render us once more great warriors?

"O divine Timour, will thy great soul soon revive?
Return! return! we await thee, O Timour!

"The young Mongol has arms wherewith to quell the wild horse, eyes wherewith he sees afar off in the desert the traces of the lost camel. Alas! his arms can no longer bend the bow of his ancestors; his eye cannot see the wiles of the enemy.

"O divine Timour, will thy great soul soon revive?
Return! return! we await thee, O Timour!

"We have burned the sweet smelling wood at the feet of the divine Timour, our foreheads bent to the earth; we have offered to him the green leaf of tea and the milk of our herds. We are ready; the Mongols are on foot, O Timour! And do thou, O Lama, send down good fortune upon our arrows and our lances.

"O divine Timour, will thy great soul soon revive?
Return! return! we await thee, O Timour!"

When the Tartar Troubadour had completed this national song, he rose, made a low bow to the company, and, having suspended his instrument upon a wooden pin, took his leave. "Our neighbors," said the old man, "are also keeping the festival, and expect the Toolholos: but, since you seem to listen with interest to Tartar songs, we will offer some other melodies to your notice. We have in our own family a brother who has in his memory a great number of airs, cherished by the Mongols; but he cannot play; he is not a Toolholos. Come, brother Nymbo, sing; you have not got Lamas of the West to listen to you every day."

A Mongol, whom, seated as he was in a corner, we had not before noticed, at once rose, and took the place of the departed *Toolholos*. The appearance of this personage was truly remarkable; his neck was completely buried in his enormous shoulders; his great dull staring eyes contrasted strangely with his dark face half-calcined as it were by the sun; his hair, or rather a coarse uncombed mane, straggling down his back, completed the savageness of his aspect. He began to sing; but his singing was a mere counterfeit, an absurd parody. His grand quality was extreme long-windedness, which enabled him to execute roulades, complicated and continuous enough to throw any rational audience into fits. We soon became desperately tired of his noise, and watched with impatience a moment's cessation, that might give us an opportunity of retiring. But this was no easy matter; the villain divined our thoughts, and was resolved to spite us. No sooner had he finished one air than he dovetailed another into it, and so started afresh. In this way he went on, until it was really quite late in the night. At length he paused for a moment to drink a cup of tea; he threw the beverage down his throat, and was just clearing his throat to commence anew, when we started up, offered to the head of the family a pinch of snuff, and having saluted the rest of the company, withdrew.

You often meet in Tartary these Toolholos, or wandering singers, who go about from tent to tent, celebrating in their melodies national events and personages. They are generally very poor; a violin and a flute, suspended from the girdle, are their only property; but they are always received by the Mongol families with kindness and honor; they often remain in one tent for several days, and on their departure are supplied with cheese, wine, tea, and so on, to support them on their way. These poet-singers, who remind us of the minstrels and rhapsodists of Greece, are also very numerous in China; but they are, probably, nowhere so numerous or so popular as in Thibet.

The day after the festival, the sun had scarcely risen, when a little boy presented himself at the entrance of our tent, carrying in one hand a wooden vessel full of milk, and in the other hand a rude rush basket, in which were some new cheese and some butter. He was followed soon after by an old Lama, attended by a Tartar who had on his shoulder a large bag of fuel. We invited them all to be seated. " Brothers of the West," said the Lama, " accept these trifling presents from my master." We bowed in token of thanks, and Samdadchiemba hastened to prepare some tea, which we pressed the Lama to stay and partake of. " I will come and see you this evening," said he; " but I cannot remain at present; for I have not set my pupil the prayer he has to learn this morning." The pupil in question was the little boy who had brought the milk. The old man then took his pupil by the hand, and they returned together to their tent.

The old Lama was the preceptor of the family, and his function consisted in directing the little boy in the study of the Thibetian prayers. The education of the Tartars is very limited. They who shave the head, the Lamas, are, as a general rule, the only persons who learn to read and pray. There is no such thing throughout the country as a public school. With the exception of a few rich Mongols, who have their children taught at home, all the young Lamas are obliged to resort to the Lamaseries, wherein is concentrated all that exists in Tartary, of arts, or sciences, or intellectual industry. The Lama is not merely a priest; he is the painter, poet, sculptor, architect, physician; the head, heart, and oracle of the laity. The training of the young Mongols, who do not resort to the Lamaseries, is limited, with the men, to perfecting the use of the bow and arrow and matchlock, and to their obtaining a thorough mastery of equestrianism. When a mere infant the Mongol is weaned, and as soon as he is strong enough he is stuck upon a horse's back behind a man, the animal is put to a gallop, and the juvenile rider, in order not to fall off, has to cling with both hands to his teacher's jacket. The Tartars thus become accustomed, from a very early age, to the movements of the horse, and by degrees and the force of habit, they identify themselves, as it were, with the animal.

There is, perhaps, no spectacle more exciting than that of Mongol riders in chase of a wild horse. They are armed with a long, heavy pole, at the end of which is a running knot. They gallop, they fly after the horse they are pursuing down rugged ravines, and up precipitous hills, in and out, twisting and twining in their rapid course, until they come up with their game. They then take the bridle of their own horses in their teeth, seize with both hands their heavy pole, and bending forward throw, by a powerful effort, the running knot round the wild horse's neck. In this exercise the greatest vigor must be combined with the greatest dexterity, in order to enable them to stop short the powerful untamed animals with which they have to deal. It sometimes happens that pole and cord are broken; but as to a horseman being thrown, it is an occurrence we never saw or heard of.

The Mongol is so accustomed to horseback that he is altogether like a fish out of water when he sets foot on the ground. His step is heavy and awkward; and his bowed legs, his chest bent forward, his constant looking around him, all indicate a person who spends the greater portion of his time on the back of a horse or a camel.

When night overtakes the traveling Tartar, it often happens that he will not even take the trouble to alight for the purpose of repose. Ask people whom you meet in the desert where they slept last night, and you will as frequently as not have for answer, in a melancholy tone, "*Temen dero*" (on the camel). It is a singular spectacle to see caravans halting at noon, when they come to a rich pasturage. The camels disperse in all directions, browsing upon the high grass of the prairie, while the Tartars, astride between the two humps of the animal, sleep as profoundly as though they were sheltered in a good bed.

This incessant activity, this constant traveling, contributes to render the Tartars very vigorous, and capable of supporting the most terrible cold without appearing to be in the least affected by it. In the deserts of Tartary, and especially in the country of the Khalkhas, the cold is so intense, that for a considerable portion of the winter the thermometer will not act, on account of the congelation of the mercury. The whole district is often covered with snow; and if at these times the southwest wind blows, the plain wears the aspect of a raging sea. The wind raises the snow in immense waves, and impels the gigantic avalanches vehemently before it. Then the Tartars hurry courageously to the aid of their herds and flocks, and you see them dashing in all directions, exciting the animals by their cries, and driving them to the shelter of some rock or mountain. Sometimes these intrepid shepherds stop short amid the tempest, and stand erect for a time, as if defying the cold and the fury of the elements.

The training of the Tartar women is not more refined than that of the men. They are not, indeed, taught the use of the bow and the matchlock; but in equitation they are as expert and as fearless as the men. Yet it is only on occasions that they mount on horseback; such, for example, as traveling, or when there is no man at home to go in search of a stray animal. As a general rule, they have nothing to do with the care of the herds and flocks.

Their chief occupation is to prepare the family meals, and to make the family clothes. They are perfect mistresses of the needle; it is they who fabricate the hats, boots, coats, and other portions of the Mongol attire. The leather boots, for example, which they make are not indeed very elegant in form, but, on the other hand, their solidity is astonishing.

It was quite unintelligible to us how, with implements so rude and coarse as theirs, they could manufacture articles almost indestructible in their quality. It is true they take their time about them, and get on very slowly with their work. The Tartar women excel in embroidery, which, for taste and variety of pattern and for excellence of manipulation, excited our astonishment. We think we may venture to say, that nowhere in France would you meet with embroidery more beautiful and more perfect in fabric than that we have seen in Tartary.

The Tartars do not use the needle in the same way as the Chinese. In China they impel the needle perpendicularly down and up; whereas the Tartars impel it perpendicularly up and down. In France the manner is different from both; if we recollect right, the French women impel the needle horizontally from right to left. We will not attempt to pronounce as to the respective merit of the three methods; we will leave the point to the decision of the respectable fraternity of tailors.

On the 17th of the moon, we proceeded very early in the morning to the Chinese station of *Chaborté*, for the purpose of laying in a store of meal. *Chaborté*, as its Mongol name intimates, is built upon a slough. The houses are all made of mud, and surrounded each by an enclosure of high walls. The streets are irregular, tortuous, and narrow; the aspect of the whole town is somber and sinister, and the Chinese who inhabit it have, if possible, a more knavish look than their countrymen anywhere else. The trade of the town comprehends all the articles in ordinary use with the Mongols—oatmeal and millet, cotton manufactures, and brick tea, which the Tartars receive in exchange for the products of the desert, salt, mushrooms, and furs. Upon our return, we hastened to prepare for our departure. While we were packing up our baggage in the tent, Samdadchiemba went in search of the animals which had been put to pasture in the vicinity. A moment afterwards he returned with the three camels. "There are the camels," said we, with gloomy anticipation, "but where are the horse and mule; they were both at hand just now, for we tied their legs to prevent their straying." "They are stolen, in all probability. It never does to encamp too near the Chinese, whom everybody knows to be arrant horse stealers." These words came upon us like a clap of thunder. However, it was not a moment for sterile lamentation; it was necessary to go in search of the thieves. We each mounted a camel, and made a circuit in search of the animals, leaving our tent under the charge of Arsalan. Our search being futile, we resolved to proceed to the Mongol encampment, and inform them that the animals had been lost near their habitation.

By a law among the Tartars, when animals are lost from a caravan, the persons occupying the nearest encampment are bound either to find them or to replace them. It seems, no doubt, very strange to European views, that because, without their consent or even knowledge, without being in the smallest degree known to them, you have chosen to pitch your tent near those of a Mongol party, you and your animals, and your baggage are to be under their responsibility; but so it is. If a thing disappears, the law supposes that your next neighbor is the thief, or at all events an accomplice. This it is which has contributed to render the Mongols so skilful in tracking animals. A mere glance at the slight traces left by an animal upon the grass, suffices to inform the Mongol pursuer how long since it passed, and whether or not it bore a rider; and the track once found, they follow it throughout all its meanderings, however complicated.

We had no sooner explained our loss to the Mongol chief, than he said to us cheerfully: "Sirs Lamas, do not permit sorrow to invade your hearts. Your animals cannot be lost; in these plains there are neither robbers nor associates of robbers. I will send in quest of your horses. If we do not find them, you may select what others you please in their place, from our herd. We would have you leave this place as happy as you came to it." While he was speaking eight of his people mounted on horseback, and dashed off in as many directions, upon the quest, each man trailing after him his lasso, attached to the long, flexible pole we have described. After a while they all collected in one body, and galloped away, as hard as they could, towards the town. "They are on the track now, holy sirs," said the chief, "who was watching their movements by our sides, and you will have your horses back very soon. Meanwhile come within my tent, and drink some tea."

In about two hours, a boy appeared at the entrance of the tent, and announced the return of the horsemen. We hastened outside, and in the track which we had pursued saw something amid a cloud of dust which seemed horsemen galloping like the wind. We presently discovered the eight Tartars, dashing along, like so many mad centaurs, our stray animals each held by a lasso, in the midst of them. On their arrival, they alighted, and with an air of satisfaction said: "We told you nothing was ever lost in our country." We thanked the generous Mongols for the great service they had rendered us; and, bidding adieu to them, saddled our horses, and departed on our way to the Blue City.

On the third day we came, in the solitude, upon an imposing and majestic monument of antiquity,—a large city utterly abandoned. Its turreted ramparts, its watch towers, its four great gates, facing the four cardinal points, were all there perfect, in preservation, except that, besides being three-fourths buried in the soil, they were covered with a thick coating of turf. Arrived opposite the southern gate, we directed Samdadchiemba to proceed quietly with the animals, while we paid a visit to the Old Town, as the Tartars designate it. Our impression, as we entered the vast enclosure, was one of mingled awe and sadness. There were no ruins of any sort to be seen, but only the outline of a large and fine town, becoming absorbed below by gradual accumulations of wind-borne soil, and above by a winding-sheet of turf. The arrangement of the streets and the position of the principal edifices, were indicated by the inequalities of ground. The only living things we found here were a young Mongol shepherd, silently smoking his pipe, and the flock of goats he tended. We questioned the former as to when the city was built, by whom, when abandoned, and why? We might as well have interrogated his goats; he knew no more than that the place was called the Old Town.

Such remains of ancient cities are of no unfrequent occurrence in the deserts of Mongolia; but everything connected with their origin and history is buried in darkness. Oh, with what sadness does such a spectacle fill the soul! The ruins of Greece, the superb remains of Egypt,— all these, it is true, tell of death; all belong to the past; yet when you gaze upon them, you know what they are; you can retrace, in memory, the revolutions which have occasioned the ruins and the decay of the country around them. Descend into the tomb, wherein was buried alive the city of Herculaneum,—you find there, it is true, a gigantic skeleton, but you have within you historical associations wherewith to galvanize it. But of these old abandoned cities of Tartary, not a tradition remains; they are tombs without an epitaph, amid solitude and silence, uninterrupted except when the wandering Tartars halt, for a while, within the ruined enclosures, because there the pastures are richer and more abundant.

Although, however, nothing positive can be stated respecting these remains, the probabilities are, that they date no earlier back than the 13th century, the period when the Mongols rendered themselves masters of the Chinese empire, of which they retained possession for more than 100 years. During their domination, say the Chinese annals, they erected in Northern Tartary many large and powerful cities. Towards the middle of the 14th century the Mongol dynasty was expelled from China; the Emperor *Young-Lo*, who desired to exterminate the Tartars, invaded their country, and burned their towns, making no fewer than three expeditions against them into the desert, 200 leagues north of the Great Wall.

After leaving behind us the Old Town, we came to a broad road crossing N. S. that along which we were traveling E. W. This road, the ordinary route of the Russian embassies to Peking, is called by the Tartars *Koutchcon-Dcham* (Road of the Emperor's Daughter), because it was constructed for the passage of a princess, whom one of the Celestial Emperors bestowed upon a King of the Khalkhas. After traversing the *Tchakar* and *Western Souniot*, it enters the country of the *Khalkhas* by the kingdom of *Mourguevan;* thence crossing N. S. the great desert of *Gobi*, it traverses the river *Toula*, near the *Great Couren*, and terminates with the Russian factories at *Kiaktha*.

This town, under a treaty of peace in 1688 between the Emperor *Khang-Hi*, and the *White Khan of the Oros*, i. e. the Czar of Russia, was established as the entrepôt of the trade between the two countries. Its northern portion is occupied by the Russian factories, its southern by the Tartaro-Chinese. The intermediate space is a neutral ground, devoted to the purposes of commerce. The Russians are not permitted to enter the Chinese quarter, nor the Chinese the Russian. The commerce of the town is considerable, and apparently very beneficial to both parties. The Russians bring linen goods, cloths, velvets, soaps, and hardware; the Chinese tea in bricks, of which the Russians use large quantities; and these Chinese tea-bricks being taken in payment of the Russian goods at an easy rate, linen goods are sold in China at a lower rate than even in Europe itself. It is owing to their ignorance of this commerce of Russia with China that speculators at Canton so frequently find no market for their commodities.

Under another treaty of peace between the two powers, signed 14th of June, 1728, by Count Vladislavitch, Ambassador Extraordinary of Russia, on the one part, and by the Minister of the Court of Peking on the other, the Russian government maintains, in the capital of the celestial empire, a monastery, to which is attached a school, wherein a certain number of young Russians qualify themselves as Chinese and Tartar-Mantchou interpreters. Every ten years, the pupils, having completed their studies, return with their spiritual pastors of the monastery to St Petersburg, and are relieved by a new settlement. The little caravan is commanded by a Russian officer, who has it in charge to conduct the new disciples to Peking, and bring back the students and the members who have completed their period. From Kiaktha to Peking the Russians travel at the expense of the Chinese government, and are escorted from station to station by Tartar troops.

M. Timkouski, who in 1820 had charge of the Russian caravan to Peking, tells us, in his account of the journey, that he could never make out why the Chinese guides led him by a different route from that which the preceding ambassadors had pursued. The Tartars explained the matter to us. They said it was a political precaution of the Chinese government, who conceived that, being taken by all sorts of roundabout paths and no-paths, the Russians might be kept from a knowledge of the regular route;—an immensely imbecile precaution, since the Autocrat of all the Russias would not have the slightest difficulty in leading his armies to Peking, should he ever take a fancy to go and beard the Son of Heaven in his celestial seat.

This road to Kiaktha, which we thus came upon unexpectedly amid the deserts of Tartary, created a deep emotion in our hearts: "Here," said we to each other, "here is a road which leads to Europe!" Our native land presented itself before our imagination, and we spontaneously entered upon the road, which connected us with our beloved France. The conversation that rose to our lips from our hearts was so pleasing, that we insensibly advanced. The sight of some Mongol tents, on an adjacent eminence, recalled us to a sense of our position, and at the same moment a loud cry came from a Tartar whom we saw gesticulating in front of the tents. Not understanding the cry to be addressed to us, we turned, and were proceeding on our route when the Tartar, jumping on his horse, galloped after us: upon reaching us, he alighted and knelt before us: "Holy sirs," said he, raising his hands before Heaven, "have pity upon me, and save my mother from death. I know your power is infinite: come and preserve my mother by your prayers." The parable of the good Samaritan came before us, and we felt that charity forbade us to pass on without doing all we could in the matter. We therefore turned once more, in order to encamp near the Tartars.

While Samdadchiemba arranged our tent, we went, without loss of time, to tend the sick woman, whom we found in a very deplorable state. "Inhabitants of the desert," said we to her friends, "we know not the use of simples, we are unacquainted with the secrets of life, but we will pray to Jehovah for this sick person. You have not heard of this Almighty God—your Lamas know him not; but, be assured, Jehovah is the master of life and of death." Circumstances did not permit us to dwell on the theme to these poor people who, absorbed in grief and anxiety, could pay little attention to our words. We returned to our tent to pray, the Tartar accompanying us. When he saw our Breviary; "Are these," asked he, "the all-powerful prayers to Jehovah, of which you spoke?" "Yes," said we; "these are the only true prayers; the only prayers that can save." Thereupon he prostrated himself successively before each of us, touching the ground with his forehead; then he took the Breviary, and raised it to his head in token of respect. During our recitation of the prayers for the sick, the Tartar remained seated at the entrance of the tent, preserving a profound and religious silence. When we had finished, "Holy men," said he, again prostrating himself, "how can I make acknowledgments for your great benefits? I am poor; I can offer you neither horse nor sheep." "Mongol brother," we replied, "the priests of Jehovah may not offer up prayers for the sake of enriching themselves; since thou art not rich, accept from us this trifling gift;" and we presented to him a fragment of a tea-brick. The Tartar was profoundly moved with this proceeding; he could not say a word, his only answer to us was tears of gratitude.

We heard next morning with pleasure that the Tartar woman was much better. We would fain have remained a few days in the place, in order to cultivate the germ of the true faith thus planted in the bosom of this family; but we were compelled to proceed. Some of the Tartars escorted us a short distance on our way.

Medicine in Tartary, as we have already observed, is exclusively practised by the Lamas. When illness attacks any one, his friends run to the nearest monastery for a Lama, whose first proceeding, upon visiting the patient, is to run his fingers over the pulse of both wrists simultaneously, as the fingers of a musician run over the strings of an instrument. The Chinese physicians feel both pulses also, but in succession. After due deliberation, the Lama pronounces his opinion as to the particular nature of the malady. According to the religious belief of the Tartars, all illness is owing to the visitation of a *Tchutgour* or demon; but the expulsion of the demon is first a matter of medicine. The Lama physician next proceeds, as Lama apothecary, to give the specific befitting the case; the Tartar pharmacopœia rejecting all mineral chemistry, the Lama remedies consist entirely of vegetables pulverized, and either infused in water or made up into pills. If the Lama doctor happens not to have any medicine with him, he is by no means disconcerted; he writes the names of the remedies upon little scraps of paper, moistens the papers with his saliva, and rolls them up into pills, which the patient tosses down with the same perfect confidence as though they were genuine medicaments. To swallow the name of a remedy, or the remedy itself, say the Tartars, comes to precisely the same thing.

The medical assault of the usurping demon being applied, the Lama next proceeds to spiritual artillery, in the form of prayers, adapted to the quality of the demon who has to be dislodged. If the patient is poor, the *Tchutgour* visiting him can evidently be only an inferior *Tchutgour*, requiring merely a brief, off-hand prayer, sometimes merely an interjectional exorcism. If the patient is very poor, the Lama troubles himself with neither prayer nor pill, but goes away, recommending the friends to wait with patience until the sick person gets better or dies, according to the decree of *Hormoustha*. But where the patient is rich, the possessor of large flocks, the proceedings are altogether different. First, it is obvious that a devil who presumes to visit so eminent a personage must be a potent devil, one of the chiefs of the lower world; and it would not be decent for a great *Tchutgour* to travel like a mere sprite; the family, accordingly, are directed to prepare for him a handsome suit of clothes, a pair of rich boots, a fine horse, ready saddled and bridled, othewise the devil will never think of going, physic or exorcise him how you may. It is even possible, indeed, that one horse will not suffice, for the demon, in very rich cases, may turn out, upon inquiry, to be so high and mighty a prince, that he has with him a number of courtiers and attendants, all of whom have to be provided with horses.

Everything being arranged, the ceremony commences. The Lama and numerous co-physicians called in from his own and other adjacent monasteries, offer up prayers in the rich man's tents for a week or a fortnight, until they perceive that the devil is gone—that is to say, until they have exhausted all the disposable tea and sheep. If the patient recovers, it is a clear proof that the prayers have been efficaciously recited; if he dies, it is a still greater proof of the efficaciousness of the prayers, for not only is the devil gone, but the patient has transmigrated to a state far better than that he has quitted.

The prayers recited by the Lamas for the recovery of the sick are sometimes accompanied with very dismal and alarming rites. The aunt of Tokoura, chief of an encampment in the Valley of Dark Waters, visited by M. Huc, was seized one evening with an intermittent fever. "I would invite the attendance of the doctor Lama," said Tokoura, "but if he finds that there is a very big *Tchutgour* present, the expenses will ruin me." He waited for some days; but as his aunt grew worse and worse, he at last sent for a Lama; his anticipations were confirmed. The Lama pronounced that a demon of considerable rank was present, and that no time must be lost in expelling him. Eight other Lamas were forthwith called in, who at once set about the construction, in dried herbs, of a great puppet, which they entitled the *Demon of Intermittent Fevers*, and which, when completed, they placed on its legs by means of a stick, in the patient's tent.

The ceremony began at eleven o'clock at night; the Lamas ranged themselves in a semicircle round the upper portion of the tent, with cymbals, sea-shells, bells, tambourines, and other instruments of the noisy Tartar music. The remainder of the circle was completed by the members of the family, squatting on the ground close to one another, the patient kneeling, or rather crouched on her heels, opposite the *Demon of Intermittent Fevers*. The Lama doctor-in-chief had before him a large copper basin filled with millet, and some little images made of paste. The dung-fuel threw, amid much smoke, a fantastic and quivering light over the strange scene.

Upon a given signal, the clerical orchestra executed an overture harsh enough to frighten Satan himself, the lay congregation beating time with their hands to the charivari of clanging instruments and ear-splitting voices. The diabolical concert over, the Grand Lama, opened the Book of Exorcisms, which he rested on his knees. As he chanted one of the forms, he took from the basin, from time to time, a handful of millet, which he threw east, west, north, and south, according to the Rubric. The tones of his voice, as he prayed, were sometimes mournful and suppressed, sometimes vehemently loud and energetic. All of a sudden, he would quit the regular cadence of prayer, and have an outburst of apparently indomitable rage, abusing the herb puppet with fierce invectives and furious gestures. The exorcism terminated, he gave a signal by stretching out his arms, right and left, and the other Lamas struck up a tremendously noisy chorus, in hurried, dashing tones; all the instruments were set to work, and meantime the lay congregation, having started up with one accord, ran out of the tent, one after the other, and tearing round it like mad people, beat it at their hardest with sticks, yelling all the while at the pitch of their voices in a manner to make ordinary hair stand on end. Having thrice performed this demoniac round, they re-entered the tent as precipitately as they had quitted it, and resumed their seats. Then all the others covering their faces with their hands, the Grand Lama rose and set fire to the herb figure. As soon as the flames rose, he uttered a loud cry, which was repeated with interest by the rest of the company. The laity immediately rose, seized the burning figure, carried it into the plain, away from the tents, and there, as it consumed, anathematized it with all sorts of imprecations; the Lamas meantime squatted in the tent, tranquilly chanting their prayers in a grave, solemn tone.

Upon the return of the family from their valorous expedition, the praying was exchanged for joyous felicitations. By and by, each person provided with a lighted torch, the whole party rushed simultaneously from the tent, and formed into a procession, the laymen first, then the patient, supported on either side by a member of the family, and lastly, the nine Lamas, making night hideous with their music. In this style the patient was conducted to another tent, pursuant to the orders of the Lama, who had declared that she must absent herself from her own habitation for an entire month.

After this strange treatment, the malady did not return. The probability is, that the Lamas, having ascertained the precise moment at which the fever-fit would recur, met it at the exact point of time by this tremendous counter-excitement, and overcame it.

Though the majority of the Lamas seek to foster the ignorant credulity of the Tartars, in order to turn it to their own profit, we have met some of them who frankly avowed that duplicity and imposture played considerable part in all their ceremonies. The superior of a Lamasery said to us one day: "When a person is ill, the recitation of prayers is proper, for Buddha is the master of life and death; it is he who rules the transmigration of beings. To take remedies is also fitting, for the great virtue of medicinal herbs also comes to us from Buddha. That the Evil One may possess a rich person is credible, but that, in order to repel the Evil One, the way is to give him dress, and a horse, and what not, this is a fiction invented by ignorant and deceiving Lamas, who desire to accumulate wealth at the expense of their brothers."

The manner of interring the dead among the Tartars is not uniform. The Lamas are only called in to assist at extremely grand funerals. Towards the Great Wall, where the Mongols are mixed up with the Chinese, the custom of the latter in this particular, as in others, has insensibly prevailed. There the corpse is placed, after the Chinese fashion, in a coffin, and the coffin in a grave. In the desert, among the true nomadic tribes, the entire ceremony consists in conveying the dead to the tops of hills or the bottoms of ravines, there to be devoured by the birds and beasts of prey. It is really horrible to travelers through the deserts of Tartary to see, as they constantly do, human remains, for which the eagles and the wolves are contending.

The richer Tartars sometimes burn their dead with great solemnity. A large furnace of earth is constructed in a pyramidical form. Just before it is completed, the body is placed inside, standing, surrounded with combustibles. The edifice is then completely covered in, with the exception of a small hole at the bottom to admit fire, and another at the top, to give egress to the smoke, and keep up a current of air. During the combustion, the Lamas surround the tomb and recite prayers. The corpse being burnt, they demolish the furnace and remove the bones, which they carry to the Grand Lama; he reduces them to a very fine powder, and having added to them an equal quantity of meal, he kneads the whole with care, and constructs, with his own hands, cakes of different sizes, which he places one upon the other, in the form of a pyramid. When the bones have been thus prepared by the Grand Lama, they are transported with great pomp to a little tower built beforehand, in a place indicated by the diviner.

They almost always give to the ashes of the Lamas a sepulture of this description. You meet with a great number of these monumental towers on the summits of the mountains, and in the neighborhood of the Lamaseries; and you may find them in countries whence the Mongols have been driven by the Chinese. In other respects these countries scarcely retain any trace of the Tartars: the Lamaseries, the pasturages, the shepherds, with their tents and flocks, all have disappeared, to make room for new people, new monuments, new customs. A few small towers raised over graves alone remain there, as if to assert the rights of the ancient possessors of these lands, and to protest against the invasion of the Kitat.

The most celebrated seat of Mongol burials is in the province of Chan-Si, at the famous Lamasery of Five Towers (*Ou-Tay*). According to the Tartars, the Lamasery of the Five Towers is the best place you can be buried in. The ground in it is so holy, that those who are so fortunate as to be interred there are certain of a happy transmigration thence. The marvelous sanctity of this place is attributed to the presence of Buddha, who for some centuries past has taken up his abode there in the interior of a mountain. In 1842 the noble Tokoura, of whom we have already had occasion to speak, conveying the bones of his father and mother to the Five Towers, had the infinite happiness to behold there the venerable Buddha. "Behind the great

Lamasery of the Five Towers.

monastery," he told us, "there is a very lofty mountain, which you must climb by creeping on your hands and feet. Just towards the summit you come to a portico cut in the rock: you lie down on the earth, and look through a small aperture not larger than the bowl of a pipe. It is some time before you can distinguish anything, but by degrees your eye gets used to the place, and you have the happiness of beholding, at length, in the depths of the mountain, the face of the ancient Buddha. He is seated cross-legged, doing nothing. There are around him Lamas of all countries, who are continually paying homage to him."

Whatever you may think of Tokura's narrative, it is certain that the Tartars and the Thibetians have given themselves up to an inconceivable degree of fanaticism, in reference to the Lamasery of the Five Towers. You frequently meet, in the deserts of Tartary, Mongols, carrying on their shoulders the bones of their parents, to the Five Towers, to purchase, almost at its weight in gold, a few feet of earth, whereupon they may raise a small mausoleum. Even the Mongols of Torgot perform journeys occupying a whole year and attended with immense difficulty, to visit for this purpose the province of Chan-Si.

The Tartar kings sometimes make use of a sepulture which is the height of extravagance and barbarism. The royal corpse is conveyed to a vast edifice, constructed of bricks, and adorned with numerous statues representing men, lions, elephants, tigers, and various subjects of Buddhic mythology. With the illustrious defunct, they bury in a large cavern, constructed in the center of the building, large sums of gold and silver, royal robes, precious stones, in short, everything which he may need in another life. These monstrous interments sometimes cost the lives of a great number of slaves. They take children of both sexes, remarkable for their beauty, and make them swallow mercury till they are suffocated; in this way they preserve, they say, the freshness and ruddiness of their countenance, so as to make them appear still alive. These unfortunate victims are placed upright, round the corpse of their master, continuing, in this fashion, to serve him as during life. They hold in their hands the pipe, fan, the small phial of snuff, and the numerous other knick-knacks of the Tartar kings.

To protect these buried treasures, they place in the cavern a kind of bow, capable of discharging a number of arrows, one after the other. This bow, or rather these several bows joined together, are all bent, and the arrows ready to fly. They place this infernal machine in such a manner that, on opening the door of the cavern, the movement causes the discharge of the first arrow at the man who enters; the discharge of the first arrow causes the discharge of the second, and so on to the last—so that the unlucky person, whom covetousness or curiosity should induce to open the door, would fall, pierced with many arrows, in the tomb he sought to profane. They sell these murderous machines, ready prepared by the bow-makers. The Chinese sometimes purchase them, to guard their houses in their absence.

After a march of two days, we entered the district called the Kingdom of Efe; it is a portion of the territory of the Eight Banners, which the Emperor Kin-Loug dismembered in favor of a prince of the Khalkhas. *Sun Tché*, founder of the Mantchou dynasty, laid down this maxim: "In the south, establish no kings; in the north, interrupt no alliances." This policy has ever since been exactly pursued by the court of Peking. The Emperor *Kien-Long*, in order to attach to his dynasty the prince in question, gave him his daughter in marriage, hoping by this means to fix him at Peking, and thus to weaken the still dreaded power of the Khalkha sovereigns. He built for him, within, the circuit of the Yellow Town itself, a large and magnificent palace, but the Mongol prince could not adapt or reconcile himself to the stiff arbitrary etiquette of a court. Amid the pomp and luxury accumulated for his entertainment, he was incessantly absorbed with the thought of his tents and his herds: even the snows and frosts of his country were matters of regret. The attentions of the court being altogether inadequate to the dissipation of his ennui, he began to talk about returning to his prairies in the Khalkhas. On the other hand, his young wife, accustomed to the refinements of the court of Peking, could not bear the idea of spending the rest of her days in the desert, amongst milkmaids and shepherds. The Emperor resorted to a compromise which sufficiently met the wishes of his son-in-law, without too violently disconcerting the feelings of his daughter. He dismembered a portion of the *Tchakar*, and assigned it to the Mongol prince; he built for him, amid these solitudes, a small but handsome city, and presented to him a hundred families of slaves skilled in the arts and manufactures of China. In this manner, while the young Mantchou princess was enabled to dwell in a city and to have a court, the Mongol prince, on his part, was in a position to enjoy the tranquillity of the Land of Grass, and to resume at will the pleasures of nomadic life, in which he had passed his boyhood.

The King of Efe brought with him into his petty dominions a great number of Mongol Khalkhas, who inhabit, under the tent, the country bestowed upon their prince. These Tartars fully maintain the reputation for strength and active vigor which is generally attributed to the men of their nation. They are considered the most powerful wrestlers in southern Mongolia. From their infancy, they are trained to gymnastic exercises, and at the public wrestling matches, celebrated every year at Peking, a great number of these men attend to compete for the prizes, and to sustain the reputation of their country. Yet, though far superior in strength to the Chinese, they are sometimes thrown by the latter, generally more active, and especially more tricky.

In the great match of 1843, a wrestler of the kingdom of Efe had overthrown all competitors, Tartars and Chinese. His body, of gigantic proportions, was fixed upon legs which seemed immovable columns; his hands, like great grappling irons, seized his antagonists, raised them, and then hurled them to the ground, almost without effort. No person had been at all able to stand before his prodigious strength, and they were about to assign him the prize, when a Chinese stepped into the ring. He was short, small, meager, and appeared calculated for no other purpose than to augment the number of the Efeian's victims. He advanced, however, with an air of firm confidence; the Goliath of Efe stretched out his brawny arms to grasp him, when the Chinese, who had his mouth full of water, suddenly discharged the liquid in the giant's face. The Tartar mechanically raised his hands to wipe his eyes, and at the instant, the cunning Chinese rushed in, caught him round the waist, threw him off his balance, and down he went, amid the convulsive laughter of the spectators.

This anecdote was told to us by a Tartar horseman who traveled with us a part of our way through the kingdom of Efe. From time to time he showed us children engaged in wrestling. "This," said he, " is the favorite exercise with all the inhabitants of our kingdom of Efe. We esteem in a man but two things,—his being a good horseman and his being a good wrestler." There was one group of youthful wrestlers whom, exercising as they were on the side of our road, we were enabled to watch closely and at leisure; their ardor redoubled when they saw we were looking at them. The tallest of the party, who did not seem more than eight or nine years old, took in his arms one of his companions, nearly his own height, and very fat, and amused himself with tossing him above his head, and catching him again, as you would a ball. He repeated this feat seven or eight times, and at every repetition we trembled for the life of the boy; but the rest of the children only gamboled about, applauding the success of the performers.

On the 22d day of the eighth moon, on quitting the petty kingdom of Efe, we ascended a mountain, on the sides of which grew thickets of fir and birch. The sight of these at first gave us great pleasure. The deserts of Tartary are in general so monotonously bare, that you cannot fail to experience a pleasurable sensation when you come upon some occasional trees on your way. Our first feelings of joy were, however, soon demolished by a sentiment of a very different nature; we were as though frozen with horror, on perceiving at a turn of the mountain, three enormous wolves, that seemed awaiting us with calm intrepidity. At sight of these villainous beasts we stopped suddenly and as it were instinctively. After a moment of general stupor, Samdadchiemba descended from his mule, and wrung the noses of our camels. The expedient succeeded marvelously; the poor beasts sent forth such piercing and terrible cries, that the scared wolves dashed off with all speed. Arsalan, who saw them flee, thinking undoubtedly that it was himself they were afraid of, pursued them at the utmost speed of his legs; soon the wolves turned round, and our tent-porter would have been infallibly devoured had not M. Gabet rushed to his aid, uttering loud cries, and wringing the nose of his camel; the wolves having taken flight a second time, disappeared without our again thinking of pursuing them.

Although the want of population might seem to abandon the interminable deserts of Tartary to wild beasts, wolves are rarely met with. This arises, no doubt, from the incessant and vindictive warfare which the Mongols wage against them. They pursue them, everywhere, to the death, regarding them as their capital enemy, on account of the great damage they may inflict upon their flocks. The announcement that a wolf has made its appearance in a neighborhood, is for every one a signal to mount his horse. As there are always near each tent horses ready saddled, in an instant the plain is covered with numerous cavalry, all armed with their long lasso-poles. The wolf in vain flees in every direction: it meets everywhere horsemen who rush upon it. There is no mountain so rugged or arduous, up which the Tartar horses, agile as goats, cannot pursue it. The horseman who is at length successful in passing round its neck the running knot, gallops, off at full speed, dragging the wolf after him to the nearest tent; there they strongly bind its muzzle, so that they may torture it securely; and then, by way of finale, skin it alive, and turn it off. In summer, the wretched brute lives in this condition several days; but in winter, exposed without a skin to the rigors of the season, it dies forthwith, frozen with cold.

Some short time after we had lost sight of our three wolves, we had a singular encounter enough. We saw advancing towards us, on the same road, two chariots each drawn by three oxen. To each chariot were fastened, with great iron chains, twelve dogs of a terrible and ferocious aspect, four on each side, and four behind. These carriages were laden with square boxes, painted red; the drivers sat on the boxes. We could not conjecture what was the nature of the load, on account of which they thought it essential to have this horrible escort of Cerberuses. In accordance with the customs of the country, we could not question them on this point. The slightest indiscretion would have made us pass in their eyes for people actuated by evil intentions. We contented ourselves with asking if we were still very far from the monastery of Tchortchi, where we hoped to arrive that day; but the baying of the dogs, and clanking of their chains, prevented us from hearing the answer.

As we were going through the hollow of a valley, we remarked on the summit of an elevated mountain before us a long line of objects without motion, and of an indefinite form. By and by these objects seemed to resemble a formidable battery of cannons, ranged in line, and the nearer we advanced, the more were we confirmed in this impression. We felt sure that we saw distinctly the wheels of the carriages, the sponge-rods, the mouths of the cannons pointed towards the plain. But how could we bring ourselves to think that an army, with all its train of artillery could be there in the desert, amid this profound solitude? Giving way to a thousand extravagant conjectures, we hastened our progress, impatient to examine this strange apparition closely. Our illusion was only completely dissipated when we arrived quite at the top of the mountain. What we had taken for a battery of cannons was a long caravan of little Mongol chariots. We laughed at our mistake, but the illusion was not an unnatural one. These small two-wheeled chariots were all standing still on their frames, each laden with a sack of salt, covered with a mat, the ends of which extended beyond the extremities of the sacks so as to resemble exactly the mouths of cannon; the Mongol wagoners were boiling their tea in the open air, whilst their oxen were feeding on the sides of the mountain. The transport of merchandise, across the deserts of Tartary, is ordinarily effected, in default of camels, by these small two-wheeled chariots. A few bars of rough wood are the only materials that enter into their construction, and they are so light that a child may lift them with ease. The oxen that draw them, have all a little iron ring passed through their nostrils; to this ring is a cord, which attaches the animal to the preceding chariot; thus all the carriages, from the first to the last, are connected together, and form a long uninterrupted line. The Mongol wagoners are generally seated on the oxen, very rarely on the carriage, and scarcely ever on foot. On all the chief roads you meet with these long lines of carriages, and long before you see them, you hear the lugubrious and monotonous sound of the iron bells, which the oxen carry suspended from their neck.

After drinking a cup of tea with the Mongols whom we had met in the mountain, we proceeded on our way; the sun was on the point of setting, when we set up our tent on the margin of a stream about a hundred yards from the Lamasery of Tchortchi.

Lamasery of Tchortchi.

CHAPTER IV.

Young Lama converted to Christianity—Lamasery of Tchortchi—Alms for the Construction of Religious Houses—Aspect of the Buddhist Temples—Recitation of Lama Prayers—Decorations, Paintings, and Sculptures of the Buddhist Temples—Topography of the *Great Kouren* in the country of the *Khalkhas*—Journey of the *Guison-Tamba* to Peking—The *Kouren* of the Thousand Lamas—Suit between the Lama-King and his Ministers—Purchase of a Kid—Eagles of Tartary—Western Toumet—Agricultural Tartars—Arrival at the Blue Town—Glance at the Mantchou Nation—Mantchou Literature—State of Christianity in Mantchouria—Topography and productions of Eastern Tartary—Skill of the Mantchous with the Bow.

ALTHOUGH we had never visited the Lamasery of Tchortchi, we, nevertheless, knew a good deal about it from the information that had been given us. It was here that the young Lama was educated who came to teach M. Gabet the Mongol language, and whose conversion to Christianity gave such great hopes for the propagation of the gospel among the Tartar tribes. He was twenty-five years of age when he quitted his Lamasery, in 1837; there he had passed fourteen years in the study of Lama books, and had become well acquainted with Mongol and Mantchou literature. He had as yet but a very superficial knowledge of the Thibetian language. His tutor, an old Lama, well-educated and much respected, not merely in the Lamasery, but throughout the whole extent of the Yellowish Banner, had cherished great hopes of his disciple; it was, therefore, very reluctantly that he had consented to a temporary separation, which he limited to a month. Before his departure the pupil prostrated himself, according to custom, at the feet of his master, and begged him to consult for him the Book of Oracles. After having turned over some leaves of a Thibetian book, the old Lama addressed to him these words: 'For fourteen years thou hast remained by thy master's side like a faithful Chabi (disciple). Now, for the first time thou art about to go from me. The future fills me with anxiety; be careful then to return at the appointed time. If thy absence is prolonged beyond one moon thy destiny condemns thee never more to set foot in our holy Lamasery." The youthful pupil departed, resolved to obey to the letter the instructions of his tutor.

When he arrived at our mission of Si-Wan, M. Gabet chose, as the subject of his Mongol studies, an historical summary of the Christian religion. The oral and written conferences lasted nearly a month. The young Lama, subdued by the force of truth, publicly abjured Buddhism, received the name of Paul, and was ultimately baptized, after a long course of study. The prediction of the old Lama had its perfect accomplishment; Paul, since his conversion, has never again set foot in the Lamasery which he quitted.

About 2,000 Lamas inhabit the Lamasery of Tchortchi, which, it is said, is the favorite Lamasery of the Emperor, who has loaded it with donations and privileges. The Lamas in charge of it each receive a pension from the court of Peking. Those who absent themselves from it by permission, and for reasons approved by the superiors, continue to share in the distributions of money and the provisions that are made during their absence; on their return they duly received the full amount of their share. Doubtless that air of ease pervading the Lamasery of Tchortchi is to be attributed to the imperial favors. The houses in it are neat, sometimes even elegant; and you never see there, as in other places, Lamas covered with dirty rags. The study of the Mantchou language is much cultivated there, an incontestable proof of the great devotion of the Lamasery to the reigning dynasty.

With some rare exceptions the imperial benefactions go very little way towards the construction of the Lamaseries.

Those grand and sumptuous monuments, so often met with in the desert, are due to the free and spontaneous zeal of the Mongols. So simple and economical in their dress and manner of living, these people are generous, we might say, astonishingly prodigal in all that concerns religious worship and expenditure. When it is resolved to construct a Buddhist temple, surrounded by its Lamasery, Lama collectors go on their way forthwith, provided with passports, attesting the authenticity of their mission. They disperse themselves throughout the kingdom of Tartary, beg alms from tent to tent in the name of the Old Buddha. Upon entering a tent and explaining the object of their journey, by showing

Buddhist Temple.

the sacred basin in which the offerings are placed, they are received with joyful enthusiasm. There is no one but gives something. The rich place in the "badir" ingots of gold and silver; those who do not possess the precious metals, offer oxen, horses, or camels. The poorest contribute according to the extent of their means; they give lumps of butter, furs, ropes made of the hair of camels and horses. Thus, in a short time, are collected immense sums. Then in these deserts, apparently so poor, you see rise up, as if by enchantment, edifices whose grandeur and wealth would defy the resources of the richest potentates. It was, doubtless, in the same manner, by the zealous co-operation of the faithful, that were constructed in Europe those magnificent cathedrals whose stupendous beauty is an abiding reproach to modern selfishness and indifference.

The Lamaseries you see in Tartary are all constructed of brick and stone. Only the poorest Lamas build for themselves habitations of earth, and these are always so well whitewashed that they closely resemble the rest. The temples are generally built with considerable elegance, and with great solidity; but these monuments always seem crushed, being too low in proportion to their dimensions. Around the Lamasery rise, numerous and without order, towers or pyramids, slender and tapering, resting generally on huge bases, little in harmony with the tenuity of the constructions they support. It would be difficult to say to what order of architecture the Buddhic temples of Tartary belong. They are always fantastical constructions of monstrous colonnades, peristyles with twisted columns, and endless ascents. Opposite the great gate is a kind of altar of wood or stone, usually in the form of a cone reversed; on this the idols are placed, mostly seated cross-legged. These idols are of colossal stature, but their faces are fine and regular, except in the preposterous length of the ears; they belong to the Caucasian type, and are wholly distinct from the monstrous, diabolical physiognomies of the Chinese Pou-Ssa.

Before the great idol, and on the same level with it, is a gilt seat where the living Fô, the Grand Lama of the Lamasery is seated. All around the temple are long tables almost level with the ground, a sort of ottomans covered with carpet; and between each row there is a vacant space, so that the Lamas may move about freely.

When the hour for prayer is come, a Lama, whose office it is to summon the guests of the convent, proceeds to the great gate of the temple, and blows, as loud as he can, a sea-conch, successively towards the four cardinal points. Upon hearing this powerful instrument, audible for a league round, the Lamas put on the mantle and cap of ceremony and assemble in the great inner court. When the time is come the sea-conch sounds again, the great gate is opened, and the living Fô enters the temple. As soon as he is seated upon the altar all the Lamas lay their red boots at the vestibule, and advance barefoot and in silence. As they pass him they worship the living Fô by three prostrations, and then place themselves upon the divan, each according to his dignity. They sit cross-legged; always in a circle.

As soon as the master of the ceremonies has given the signal, by tinkling a little bell, each murmurs in a low voice a preliminary prayer, whilst he unrolls, upon his knees, the prayers directed by the rubric. After this short recitation, follows a moment of profound silence; the bell is again rung, and then commences a psalm in double chorus, grave and melodious. The Thibetian prayers, ordinarily in verse, and written in a metrical and well-cadenced style, are marvelously adapted for harmony. At certain pauses, indicated by the rubric, the Lama musicians execute a piece of music, little in concert with the melodious gravity of the psalmody. It is a confused and deafening noise of bells, cymbals, tambourines, sea-conches, trumpets, pipes, etc., each musician playing on his instrument with a kind of ecstatic fury, trying with his brethren who shall make the greatest noise.

The interior of the temple is usually filled with ornaments, statues, and pictures, illustrating the life of Buddha, and the various transmigrations of the more illustrious Lamas. Vases in copper, shining like gold, of the size and form of teacups, are placed in great numbers on a succession of steps, in the form of an amphitheater, before the idols. It is in these vases that the people deposit their offerings of milk, butter, Mongol wine, and meal. The extremities of each step consist of censers, in which are ever burning aromatic plants, gathered on the sacred mountains of Thibet. Rich silk stuffs, covered with tinsel and gold embroidery, form, on the heads of the idols, canopies from which hang pennants and lanterns of painted paper or transparent horn.

The Lamas are the only artists who contribute to the ornament and decoration of the temples. The paintings are quite distinct from the taste and the principles of art as understood in Europe. The fantastical and the grotesque

Interior of Buddhist Temple.

predominate inside and out, both in carvings and statuary, and the personages represented, with the exception of Buddha, have generally a monstrous and satanic aspect. The clothes seem never to have been made for the persons upon whom they are placed. The idea given is that of broken limbs concealed beneath awkward garments.

Amongst these Lama paintings, however, you sometimes come across specimens by no means destitute of beauty. One day, during a visit in the kingdom of Gechekten to the great temple called *Alton-Somné* (Temple of Gold), we saw a picture which struck us with astonishment. It was a large piece representing, in the center, Buddha seated on a rich carpet. Around this figure, which was of life size, there was a sort of glory, composed of miniatures, allegorically expressing the Thousand Virtues of Buddha. We could scarcely withdraw ourselves from this picture, remarkable as it was, not only for the purity and grace of the design, but also for the expression of the faces and the splendor of the coloring. All the personages seemed full of life. We asked an old Lama, who was attending us over the place, what he knew about this admirable work. "Sirs," said he, raising his joined hands to his forehead in token of respect, " this picture is a treasure of the remotest antiquity; it comprehends within its surface the whole doctrine of Buddha. It is not a Mongol painting; it came from Thibet, and was executed by a saint of the *Eternal Sanctuary.*"

The artists here are, in general, more successful in the landscapes than in the epic subjects. Flowers, birds, trees, mythological animals, are represented with great truth and with infinitely pleasing effect. The coloring is wonderfully full of life and freshness. It is only a pity that the painters of these landscapes have so very indifferent a notion as to perspective and chiaro-oscuro.

The Lamas are far better sculptors than painters, and they are accordingly very lavish of carvings in their Buddhist temples. Everywhere in and about these edifices you see work of this class of art, in quantity bespeaking the fecundity of the artist's chisel, but of a quality which says little for his taste. First, outside the temples are an infinite number of tigers, lions, and elephants crouching upon blocks of granite; then the stone balustrades of the steps leading to the great gates are covered with fantastic sculptures representing birds, reptiles, and beasts, of all kinds, real and imaginary. Inside, the walls are decorated with *rilievos* in wood or stone, executed with great spirit and truth.

Though the Mongol Lamaseries cannot be compared, in point either of extent or wealth, with those of Thibet, there are some of them which are highly celebrated and greatly venerated among the adorers of Buddha.

The most famous of all is that of the Great Kouren (enclosure), in the country of the Khalkhas. As we had an opportunity of visiting this edifice in one of our journeys into Northern Tartary, we will here give some details respecting it. It stands on the bank of the river Toula, at the entrance to an immense forest, which extends thence

northwards, six or seven days' journey to the confines of
Russia, and eastward, nearly five hundred miles to the land
of the Solons, in Mantchouria. On your way to the Great
Kouren, over the desert of Gobi, you have to traverse, for
a whole month, an ocean of sand, the mournful monotony
of which is not relieved by a single stream or a single
shrub; but on reaching the Kougour mountains, the western
boundary of the states of the Guison-Tamba, or King-
Lama, the scene changes to picturesque and fertile valleys,
and verdant pasture-hills, crowned with forests that seem
as old as the world itself. Through the largest valley flows
the river Toula, which, rising in the Barka mountains, runs
from east to west through the pastures of the Lamasery,
and then entering Siberia, falls into Lake Balkal.

*The Lamasery stands on the northern bank of the river,
on the slope of a mountain. The various temples inhabited
by the Guison-Tamba, and other Grand Lamas, are distinguishable
from the rest of the structure by their elevation
and their gilded roofs. Thirty thousand Lamas dwell in
the Lamasery itself, or in smaller Lamaseries erected about
it. The plain adjoining it is always covered with the tents
of the pilgrims who resort hither from all parts to worship
Buddha. Here you find the U-Pi-Ta-Dze, or "Fish-skin
Tartars," encamped beside the Torgot Tartars from the
summits of the sacred mountains (Bokte-Oula), the
Thibetians and the Péboum of the Himalaya, with their
long-haired oxen, mingling with the Mantchous from the
banks of the Songari and Amor. There is an incessant
movement of tents set up and taken down, and of pilgrims
coming and going on horses, camels, oxen, mules, or
wagons, and on foot.

Viewed from the distance, the white cells of the Lamas,
built in horizontal lines one above the other on the sides of
the mountain, seem the steps of a grand altar, of which the
tabernacle is the temple of the Guison-Tamba. In the
depths of that sanctuary, all resplendent with gold and
bright coloring, the Lama-King, The Holy, as he is called,
par excellence, receives the homage of the faithful, ever
prostrate, in succession, before him. There is not a Khalkha Tartar who does not glory in the title of the *Holy One's
Disciple*. Wherever you meet a man from the district of
the Great Kouren, and ask him who he is, his proud reply

is always this: *Koure Bokte-Ain Chabi* (I am a disciple of the Holy Kouren).

Half a league from the Lamasery, on the banks of the Toula, is a commercial station of Chinese. Their wooden or mud huts are fortified by a circle of high palisades to keep out the pilgrims, who, despite their devotion, are extremely given to thieving whenever the opportunity occurs. A watch and some ingots of silver, stolen during the night from M. Gabet, left us no doubt as to the want of probity in the Holy One's disciples.

A good deal of trade is carried on here, Chinese and Russian goods changing hands to a very large extent. The payments of the former are invariably made in tea-bricks. Whether the article sold be a house, a horse, a camel, or a bale of goods, the price is settled for in bricks of tea. Five of these represent, in value, an ounce of silver; the monetary system, therefore, which Franklin so much disliked, is not in use by these Northern Tartars.

The Court of Peking entertains several Mandarins at the Great Kouren, ostensibly for the purpose of preserving order among the Chinese traders, but in reality to keep a watch upon the Guison-Tamba, always an object of suspicion to the Chinese Emperors, who bear in mind that the famous Tching-Kis-Khan was a Khalkha, and that the memory of his conquests has not passed away from the hearts of this warlike people. The slightest movement at the Great Kouren excites alarm at Peking.

In 1839 the Guison-Tamba announced his intention of paying a visit to the Emperor Tao-Kouan. The Court of Peking became horribly alarmed, and negotiators were dispatched to divert, if possible, the Guison-Tamba from his journey; but all they could effect was, that he should be attended by only 3,000 Lamas, and that three other Khalkha sovereigns who were to have accompanied him should be left behind.

Immediately upon the Guison-Tamba's departure on his progress, all the tribes of Tartary put themselves in motion, and took up positions on the road he was to travel, in vast multitudes, each tribe bringing for his acceptance offerings of horses, oxen, sheep, gold and silver bullion, and precious stones. Wells were dug for him at intervals throughout the length of the great desert of Gobi, and at each of these were placed for his use, by the chieftain of the particular locality, a store of provisions of all sorts. The Lama King was in a yellow palanquin, carried by four horses, each led by a dignitary of the Lamasery. The escort of 3,000 Lamas were before, behind, and on each side of the palanquin, jovially dashing about on horses and camels. The road almost throughout was lined with spectators, or rather with worshippers, eagerly awaiting the arrival of the Holy, and upon his approach, falling, first on their knees, and then on their faces, before him, their hands crossed over the head. It seemed the progress of a divinity come upon earth to bless its people. On reaching the Great Wall, the Guison-Tamba, ceasing to be a divinity, became only the chief of some nomad tribes, scorned by the people of China, but feared by the Court of China, more alive to political contingencies. Only one half of the 3,000 Lamas were permitted to attend their chief further, the rest remaining encamped north of the Great Wall.

The Guison-Tamba sojourned at Peking for three months, receiving an occasional visit from the Emperor, and from the Grand Dignitaries. He then relieved the celestial city from his troublesome presence, and after paying visits to the Lamaseries of the Five Towers, and of the Blue Town, set out on his return to his own states when he died, the victim, it was asserted, of a slow poison that had been administered to him by order of the Emperor. The Khalkhas, however, were more irritated than intimidated by his death, for they are persuaded that their Guison-Tamba never actually dies. All he does, when he appears to die, is to transmigrate to some other country, whence he returns to them younger, more vigorous, more active than ever. In 1844, accordingly, they were told that their living Buddha was incarnate in Thibet, and they went thither, in solemn procession, to fetch the child of five years old who was indicated to them, and to place him on his imperishable throne. While we were encamped at Kou-Kou-Noor, on the banks of the Blue Sea, we saw pass by us the great caravan of Khalkhas, who were on their way to Lha-Ssa to bring home the Lama-King of the Great Kouren.

The Kouren of the Thousand Lamas—*Mingan Lamané Kouré*—is also a celebrated Lamasery, which dates from the invasion of China by the Mantchous. When Tchun-

Tche,[1] founder of the dynasty now reigning in China, descended from the forests of Mantchouria to march upon Peking, he met on his way a Lama of Thibet, whom he consulted as to the issue of his enterprise. The Lama promised him complete success, where upon Tchun-Tche ordered him to come and see him when he should be installed at Peking. After the Mantchous had rendered themselves masters of the capital of the empire, the Lama did not fail to keep his appointment. The Emperor at once recognized the person who had favored him with such an auspicious horoscope; and, in token of his gratitude, allotted to him a large extent of land whereon to construct a Lamasery, and revenues sufficient for the support of a thousand Lamas. From the time of its erection, however, the Lamasery of the Thousand Lamas has grown and grown, so that at present it contains more than four thousand Lamas, though its original designation still remains. By degrees, traders have established themselves around it, and have built a considerable town, jointly occupied by Chinese and by Tartars. The principal commerce of the place is in beasts.

The Grand Lama of the Lamasery is, at the same time, sovereign of the district. It is he who makes laws, who administers justice, and who appoints magistrates. When he dies, his subjects go and seek for him in Thibet, where he is always understood to metempsychose himself.

At the time of our visit to the Kouren of the Thousand Lamas, everything was in utter confusion, by reason of a suit between the Lama King and his four ministers, who are called, in the Mongol language, Dchassak. The latter had taken upon themselves to marry, and to build houses for themselves apart from the Lamasery, things altogether subversive of Lama discipline. The Grand Lama essayed to bring them to order; the four Dchassak, instead of submitting, had collected a whole heap of grievances, upon which they framed an accusation against their chief before the Tou-Toun, the high Mantchou Mandarin, who acts as Secretary-of-State for the Tartar department.

The suit had been under prosecution two months when

---

[1] The anecdote, which we give as we heard it, must have reference to Tchun-Tche's father, who died immediately after the conquest. Tchun-Tche himself was only four years old at the time.

we visited the Lamasery, and we soon saw how the establishment was suffering from the absence of its principals. Study or prayer there was none; the great outer gate was open, and seemed not to have been closed at all for some time past. We entered the interior; all we found there was silence and solitude. The grass was growing in the courts, and upon the walls. The doors of the temples were padlocked, but through the gratings we could see that the seats, the altars, the paintings, the statues, were all covered with dust; everything manifested that the Lamasery had been for some time in a state of utter neglect. The absence of the superiors, and the uncertainty as to the result of the suit, had unloosened all the bonds of discipline. The Lamas had dispersed, and people began to regard the very existence of the Lamasery as extremely compromised. We have since heard that, thanks to enormous bribery, the suit terminated in favor of the Lama King, and the four Dchassak were compelled to conform themselves in all respects to the orders of their sovereign.

We may add to the enumeration of the many celebrated Lamaseries, those of Blue Town, of Tolon-Noor, of Gé-Ho-Eul; and within the Great Wall, that of Peking, and that of the Five Towers in Chan-Si.

After quitting the Lamasery of Tchortchi, just as we were entering upon the Red Banner, we met a Mongol hunter, who was carrying behind him, on his horse, a fine roebuck he had just killed. We had been so long reduced to our insipid oatmeal, seasoned with a few bits of mutton fat, that the sight of the venison inspired us with a somewhat decided desire to vary our entertainment; we felt, moreover, that our stomachs, weakened by our daily privations, imperiously demanded a more substantial alimentation. After saluting the hunter, therefore, we asked him if he was disposed to sell his venison. "Sirs Lamas," replied he, "when I placed myself in ambush to await the deer, I had no thought of trading in my head. The Chinese carmen, stationed up yonder beyound Tchortchi, wanted to buy my game for four hundred sapeks, but I said no! But to you, Sirs Lamas, I speak not as to Kitat; there is my roebuck: give me what you please for it." We told Samdadchiemba to pay the hunter five hundred sapeks; and hanging the venison over the neck of one of the camels, we proceeded on our way.

Five hundred sapeks are equivalent to about 2s. 1d., and this is the ordinary price of a roebuck in Tartary; the price of a sheep is thrice that amount. Venison is little esteemed by the Tartars, and still less by the Chinese; black meat, say they, is never so good as white. Yet in the larger cities of China, and especially at Peking, black meat has an honorable place on the tables of the rich and of the mandarins; a circumstance, however, to be attributed to the scarcity of the article, and a desire for variety. The Mantchous, indeed, do not come within the preceding observation; for, great lovers of hunting, they are also great lovers of its produce, and especially of bears, stags, and pheasants.

It was just past noon when we came to a spot marvelously beautiful. After passing through a narrow opening between two rocks, whose summits seemed lost in the clouds, we found ourselves in a large enclosure, surrounded by lofty hills, on which grew a number of scattered pines. An abundant fountain supplied a small stream, whose banks were covered with angelica and wild mint. The rivulet, after making the circuit of the enclosure, amid rich grass, had its issue thence by an opening similar to that by which we had entered the place. No sooner had a glance comprehended the attractions of the spot, than Samdadchiemba moved that we should at once set up our tent there. "Let us go no further to-day," said he; "let us encamp here. We have not gone far this morning, it is true, and the sun is still very high; but we have got the venison to prepare, and should therefore encamp earlier than usual." No one opposing the honorable gentleman's motion, it was put and carried unanimously, and we proceeded to set up our tent by the side of the spring.

Samdadchiemba had often talked of his great dexterity in the dissection of animals, and he was delighted with this opportunity of displaying his excellence in this respect. Having suspended the roebuck from a pine-branch, sharpened his knife upon a tent-pin, and turned up his sleeves to the elbow, he asked whether we would have the animal dismembered *à la Chinoise, à la Turque,* or *à la Tartare.* Unprovided with any reason for preferring any one of these modes to the other two, we left it to Samdadchiemba to obey the impulse of his genius in the matter. In a minute he had skinned and gutted the animal, and he then cut away the flesh from the bones, in one piece, without separating the limbs, so as to leave suspended from the tree merely the skeleton of the deer. This, it appeared, was the Turkish fashion, in use upon long journeys, in order to relieve travelers from the useless burden of bones.

This operation completed, Samdadchiemba cut some slices of venison and proceeded to fry them in mutton fat, a manner of preparing venison not perhaps in strict accordance with the rules of the culinary art; but the difficulty of the circumstances did not allow us to do better. Our banquet was soon ready, but, contrary to our expectations, we were not the first to taste it; we had seated ourselves triangularly on the grass, having in the midst the lid of the pot, which served us as a dish, when all of a sudden we heard, as it were, the rushing of a storm over our heads: a great eagle dashed, like a lightning stroke, upon our entertainment, and immediately rose with equal rapidity, bearing off in each claw a large slice of venison. Upon recovering from our fright at this sudden incident, we ourselves were fain to laugh at the ludicrous aspect of the matter, but Samdadchiemba did not laugh by any means; he was in a paroxysm of fury, not indeed at the loss of the venison, but because the eagle, in its flight, insolently dealt him a sound box on the ear with the extremity of its great wings.

This event served to render us more cautious on the following venison days. During our previous journeyings we had, indeed, on several occasions observed eagles hovering over our heads at meal-times, but no accident of this kind had occurred; probably the royal birds had scorned our mere oatmeal repasts.

You see the eagle almost everywhere throughout the deserts of Tartary; sometimes hovering and making large circles in the air, sometimes perched upon a rising ground, motionless as the hillock itself. No one in these countries hunts the eagle or molests it in any way; it may make its nest where it pleases, and there bring up its eaglets, and itself grow old, without being in the smallest degree interfered with by man. You often see before you an eagle resting on the plain, and looking there larger than a sheep; as you approach, before rising, it leisurely moves along the ground, beating its wings, and then, by degrees ascending, it attains the altitude where it can fly in all its grandeur and power.

After several days' journey we quitted the country of the Eight Banners and entered Western Toumet. At the time of the conquest of China by the Mantchous, the king of Toumet, having distinguished himself in the expedition as an auxiliary of the invaders, the conqueror, in order to evince his gratitude for the services which the prince had rendered him, gave him the fine districts situated north of Peking, beyond the Great Wall. From that period they have borne the name of Eastern Toumet, and Old Toumet took that of Western Toumet; the two Toumets are separated from each other by the Tchakar River.

The Mongol Tartars of Western Toumet do not lead the pastoral and nomadic life: they cultivate their lands and apply themselves to the arts of civilized nations. We had been for nearly a month traversing the desert, setting up our tent for the night in the first convenient place we found, and accustomed to see nothing but, above us the sky, and below and around us interminable prairies. We had long, as it were, broken with the world, for all we had seen of mankind had been a few Tartar horsemen dashing across the Land of Grass, like so many birds of passage. Without suspecting it, our tastes had insensibly become modified, and the desert of Mongolia had created in us a temperament friendly to the tranquillity of solitude. When, therefore, we found ourselves amid the cultivation, the movement, the bustle, the confusion of civilized existence, we felt, as it were, oppressed, suffocated; we seemed gasping for breath, and as though every moment we were going to be stifled. This impression, however, was evanescent; and we soon got to think that, after all, it was more comfortable and more agreeable, after a day's march, to take up our abode in a warm, well-stored inn, than to have to set up a tent, to collect fuel, and to prepare our own very meager repast, before we could take our rest.

The inhabitants of Western Toumet, as may well be imagined, have completely lost the stamp of their original Mongol character; they have all become, more or less, Chinese; many of them do not even know a word of the Mongol language. Some, indeed, do not scruple to express contempt for their brothers of the desert, who refuse to

Tartar Agriculturist.

subject their prairies to the ploughshare; they say, how ridiculous is it for men to be always vagabondizing about, and to have merely wretched tents wherein to shelter their heads, when they might so easily build houses, and obtain wealth and comforts of all kinds from the land beneath their feet. And, indeed, the Western Toumetians are perfectly right in preferring the occupation of agriculturist to that of shepherd, for they have magnificent plains, well watered, fertile, and favorable to the production of all kinds of grain crops. When we passed through the country, harvest was over; but the great stacks of corn that we saw in all directions told us that the produce had been abundant and fine. Everything throughout Western Toumet bears the impress of affluence; nowhere, go in what direction you may, do you see the wretched tumble-down houses that disfigure the highways and by-ways of China; nowhere do you see the miserable, half-starved, half-clothed creatures that pain the hearts of travelers in every other country: all the peasants here are well fed, well lodged, and well clothed. All the villages and roads are beautified with groups and avenues of fine trees; whereas, in the other Tartar regions, cultivated by the Chinese, no trees are to be seen; trees are not even planted, for everybody knows they would be pulled up next day by some miserable pauper or other, for fuel.

We had made three days' journey through the cultivated lands of the Toumet, when we entered *Kou-Kou-Hote* (Blue Town), called in Chinese *Koui-Hoa-Tchen*. There are two towns of the same name, five *lis* distant from one another. The people distinguish them by calling the one "Old Town," and the other "New Town," or "Commercial Town," and "Military Town." We first entered the latter, which was built by the Emperor Khang-Hi, to defend the empire against its northern enemies. The town has a beautiful, noble appearance, which might be admired in Europe itself. We refer, however, only to its circuit of embattled walls, made of brick: for inside, the low houses, built in the Chinese style, are little in unison with the lofty, huge ramparts that surround them. The interior of the town offers nothing remarkable but its regularity, and a large and beautiful street, which runs through it from east to west. A Kiang-Kian, or military commandant, resides here with 10,000 soldiers, who are drilled every day; so that the town may be regarded as a garrison town.

The soldiers of the New Town of Koukou Khoton are Mantchou Tartars; but if you did not previously know the fact, you would scarcely suspect it from hearing them speak. Amongst them there is perhaps not a single man who understands the language of his own country. Already two ages have passed away since the Mantchous made themselves masters of the vast empire of China, and you would say that during these two centuries they have been unceasingly working out their own annihilation. Their manners, their language, their very country—all has become Chinese. It may now be affirmed that Mantchou nationality has become irremediably annihilated. In order to account for this strange counter-revolution, and to understand how the Chinese have been able to fuse their conquerors with themselves, and to get possession of Mantchouria, we must look some way back, and enter somewhat into detail.

In the time of the Ming dynasty, which flourished in China from 1368 to 1644, the Mantchous, or Eastern Tartars, after a long series of internal wars, concurred in the selection of a chief, who united all the tribes into one, and

Chinese Soldier.

established a kingdom. From that time this ferocious and barbarian people insensibly acquired an importance which gave great umbrage to the Court of Peking; and in 1618 its power was so well established, that its king did not fear to transmit to the Emperor of China the statement of seven grievances which, he said, he had to avenge. The daring manifesto finished with these words: "*And in order to avenge these seven injuries, I will reduce and subjugate the dynasty of the Ming.*" Shortly afterwards the empire was convulsed with revolts in all directions; the rebel chief besieged Peking, and took it. Thereupon the Emperor, despairing of his fortune, hanged himself from a tree in the Imperial garden, leaving near him these words, written in his own blood : "*Since the empire is falling, the Emperor, too, must fall.*" Ou-San-Koueï, the Imperial general, called in the Mantchous to aid him in reducing the rebels. The latter were put to flight, and while the Chinese general was pursuing them southward, the Tartar chief returned to Peking, and finding the throne vacant, assumed it.

Previous to this event, the Great Wall, carefully maintained by the Ming dynasty, had kept the Mantchous from entering China, while, reciprocally, the Chinese were forbidden to enter Mantchouria. After the Mantchou conquest of the empire, however, there was no longer any frontier separating the two nations. The Great Wall was freely passed, and the communication between the two countries once thrown open, the Chinese populations of Pe-Tchi-Li and Chan-Toung, hitherto confined within their narrow provinces, burst like torrents upon Mantchouria. The Tartar chief had been considered the sole master, the sole possessor of the lands of his kingdom; but, established as Emperor of China, he distributed his vast possessions among the Mantchous, upon the condition that they should pay him heavy rents for them every year. By means of usury and cunning, and persevering machinations, the Chinese have since rendered themselves masters of all the lands of their conquerors, leaving to them merely their empty titles, their onerous statutory labor, and the payment of oppressive rents. The quality of Mantchou has thus by degrees become a very costly affair, and many, of consequence, seek altogether to abnegate it. According to the law, there is, every third year, a census made of the population of each banner, and all persons who do not cause their names to be inscribed on the roll, are deemed no longer to belong to the Mantchou nation; those, therefore, of the Mantchous whose indigence induces them to desire exemption from statute labor and military service, do not present themselves to the census enumerators, and by that omission enter the ranks of the Chinese people. Thus, while, on the one hand, constant migration has carried beyond the Great Wall a great number of Chinese, on the other, a great number of Mantchous have voluntarily abdicated their nationality.

The decline, or rather the extinction of the Mantchou nation, is now progressing more rapidly than ever. Up to the reign of Tao-Kouan, the regions watered by the Songari were exclusively inhabited by Mantchous: entrance into those vast districts was prohibited to the Chinese, and no man was permitted to cultivate the soil within their range. At the commencement of the present reign, these districts were put up for public sale, in order to supply the deficiency in the Imperial treasury. The Chinese rushed upon them like birds of prey, and a few years sufficed to remove everything that could in any way recall the memory of their ancient possessors. It would be vain for any one now to seek in Mantchouria a single town, a single village, that is not composed entirely of Chinese.

Yet, amid the general transformation, there are still a few tribes, such as the Si-Po and the Solon, which faithfully retain the Mantchou type. Up to the present day their territories have been invaded neither by the Chinese nor by cultivation; they continue to dwell in tents and to furnish soldiers to the Imperial armies. It has been remarked, however, that their frequent appearance at Peking, and their long periods of service in the provincial garrisons, are beginning to make terrible inroads upon their habits and tastes.

When the Mantchous conquered China, they imposed upon the conquered people a portion of their dress and many of their usages. Tobacco smoking, for example, and the manner of dressing the hair, now in use by the Chinese, came to them from the Mantchou Tartars. But the Chinese, in their turn, did far more than this; they managed to make their conquerors adopt their manners and their language. You may now traverse Mantchouria to the river Amour, without being at all aware that you are not traveling in a province of China. The local coloring has become totally effaced. With the exception of a few nomadic tribes no one speaks Mantchou: and there would, perhaps, remain no trace of this fine language, had not the Emperors Khang-Hi and Kien-Loung erected, in its honor, monuments imperishable in themselves, and which will ever attract the attention of European orientalists.

At one time the Mantchous had no writing of their own; it was not until 1624, that Tai-Tsou-Kao-Hoang-Ti, chief of the Eastern Tartars, directed several learned persons of his nation to design a system of letters for the Mantchous, upon the model of those of the Mongols. Subsequently, in, 1641, a man of great genius, named Tahai, perfected the work, and gave to the Mantchou system of letters the elegance, clearness, and refinement which now characterize it.

Chun-Tche had the finest productions of Chinese literature translated into Mantchou. Khang-Hi established an academy of learned persons, equally versed in the Chinese and Tartar languages, whom he employed upon the translation of classical and historical works, and in the compilation of several dictionaries. In order to express novel objects and the various conceptions previously unknown to the Mantchous, it was necessary to invent terms, borrowed, for the most part, from the Chinese, and adapted, by slight alterations, as closely as possible, to the Tartar idiom. This process, however, tending to destroy, by imperceptible degrees, the originality of the Mantchou language, the Emperor Kien-Loung, to avert the danger had a Mantchou dictionary compiled, from which all Chinese words were excluded. The compilers went about questioning old men and other Mantchous deemed most conversant with their mother-tongue, and rewards were given to such as brought forward an obsolescent word or expression which was deemed worthy of revival and perpetuation in the dictionary.

Thanks to the solicitude and enlightened zeal of the first sovereigns of the present dynasty, there is now no good Chinese book which has not been translated into Mantchou; and all these translations are invested with the greatest possible authenticity, as having been executed by learned academies, by order and under the immediate auspices of several emperors: and as having, moreover, been subsequently revised and corrected by other academies, equally learned, and whose members were versed alike in the Chinese language and in the Mantchou idiom.

The Mantchou language has attained, by means of all these learned labors, a solid basis; it may, indeed, become no longer spoken, but it will ever remain a classic tongue, and ever be of most important aid to philologers applying their studies to the Asiatic tongues. Besides numerous and faithful translations of the best Chinese books, the Mantchou language possesses versions of the principal productions in the Lamanesque, Thibetian, and Mantchou literature. A few years' labor will thus suffice to place the diligent student of Mantchou in full possession of all the most precious monuments of Eastern Asiatic literature.

The Mantchou language is sonorous, harmonious, and, above all, singularly clear. Its study is now rendered easy and agreeable by H. Conon de la Gabelentz's "Elemens de la Grammaire Mantchou," published at Altemburg, in Saxony, and which develops, with happy lucidity, the mechanism and rules of the language. The excellent work of this learned orientalist cannot fail to be of great assistance to all who desire to apply themselves to the study of a language menaced with extinction in the very country which gave it birth, but which France, at least, will preserve for the use of the world of letters. M. Conon de la Gabelentz says, in the preface to his grammar: "I have selected the French language in the preparation of my work, because France is, as yet, the only European country in which Mantchou has been cultivated, so that it seems to me indispensable that all who desire to study this idiom should first know French, as being the tongue in which are composed the only European works which relate to Mantchou literature."

While the French missionaries were enriching their country with the literary treasures which they found in these remote regions, they were, at the same time, ardently engaged in diffusing the light of Christianity amid these idolatrous nations, whose religion is merely a monstrous medley of doctrines and practises borrowed at once from Lao-Tseu, Confucius, and Buddha.

It is well known that in the earlier years of the present dynasty, these missionaries had, by their talents, acquired great influence at court; they always accompanied the Emperors in the long and frequent journeys which at that period they were accustomed to make into the regions of their ancient rule. These zealous preachers of the gospel never failed on all such occasions to avail themselves of the protection and influence they enjoyed, as a means for sowing, wherever they went, the seeds of the true faith. Such was the first origin of the introduction of Christianity into Mantchouria. They reckoned at first but few neophytes; but the number of these was insensibly augmented afterwards by the migrations of the Chinese, in which were always to be found several Christian families. These missions formed part of the diocese of Peking until within a few years past; then the Bishop of Nanking, administrator of the diocese of Peking, finding himself nigh the close of his career, and fearing that the political commotions of which Portugal, his native country, was at that time the theater, would preclude the Portuguese church from sending an adequate number of laborers to cultivate the vast field which had been confided to him, communicated his apprehensions to the Sacred College de Propagandâ Fide, and earnestly entreated its members to take under their especial attention a harvest, already ripe, but which was under peril of destruction, for want of husbandmen to gather it in. The sacred congregation, touched with the anxiety of this venerable and zealous old man, among its other arrangements for meeting the requirements of these unfortunate missions, dismembered Mantchouria from the diocese of Peking, and erected it into an Apostolic Vicariat, which was confided to the charge of the Foreign Missionary Society. M. Verolles, Bishop of Colombia, was made the new Vicar Apostolic. Nothing less than the patience, the devotion, the every virtue of an apostle, was essential for the due administration of this Christendom. The prejudices of the neophytes, not as yet brought within the rules of ecclesiastical discipline, were, for M. Verolles, obstacles more difficult to overcome than even the ruggedness of heart of the pagans; but his experience and his wisdom soon triumphed over all impediments. The mission has assumed a new form; the number of Christians is annually augmenting; and there is now every hope that the Apostolic Vicariat of Mantchouria will become one of the most flourishing missions in Asia.

Mantchouria is bounded on the north by Siberia, on the south by the Gulf Phou-Hai and Corea, on the east by the sea of Japan, and on the west by Russian Dauria and Mongolia.

Moukden, in Chinese Chen-Yan, is the chief town of Mantchouria, and may be considered the second capital of the Chinese empire. The Emperor has a palace and courts of justice there on the model of those at Peking. Moukden is a large and fine city, surrounded by thick and lofty ramparts; the streets are broad and regular, and less dirty and tumultuous than those of Peking. One entire quarter is appropriated to the princes of the Yellow Girdle ; that is, to the members of the Imperial family. They are all under the direction of a grand Mandarin, who is entrusted with the inspection of their conduct, and empowered summarily to punish any offenses they may commit.

After Moukden, the most remarkable towns are Ghirin, surrounded by high wooden palisades, and Ningouta, the native place of the reigning Imperial family. Lao-yan, Kai-Tcheou, and Kin-Tcheou, are remarkable for the extensive commerce their maritime position brings them.

Mantchouria, watered by a great number of streams and rivers, is a country naturally fertile. Since the cultivation has been in the hands of the Chinese, the soil has been enriched by a large number of the products of the interior. In the southern part, they cultivate successfully the dry rice, or that which has no need of watering, and the Imperial rice, discovered by the Emperor Khang-Hi. These two sorts of rice would certainly succeed in France. They have also abundant harvests of millet, of Kao-Léang or Indian corn (*Holcus Sorghum*), from which they distil excellent brandy : sesamum, linseed, hemp, and tobacco, the best in the whole Chinese empire.

The Mantchourians pay especial attention to the cultivation of the herbaceous-stemmed cotton plant, which produces cotton in extraordinary abundance. A Meou of these plants, a space of about fifteen square feet, ordinarily produces 2,000 lbs. of cotton. The fruit of the cotton tree grows in the form of a cod or shell, and attains the size of a hazelnut. As it ripens, the cod opens, divides into three parts, and develops three or four small tufts of cotton which contain the seeds. In order to separate the seed, they make use of a sort of little bow, firmly strung, the cord of which vibrating under the cotton tufts removes the seeds, of which a portion is retained for next year's sowing, and the rest is made into oil, resembling linseed oil. The upper portion of Mantchouria, too cold to grow cotton, has immense harvests of corn.

Besides these productions, common to China, Mantchouria possesses three treasures [1] peculiar to itself : jinseng, sable fur, and the grass Oula.

---

[1] The Chinese designate them San Pao: the Mantchous, Ilan Baobai: the Mongols, Korbanerdeni ; and the Thibetans, Tchok-Soum.

The first of these productions has been long known in Europe, though our learned Academy there ventured some years ago to doubt its existence. Jin-seng is perhaps the most considerable article of Mantchourian commerce. Throughout China there is no chemist's shop unprovided with more or less of it.

The root of jin-seng is straight, spindle-shaped, and very knotty; seldom so large as one's little finger, and in length from two to three inches. When it has undergone its fitting preparation, its color is a transparent white, with sometimes a slight red or yellow tinge. Its appearance, then, is that of a branch of stalactite.

The Chinese report marvels of the jin-seng, and no doubt it is, for Chinese organization, a tonic of very great effect for old and weak persons; but its nature is too healing, the Chinese physicians admit, for the European temperament, already, in their opinion, too hot. The price is enormous, and doubtless its dearness contributes, with a people like the Chinese, to raise its celebrity so high. The rich and the Mandarins probably use it only because it is above the reach of other people, and out of pure ostentation.

The jin-seng, grown in Corea, and there called Kao-li-seng, is of very inferior quality to that of Mantchouria.

The second special treasure of Eastern Tartary is the fur of the sable, which, obtained by the hunters with immense labor and danger, is of such excessive price that only the princes and great dignitaries of the empire can purchase it. The grass called Oula, the third specialty of Mantchouria, is, on the contrary, of the commonest occurrence; its peculiar property is, that if put into your shoes, it communicates to the feet a soothing warmth, even in the depth of winter.

As we have said above, the Mantchou Tartars have almost wholly abdicated their own manners, and adopted instead those of the Chinese; yet, amid this transformation of their primitive characters, they have still retained their old passion for hunting, for horse exercise, and for archery. At all periods of their history, they have attached an astonishing importance to these various exercises; any one may convince himself of this by merely running his eye over a Mantchou dictionary. Every thing, every incident, every attribute relating to these exercises, has its special expression, so as to need no circumlocution to convey it. There are different names, not only for the different colors of the horse, for example, for its age and qualities, but for all its movements; and it is just the same with reference to hunting and archery.

The Mantchous are excellent archers, and among them the tribe Solon is particularly eminent in this respect. At all the military stations, trials of skill with the bow take place on certain periodical occasions, in presence of the Mandarins and of the assembled people. Three straw men, of the size of life, are placed in a straight line, at from twenty to thirty paces distance from one another; the archer is on a line with them, about fifteen feet off from the first figure, his bow bent, and his finger on the string. The signal being given, he puts his horse to a gallop, and discharges his arrow at the first figure; without checking his horse's speed, he takes a second arrow from his quiver, places it in the bow, and discharges it against the second figure, and so with the third; all this while the horse is dashing at full speed along the line of the figures, so that the rider has to keep himself firm in the stirrups while he maneuvers with the promptitude necessary to avoid the getting beyond his mark. From the first figure to the second, the archer has bare time for drawing his arrow, fixing and discharging it, so that when he shoots, he has generally to turn somewhat on his saddle; and as to the third shot, he has to discharge it altogether in the old Parthian fashion. Yet, for a competitor to be deemed a good archer, it is essential that he should fire an arrow into every one of the three figures. "To know how to shoot an arrow," writes a Mantchou author, "is the first and most important knowledge for a Tartar to acquire. Though success therein seems an easy matter, success is of rare occurrence. How many are there who practise day and night? How many are there who sleep with the bow in their arms? and yet how few are there who have rendered themselves famous. How few are there whose names are proclaimed at the matches! Keep your frame straight and firm; avoid vicious postures; let your shoulders be immovable. Fire every arrow into its mark, and you may be satisfied with your skill.

The day after our arrival at the military town of Koukou-Khoton, we repaired on a visit to the mercantile district. Our hearts were painfully affected at finding ourselves in a Mantchou town, and hearing any language spoken there but the Mantchou. We could not reconcile to our minds the idea of a nation renegade of its nationality, of a conquering people, in nothing distinguishable from the conquered, except, perhaps, that they have a little less industry and a little more conceit. When the Thibetian Lama promised to the Tartar chief the conquest of China, and predicted to him that he should soon be seated on the throne at Peking, he would have told him more of truth, had he told him that his whole nation, its manners, its language, its country, was about to be engulfed forever in the Chinese empire. Let any revolution remove the present dynasty, and the Mantchou will be compelled to complete fusion with the empire. Admission to their own country, occupied entirely by the Chinese, will be forbidden to them. In reference to a map of Mantchouria, compiled by the Fathers Jesuits, upon the order of the Emperor Khang-Hi, Father Duhalde says that he abstained from giving the Chinese names of places in the map; and he assigns for this the following reason: "Of what use would it be to a traveler through Mantchouria to be told, for example, that the river Sakhalien-Oula is called by the Chinese Hé-Loung-Kiang, since it is not with Chinese he has there to do; and the Tartars, whose aid he requires, have never heard the Chinese name." This observation might be just enough in the time of Khang-Hi, but now the precise converse would hold good; for in traversing Mantchouria it is always with Chinese you have to deal, and it is always of the Hé-Loung-Kiang that you hear, and never of the Sakhalien-Oula.

Chinese Money Changers.

CHAPTER V.

The Old Blue Town—Quarter of the Tanners—Knavery of the Chinese Traders—Hotel of the Three Perfections—Spoliation of the Tartars by the Chinese—Money Changer's Office—Tartar Coiner—Purchase of two Sheep-skin Robes—Camel Market—Customs of the Cameleers—Assassination of a Grand Lama of the Blue Town—Insurrection of the Lamaseries—Negotiation between the Court of Peking and that of Lha-Ssa—Domestic Lamas—Wandering Lamas—Lamas in Community—Policy of the Mantchou Dynasty with reference to the Lamaseries—Interview with a Thibetian Lama—Departure from the Blue Town.

FROM the Mantchou town to the Old Blue Town is not more than half an hour's walk, along a broad road, constructed through the large market, which narrowed the town. With the exception of the Lamaseries, which rise above the other buildings, you see before you merely an immense mass of houses and shops huddled confusedly together, without any order or arrangement whatever. The ramparts of the old town still exist in all their integrity; but the increase of the population has compelled the people by degrees to pass this barrier. Houses have risen outside the walls one after another until large suburbs have been formed, and now the extra-mural city is larger than the intra-mural.

We entered the city by a broad street, which exhibited nothing remarkable except the large Lamasery, called, in common with the more celebrated establishment in the province of Chan-Si, the Lamasery of the Five Towers. It derives this appellation from a handsome square tower with five turrets, one, very lofty, in the center and one at each angle.

Just beyond this the broad street terminated, and there was no exit but a narrow lane running right and left. We turned down what seemed the least dirty of these, but soon found ourselves in a liquid slough of mud and filth, black, and of suffocating stench—we had got into the Street of the Tanners. We advanced slowly and shudderingly, for beneath the mire lay hid, now a great stone, over which we stumbled, now a hole, into which we sank. To complete our misfortune, we all at once heard before us deafening cries and shouts, indicating that along the tortuosities of the lane in which we were horsemen and carts were about to meet us. To draw back, or to stand aside, were equally impossible, so that our only resource was to bawl on our own account, and, advancing, take our chance. At the next turning we met the cavalcade, and something extremely disagreeable seemed threatening us, when upon sight of our camels, the horses of the other party took fright, and turning right round, galloped off in utter confusion, leaving the way clear before us. Thus, thanks to our beasts of burden, we were enabled to continue our journey without giving the way to any one, and we at last arrived, without any serious accident, in a spacious street, adorned on each side with fine shops.

We looked about for an inn, but fruitlessly; we saw several inns, indeed, but these were not of the kind we sought. In the great towns of Northern China and Tartary each inn is devoted to a particular class of travelers, and will receive no other. "The Corndealers' Arms" inn, for example, will not admit a horse dealer, and so on. The inns which devote themselves to the entertainment of mere travelers are called the taverns of the Transitory Guests. We were pausing, anxiously looking about for one of these, when a young man, hastening from an adjacent shop, came up to us: "You seek an inn, gentlemen travelers," said he; "suffer me to guide you to one; yet I scarcely know one in the Blue City worthy of you. Men are innumerable here, my Lords Lamas; a few good, but, alas! most bad. I speak it from my heart. In the Blue City you would with difficulty find one man who is guided by his conscience; yet conscience is a treasure! You Tartars, you, indeed, know well what conscience is. Ah! I know the Tartars well! excellent people, right-hearted souls! We Chinese are altogether different—rascals, rogues. Not one Chinaman in ten thousand heeds conscience. Here, in this Blue City, everybody, with the merest exceptions, makes it his business to cheat the worthy Tartars, and rob them of their goods. Oh! it's shameful!"

And the excellent creature threw up his eyes as he denounced the knavery of his townsmen. We saw very clearly, however, that the direction taken by the eyes thus thrown up was the camel's back, whereon were two large cases, which our disinterested adviser no doubt took to contain precious merchandise. However, we let him lead us on and chatter as he pleased. When we had been wandering about under his escort for a full hour, and yet had reached no inn, we said to him: "We cannot think of troubling you further, since you yourself seem not to know where we may find that which we need." "Be perfectly easy, my lords," replied he; "I am guiding you to an excellent, a superexcellent hotel. Don't mention a word as to troubling me: you pain me by the idea. What! are we not all brothers? Away with the distinction between Tartar and Chinese! True, the language is not the same, nor the dress; but men have but one heart, one conscience, one invariable rule of justice. Just wait one moment for me, my lords; I will be with you again before you can look round," and so saying he dived into a shop on the left. He was soon back with us, making a thousand apologies for having detained us. "You must be very tired, my lords; one cannot be otherwise when one is traveling. 'Tis quite different from being with one's own family." As he spoke, we were accosted by another Chinese, a ludicrous contrast with our first friend, whose round shining, smiling face was perfectly intense in its aspect of benevolence. The other fellow was meager and lanky, with thin, pinched lips and little black eyes, half buried in the head, that gave to the whole physiognomy a character of the most thorough knavery. "My Lords Lamas," said he, "I see you have just arrived! Excellent! And you have journeyed safely. Well, well! Your camels are magnificent; 'tis no wonder you travel fast and securely upon such animals. Well, you have arrived: that's a great happiness. Se-Eul," he continued, addressing the Chinese who had first got hold of us, "you are guiding these noble Tartars to an hotel. 'Tis well! Take care that the hotel is a good one, worthy of the distinguished strangers. What think you of the 'Tavern of Eternal Equity?'" "The very hotel whither I was leading the Lords Lamas." "There is none better in the empire. By the way, the host is an acquaintance of mine. I cannot do better than accompany you and recommend these noble Tartars to his best care. In fact, if I were not to go with you, I should have a weight upon my heart. When we are fortunate enough to meet brothers who need our aid, how can we do too much for them, for we are all brothers! My lords, you see this young man and myself; well, we two are clerks in the same establishment, and we make it our pride to serve our brothers the Tartars; for, alas! in this dreadful city there is but too little virtue."

Any one, hearing their professions of devoted zeal, would have imagined these two personages to have been the friends of our childhood; but we were sufficiently acquainted with Chinese manners to perceive at once that we were the mark of a couple of swindlers. Accordingly, when we saw inscribed on a door, " Hotel of the Three Perfections; transitory guests on horse and camel entertained, and their affairs transacted with infallible success," we at once directed our course up the gateway, despite the vehement remonstrances of our worthy guides, and rode down a long avenue to the great square court of the hotel. The little blue cap worn by the attendants indicated that we were in a Turkish establishment.

This proceeding of ours was not at all what the two Chinese desired; but they still followed us, and, without appearing disconcerted, continued to act their parts. "Where are the people of the hotel," cried they, with an immense air; "let them prepare a large apartment, a fine, clean apartment? Their Excellencies have arrived, and must be suitably accommodated." One of the principal waiters presented himself, holding by his teeth a key, in one hand a broom, and in the other a watering-pot. Our two protectors immediately took possession of these articles. "Leave everything to us," said they; "it is we who claim the honor of personally waiting upon our illustrious friends; you, attendants of the hotel, you only do things by halves, actuated as you are merely by mercenary considerations." And thereupon they set to work sprinkling, sweeping, and cleaning the room to which the waiter guided us. When this operation was concluded, we seated ourselves on the khang; the two Chinese "knew themselves better than to sit by the side of our Eminent Distinctions," and they accordingly squatted on the floor. As tea was being served, a young man, well attired and of exceedingly elegant address, came into the room, carrying by the four corners a silk handkerchief. "Gentlemen Lamas," said the elder of our previous companions, "this young man is the son of our principal, and doubtless has been sent by his father to inquire after your health, and whether you have so far journeyed in peace." The young man placed his handkerchief upon the table that stood before us. "Here are some cakes my father has sent to be eaten with your tea. When you have finished that meal, he entreats you will come and partake of an humble repast in our poor dwelling." "But why wear your hearts out thus for us mere strangers?" "Oh!" exclaimed all three in chorus, "the words you utter cover us with blushes! What! can we do anything in excess for brothers who have thus honored us with their presence in our poor city!" "Poor Tartars!" said I in French to my colleague, "how thoroughly eaten up they must be when they fall into such hands as these!" These words, in an unknown tongue, excited considerable surprise in our worthy friends. "In which of the illustrious kingdoms of Tartary dwell your Excellencies?" asked one of them. "We are not Tartars at all," was the reply. "Ah! we saw that at once; the Tartars have no such majesty of aspect as yours; their mien has no grandeur about it! May we ask what is the noble country whence you come?" "We are from the West; our native land is far hence." "Quite so," replied the eldest of the three knaves. I knew it, and I said so to these young men, but they are ignorant; they know nothing about physiognomy. Ah! you are from the West. I know your country well; I have been there more than once." "We are delighted to hear this: doubtless, then, you are acquainted with our language?" "Why, I cannot say I know it thoroughly; but there are some few words I understand. I can't speak them, indeed; but that does not matter. You western people are so clever, you know everything, the Chinese language, the Tartarian, the western—you can speak them all. I have always been closely mixed up with your countrymen, and have invariably been selected to manage their affairs for them whenever they come to the Blue Town. It is always I who make their purchases for them."

We had by this time finished our tea; our three friends rose, and with a simultaneous bow, invited us to accompany them. "My lords, the repast is by this time prepared, and our chief awaits you." "Listen," said we, gravely, "while we utter words full of reason. You have taken the trouble to guide us to an inn, which shows you to be men of warm hearts; you have here swept for us and prepared our room; again, in proof of your excellent dispositions, your master has sent us pastry, which manifests in him a benevolence incapable of exhaustion towards the wayfaring stranger. You now invite us to go and dine with you: we cannot possibly trespass so grossly upon your kindness. No, dear friends, you must excuse us; if we desire to make some purchases in your establishment, you may rely upon us. For the present we will not detain you. We are going to dine at the Turkish Eating House." So saying, we rose and ushered our excellent friends to the door.

The commercial intercourse between the Tartars and the Chinese is revoltingly iniquitous on the part of the latter. So soon as Mongols, simple, ingenuous men, if such there be at all in the world, arrive in a trading town, they are snapped up by some Chinese, who carry them off, as it were, by main force, to their houses, give them tea for themselves and forage for their animals, and cajole them in every conceivable way. The Mongols, themselves without guile and incapable of conceiving guile in others, take all they hear to be perfectly genuine, and congratulate themselves, conscious as they are of their inaptitude for business, upon their good fortune in thus meeting with brothers, *Ahatou*, as they say, in whom they can place full confidence, and who will undertake to manage their whole business for them. A good dinner provided gratis in the back shop, completes the illusion. "If these people wanted to rob me," says the Tartar to himelf, "they would not go to all this expense in giving me a dinner for nothing." When once the Chinese has got hold of the Tartar, he employs over him all the resources of the skilful and utterly unprincipled knavery of the Chinese character. He keeps him in his house, eating, drinking, and smoking, one day after another, until his subordinates have sold all the poor man's cattle, or whatever else he has to sell, and bought for him, in return, the commodities he requires, at prices double and triple the market value. But so plausible is the Chinese, and so simple is the Tartar, that the latter invariably departs with the most entire conviction of the immense philanthropy of the former, and with a promise to return, when he has other goods to sell, to the establishment where he has been treated so fraternally.

The next morning we went out to purchase some winter clothing, the want of which began to make itself sensibly felt. But first, in order to facilitate our dealings, we had to sell some ounces of silver. The money of the Chinese consists entirely of small round copper coins, of the size of our halfpenny, with a square hole in the center, through which the people string them, so that they may be more conveniently carried. These coins the Chinese call, tsien; the Tartars, dehos; and the Europeans, sapeks. Gold and silver are not coined at all; they are melted into ingots of various sizes, and thus put into circulation. Gold-dust and gold leaf are also current in commerce, and they also possess bank-notes. The ordinary value of the ounce of silver is 1,700 or 1,800 sapeks, according to the scarcity or abundance of silver in the country.

The money changers have two irregular modes of making a profit by their traffic: if they state the fair price of silver to the customer, they cheat him in the weight; if their scales and their method of weighing are accurate, they diminish the price of the silver accordingly. But when they have to do with Tartars, they employ neither of these methods of fraud; on the contrary, they weigh the silver scrupulously, and sometimes allow a little overweight, and even they pay them above the market price; in fact, they appear to be quite losers by the transaction, and so they would be, if the weight and the price of the silver alone were considered; their advantage is derived, in these cases, from their manner of calculating the amount. When they come to reduce the silver into sapeks, they do indeed reduce it, making the most flagrant miscalculations, which the Tartars, who can count nothing beyond their beads, are quite incapable of detecting, and which they, accordingly, adopt implicitly, and even with satisfaction, always considering they have sold their bullion well, since they know the full weight has been allowed, and that the full market price has been given.

At the money changers in the Blue Town, to which we went to sell some silver, the Chinese dealers essayed, according to custom, to apply this fraud to us, but they were disconcerted. The weight shown by their scales was perfectly correct, and the price they offered us was rather above the ordinary course of exchange, and the bargain between us was so far concluded. The chief clerk took the souan-pan, the calculation table used by the Chinese, and after calculating with an appearance of intense nicety, announced the result of his operation. "This is an exchange-office," said we; "you are the buyers, we the sellers; you have made your calculation, we will make ours: give us a pencil and a piece of paper."—" Nothing can be more just; you have enunciated a fundamental law of commerce," and so saying, they handed us a writing-case. We took the pencil, and a very short calculation exhibited a difference in our favor of a thousand sapeks. "Superintendent of the bank," said we, "your souan-pan is in error by a thousand sapeks."—" Impossible! Do you think that all of a sudden I've forgotten my souan-pan? Let me go over it again;" and he proceeded with an air of great anxiety to appear correct, to set his calculating machine once more in operation, the other customers by our side looking on with great amazement at all this. When he had done: "Yes," said he, " I knew I was right; see, brother;" and he passed the machine to a colleague behind the counter, who went over his calculation; the result of their operations was exactly the same to a fraction. "You see," said the principal, " there is no error. How is it that our calculation does not agree with that which you have written down here?"—" It is unimportant to inquire why your calculation does not agree with ours; this is certain, that your calculation is wrong and ours right. You see these little characters that we have traced on this paper; they are a very different thing from your souan-pan; it is impossible for them to be wrong. Were all the calculators in the world to work the whole of their lives upon this operation, they could arrive at no other result than this; that your statement is wrong by a thousand sapeks."

The money-changers were extremely embarrassed, and began to turn very red, when a bystander, who perceived that the affair was assuming an awkward aspect, presented himself as umpire. "I'll reckon it up for you," said he, and taking the souan-pan, his calculation agreed with ours. The superintendent of the bank hereupon made us a profound bow: "Sirs Lamas," said he, "your mathematics are better than mine." "Oh, not at all," replied we, with a bow equally profound; "your souan-pan is excellent, but who ever heard of a calculator always exempt from error? People like you may very well be mistaken once and a way, whereas poor simple folks like us make blunders ten thousand times. Now, however, we have fortunately concurred in our reckoning, thanks to the pains you have taken." These phrases were rigorously required under the circumstances, by Chinese politeness. Whenever any person in China is compromised by any awkward incident, those present always carefully refrain from any observation which may make him blush, or as the Chinese phrase it, take away his face.

After our conciliatory address had restored self-possession to all present, everybody drew round the piece of paper on which we had cast up our sum in Arabic numerals. "That is a fine souan-pan," said one to another; "simple, sure, and speedy."—"Sirs Lamas," asked the principal, "what do these characters mean? What souan-pan is this?" "This souan-pan is infallible," returned we; "the characters are those which the Mandarins of Celestial Literature use in calculating eclipses, and the course of the seasons."[1] After a brief conversation on the merits of the Arabic numerals, the cashier handed us the full amount of sapeks, and we parted good friends.

[1] The Fathers Jesuits introduced the use of Arabic numerals into the Observatory at Peking.

The Chinese are sometimes victims to their own knavery, and we have known even Tartars catch them in a snare. One day a Mongol presented himself at the counter of a Chinese money-changer, with a youen-pao carefully packed and sealed. A youen-pao is an ingot of silver weighing three pounds—in China there are sixteen ounces to the pound; the three pounds are never very rigorously exacted; there being generally four or five ounces over, so that the usual weight of an ingot of silver is fifty-two ounces. The Tartar had no sooner unpacked his youen-pao than the Chinese clerk resolved to defraud him of an ounce or two, and weighing it, he pronounced it to be fifty ounces. "My youen-pao weighs fifty-two ounces," exclaimed the Tartar. "I weighed it before I left home." "Oh, your Tartar scales are all very well for sheep; but they don't do for weighing bullion." After much haggling, the bargain was concluded, the youen-pao was purchased as weighing fifty ounces, and the Tartar, having first required and obtained a certificate of the stated weight and value of the ingot, returned to his tent with a good provision of sapeks and bank notes.

In the evening the principal of the establishment received the usual report from each clerk of the business done in the course of the day. "I," said one of them with a triumphant air, "bought a youen-pao of silver, and made two ounces by it." He produced the ingot, which the chief received with a smile, soon changing into a frown. "What have you got here?" cried he. "This is not silver!" The ingot was handed round, and all the clerks saw that indeed it was base bullion. "I know the Tartar," said the clerk who had purchased it, "and will have him up before the Mandarin."

The satellites of justice were forthwith dispatched after the roguish Tartar, whose offense, proved against him, was matter of capital punishment. It was obvious that the ingot was base bullion, and on the face of the affair there was clear proof that the Tartar had sold it. The Tartar, however, stoutly repudiated the imputation. "The humblest of the humble," said he, "craves that he may be allowed to put forth a word in his defense." "Speak," said the Mandarin, "but beware how you say aught other than the exact truth." "It is true," proceeded the Tartar, "that I sold a youen-pao at this person's shop, but it was all pure silver. I am a Tartar, a poor, simple man, and these people, seeking to take advantage of me, have substituted a false for my genuine ingot. I cannot command many words, but I pray our father and mother (*i.e.* the Mandarin), to have this false youen-pao weighed." The ingot was weighed, and was found to contain fifty-two ounces. The Tartar now drew from one of his boots a small parcel, containing, wrapped in rags, a piece of paper, which he held up to the Mandarin. "Here is a certificate," cried he, "which I received at the shop, and which attests the value and weight of the youen-pao that I sold." The Mandarin looked over the paper with a roguish smile, and then said: "According to the testimony of the clerk himself who wrote this certificate, this Mongol sold to him a youen-pao weighing fifty ounces; this youen-pao of base bullion weighs fifty-two ounces; this, therefore, cannot be the Mongol's youen-pao; but now comes the question, whose is it? Who are really the persons that have false bullion in their possession?" Every body present, the Mandarin included, knew perfectly well how the case stood; but the Chinese magistrate, tickled with the Tartar's ingenuity, gave him the benefit of the clerk's dull roguery, and dismissed the charge; but not so the accusers, who were well bastinadoed, and would have been put to death as coiners, had they not found means to appease justice by the present of some ingots of purer metal. It is only, however, upon very rare and extraordinary occasions that the Mongols get the better of the Chinese. In the ordinary course of things, they are everywhere, and always, and in every way, the dupes of their neighbors who by dint of cunning and unprincipled machinations, reduce them to poverty.

Upon receiving our sapeks, we proceeded to buy the winter clothing we needed. Upon a consideration of the meagerness of our exchequer, we came to the resolution that it would be better to purchase what we required at some second-hand shop. In China and Tartary no one has the smallest repugnance to wear other people's clothes; he who has not himself the attire wherein to pay a visit or make a holiday, goes without ceremony to a neighbor and borrows a hat, or a pair of trousers, or boots, or shoes, or whatever else he wants, and nobody is at all surprised at these borrowings, which are quite a custom. The only hesitation any one has in lending his clothes to a neighbor, is lest the borrower should sell them in payment of some debt, or, after using them, pawn them. People who buy clothes buy them indifferently, new or second-hand. The question of price is alone taken into consideration, for there is no more delicacy felt about putting on another man's hat or trousers, than there is about living in a house that some one else has occupied before you.

This custom of wearing other people's things was by no means to our taste, and all the less so, that ever since our arrival at the mission of Si-Wang, we had not been under the necessity of departing from our old habits in this respect. Now, however, the slenderness of our purse compelled us to waive our repugnance. We went out, therefore, in search of a second-hand clothes shop, of which, in every town here, there are a greater or less number, for the most part in connection with pawnshops, called in these countries Tang-Pou. Those who borrow upon pledges are seldom able to redeem the articles they have deposited, which they accordingly leave to die, as the Tartars and Chinese express it; or in other words, they allow the period of redemption to pass, and the articles pass altogether from them. The old clothes shops of the Blue Town were filled in this way with Tartar spoils, so that we had the opportunity of selecting exactly the sort of things we required, to suit the new costume we had adopted.

At the first shop we visited they showed us a quantity of wretched garments turned up with sheep-skin; but though these rags were exceedingly old, and so covered with grease that it was impossible to guess at their original color, the price asked for them was exorbitant. After a protracted haggling, we found it impossible to come to terms, and we gave up this first attempt; and we gave it up, be it added, with a certain degree of satisfaction, for our self-respect was somewhat wounded at finding ourselves reduced even to the proposition of wearing such filthy rags. We visited another shop, and another, a third, and a fourth, and still several more. We were shown magnificent garments, handsome garments, fair garments, endurable garments, but the consideration of expense was, in each instance, an impracticable stumbling-block. The journey we had undertaken might endure for several years, and extreme economy, at all events in the outset, was indispensable. After going about the whole day, after making the acquaintance of all the rag-merchants in the Blue Town, after turning over and over all their old clothes, we were fain to return to the second-hand dealer whom we had first visited, and to make the best bargain we could with him. We purchased from him, at last, two ancient robes of sheep-skin, covered with some material, the nature of which it was impossible to identify, and the original color of which we suspected to have been yellow. We proceeded to try them on, and it was at once evident that the tailor in making them had by no means had us in his eye. M. Gabet's robe was too short, M. Huc's too long; but a friendly exchange was impracticable, the difference in height between the two missionaries being altogether too disproportionate. We at first thought of cutting the excess from the one, in order to make up the deficiency of the other; but then we should have had to call in the aid of a tailor, and this would have involved another drain upon our purse; the pecuniary consideration decided the question, and we determined to wear the clothes as they were, M. Huc adopting the expedient of holding up, by means of a girdle, the surplus of his robe, and M. Gabet resigning himself to the exposure to the public gaze of a portion of his legs: the main inconvenience, after all, being the manifestation to all who saw us that we could not attire ourselves in exact proportion to our size.

Provided with our sheep-skin coats, we next asked the dealer to show us his collection of second-hand winter hats. We examined several of these, and at last selected two caps of fox-skin, the elegant form of which reminded us of the shakos of our sappers. These purchases completed, each of us put under his arm his packet of old clothes, and we returned to the hotel of the "Three Perfections."

We remained two days longer at Koukou-Khoton; for, besides that we needed repose, we were glad of the opportunity of seeing this great town, and of becoming acquainted with the numerous and celebrated Lamaseries established there.

The Blue Town enjoys considerable commercial importance, which it has acquired chiefly through its Lamaseries, the reputation of which attracts thither Mongols from the most distant parts of the empire. The Mongols bring hither large herds of oxen, camels, horses, sheep, and loads of furs, mushrooms, and salt, the only produce of the deserts of Tartary. They receive, in return, brick-tea, linen, saddlery, odoriferous sticks to burn before their idols, oatmeal, millet, and kitchen utensils.

The Blue Town is especially noted for its great trade in camels. The camel market is a large square in the center of the town; the animals are ranged here in long rows, their front feet raised upon a mud elevation constructed for that purpose, the object being to show off the size and height of the creatures. It is impossible to describe the uproar and confusion of this market, what with the incessant bawling of the buyers and sellers as they dispute, their noisy chattering after they have agreed, and the horrible shrieking of the camels at having their noses pulled for the purpose of making them show their agility in kneeling and rising. In order to test the strength of the camel, and the burden it is capable of bearing, they make it kneel, and then pile one thing after another upon its back, causing it to rise under each addition, until it can rise no longer. They sometimes use the following expedient: While the camel is kneeling, a man gets upon its hind heels, and holds on by the long hair of its hump; if the camel can rise then, it is considered an animal of superior power.

The trade in camels is entirely conducted by proxy: the seller and the buyer never settle the matter between themselves. They select indifferent persons to sell their goods, who propose, discuss, and fix the price; the one looking to the interests of the seller, the other to those of the purchaser. These "sale-speakers" exercise no other trade; they go from market to market to promote business, as they say. They have generally a great knowledge of cattle, have much fluency of tongue, and are, above all, endowed with a knavery beyond all shame. They dispute, by turns, furiously and argumentatively, as to the merits and defects of the animal; but as soon as it comes to a question of price, the tongue is laid aside as a medium, and the conversation proceeds altogether in signs. They seize each other by the wrist, and beneath the long wide sleeve of their jackets, indicate with their fingers the progress of the bargain. After the affair is concluded they partake of the dinner, which is always given by the purchaser, and then receive a certain

The Camel Market.

number of sapeks, according to the custom of different places.

In the Blue Town there exist five great Lamaseries, each inhabited by more than 2,000 Lamas; besides these, they reckon fifteen less considerable establishments—branches, as it were, of the former. The number of regular Lamas resident in this city may fairly be stated at 20,000. As to those who inhabit the different quarters of the town, engaged in commerce and horse-dealing, they are innumerable. The Lamasery of the Five Towers is the finest and the most famous: here it is that the Hobilgan lives—that is, a Grand Lama—who, after having been identified with the substance of Buddha, has already undergone several times the process of transmigration. He sits here upon the altar once occupied by the Guison-Tamba, having ascended it after a tragical event, which very nearly brought about a revolution in the empire.

The Emperor Khang-Hi, during the great military expedition which he made in the West against the Oelets, one day, in traversing the Blue Town, expressed a wish to pay a visit to the Guison-Tamba, at that time the Grand Lama of the

Five Towers. The latter received the Emperor without rising from the throne, or manifesting any kind of respect. Just as Khang-Hi drew near to speak to him, a Kian-Kan, or high military Mandarin, indignant at this unceremonious treatment of his master, drew his saber, fell upon the Guison-Tamba, and laid him dead on the steps of his throne. This terrible event roused the whole Lamasery, and indignation quickly communicated itself to all the Lamas of the Blue Town.

They ran to arms in every quarter, and the life of the Emperor, who had but a small retinue, was exposed to the greatest danger. In order to calm the irritation of the Lamas, he publicly reproached the Kian-Kan with his violence. "If the Guison-Tamba," answered the Kian-Kan, "was not a living Buddha, why did he not rise in the presence of the master of the universe? If he was a living Buddha, how was it he did not know I was going to kill him?" Meanwhile the danger to the life of the Emperor became every moment more imminent; he had no other means of escape than that of taking off his imperial robes, and attiring himself in the dress of a private soldier. Under favor of this disguise, and the general confusion, he was enabled to rejoin his army, which was near at hand. The greater part of the men who had accompanied the Emperor into the Blue Town were massacred, and among the rest, the murderer of the Guison-Tamba.

The Mongols sought to profit by this movement. Shortly afterwards it was announced that the Guison-Tamba had reappeared, and that he had transmigrated to the country of the Khalkhas, who had taken him under their protection, and had sworn to avenge his murder. The Lamas of the Great Kouren set actively to the work of organization. They stripped off their red and yellow robes, clothed themselves in black, in memory of the disastrous event of the Blue Town, and allowed the hair and beard to grow, in sign of grief. Everything seemed to presage a grand rising of the Tartar tribes. The great energy and rare diplomatic talents of the Emperor Khang-Hi alone sufficed to arrest its progress. He immediately opened negotiations with the Talé-Lama, Sovereign of Thibet, who was induced to use all his influence with the Lamas for the re-establishment of order whilst Khang-Hi was intimidating the Khalkha kings by means of his troops. Gradually peace was restored; the Lamas resumed their red and yellow robes; but, as a memorial of their coalition in favor of the Guison-Tamba, they retained a narrow border of black on the collar of their robes. Khalkha Lamas alone bear this badge of distinction.

Ever since that period, a Hobilgan has taken the place in the Blue Town of the Guison-Tamba, who himself is resident at the great Kouren, in the district of the Khalkhas. Meanwhile, the Emperor Khang-Hi, whose penetrating genius was always occupied with the future, was not entirely satisfied with these arrangements. He did not believe in all these doctrines of transmigration, and clearly saw that the Khalkhas, in pretending that the Guison-Tamba had reappeared among them, had no other end than that of keeping at their disposal a power capable of contending, upon occasion, with that of the Chinese Emperor. To abolish the office of Guison-Tamba would have been a desperate affair; the only course was, whilst tolerating him, to neutralize his influence. It was decreed, with the concurrence of the Court of Lha-Ssa, that the Guison-Tamba should be recognized legitimate sovereign of the great Kouren; but that after his successive deaths, he should always be bound to make his transmigration to Thibet. Khang-Hi had good reason to believe that a Thibetian by origin would espouse with reluctance the resentments of the Khalkhas against the Court of Peking.

The Guison-Tamba, full of submission and respect for the orders of Khang-Hi and of the Talé-Lama, has never failed since that to go and accomplish his metempsychosis in Thibet. Still, as they fetch him whilst he is yet an infant, he must necessarily be influenced by those about him; and it is said, that as he grows up, he imbibes sentiments little favorable to the reigning dynasty. In 1839, when the Guison-Tamba made that journey to Peking, of which we have spoken, the alarm manifested by the Court arose from the recollection of these events. The Lamas who flock from all the districts of Tartary to the Lamaseries of the Blue Town, rarely remain there permanently. After taking their degrees, as it were, in these quasi universities, they return, one class of them, to their own countries, where they either settle in the small Lamaseries, wherein they can be more independent, or live at home with their families; retaining of their order little more than its red and yellow habit.

Another class consists of those Lamas who live neither in Lamaseries nor at home with their families, but spend their time vagabondizing about like birds of passage, traveling all over their own and the adjacent countries, and subsisting upon the rude hospitality which, in Lamasery and in tent they are sure to receive, throughout their wandering way. Lamasery or tent, they enter without ceremony, seat themselves, and while the tea is preparing for their refreshment, give their host an account of the places they have visited in their rambles. If they think fit to sleep where they are, they stretch themselves on the floor and repose until the morning. After breakfast, they stand at the entrance of the tent, and watch the clouds for a while, and see whence the wind blows; then they take their way, no matter whither, by this path or that, east or west, north or south, as their fancy or a smoother turf suggests, and lounge tranquilly on, sure at least, if no other shelter presents itself by and by, of the shelter of the cover, as they express it, of that great tent, the world; and sure, moreover, having no destination before them, never to lose their way.

The wandering Lamas visit all the countries readily accessible to them:—China, Mantchouria, the Khalkhas, the various kingdoms of Southern Mongolia, the Ourianghai, the Koukou-Noor, the northern and southern slopes of the Celestial Mountains, Thibet, India, and sometimes even Turkestan. There is no stream which they have not crossed, no mountains they have not climbed, no Grand Lama before whom they have not prostrated themselves, no people with whom they have not associated, and whose customs and language are unknown to them. Traveling without any end in view, the places they reach are always those they sought. The story of the Wandering Jew, who is forever a wanderer, is exactly realized in these Lamas. They seem influenced by some secret power, which makes them wander unceasingly from place to place. God seems to have infused into the blood which flows in their veins, something of that motive power which propels them on their way, without allowing them to stop.

The Lamas living in community are those who compose the third class. A Lamasery is a collection of small houses

Vagabond Lamas.

built around one or more Buddhic temples. These dwellings are more or less large and beautiful, according to the means of the proprietor. The Lamas who live thus in community, are generally more regular than the others; they pay more attention to prayer and study. They are allowed to keep a few animals; some cows to afford them milk and butter, the principal materials of their daily food; horses; and some sheep to be killed on festivals.

Generally speaking, the Lamaseries have endowments, either royal or imperial. At certain periods of the year, the revenues are distributed to the Lamas according to the station which they have obtained in the hierarchy. Those who have the reputation of being learned physicians, or able fortune-tellers, have often the opportunity of acquiring possession of the property of strangers; yet they seldom seem to become rich. A childish and heedless race, they cannot make a moderate use of the riches they acquire; their money goes as quickly as it comes. The same Lama whom you saw yesterday in dirty, torn rags, to-day rivals in the magnificence of his attire the grandeur of the highest dignitaries of the Lamasery. So soon as animals or money are placed within his disposition, he starts off to the next trading town, sells what he has to sell, and clothes himself in the richest attire he can purchase. For a month or two he plays the elegant idler, and then, his money all gone, he repairs once more to the Chinese town, this time to pawn his fine clothes for what he can get, and with the certainty that once in the Tang-Pou, he will never, except by some chance, redeem them. All the pawnbrokers' shops in the Tartar Chinese towns are full of these Lama relics. The Lamas are very numerous in Tartary; we think we may affirm, without exaggeration, that they compose at least a third of the population. In almost all families, with the exception of the eldest son, who remains a layman, the male children become Lamas.

The Tartars embrace this profession compulsorily, not of their own free will; they are Lamas or laymen from their birth, according to the will of the parents. But as they grow up, they grow accustomed to this life; and, in the end, religious exaltation attaches them strongly to it.

It is said that the policy of the Mantchou dynasty is to increase the number of Lamas in Tartary; the Chinese Mandarins so assured us, and the thing seems probable enough. It is certain that the government of Peking, whilst it leaves to poverty and want the Chinese Bonzes, honors and favors Lamaism in a special degree. The secret intention of the government, in augmenting the number of the Lamas, who are bound to celibacy, is to arrest, by this means, the progress of the population of Tartary. The recollection of the former power of the Mongols ever fills its mind; it knows that they were formerly masters of the empire,—and in the fear of a new invasion, it seeks to enfeeble them by all the means in its power. Yet, although Mongolia is scantily peopled, in comparison with its immense extent, it could, at a day's notice, send forth a formidable army. A high Lama, the Guison-Tamba, for instance, would have but to raise his finger, and all the Mongols, from the frontier of Siberia to the extremities of Thibet, rising as one man, would precipitate themselves like a torrent wherever their sainted leader might direct them. The profound peace which they have enjoyed for more than two centuries, might seem to have necessarily enervated their warlike character: nevertheless, you may still observe that they have not altogether lost their taste for warlike adventures. The great campaigns of Tsing-Kis-Khan, who led them to the conquest of the world, have not escaped their memory during the long period of leisure of their nomadic life; they love to talk of them, and to feed their imagination with vague projects of invasion.

During our short stay at the Blue Town we had constant conversation with the Lamas of the most celebrated Lamaseries, endeavoring to obtain fresh information on the state of Buddhism in Tartary and Thibet. All they told us only served to confirm us more and more in what we had before learnt on this subject. In the Blue Town, as at Tolon-Noor, every one told us that the doctrine would appear more sublime and more luminous as we advanced towards the West. From what the Lamas said, who had visited Thibet, Lha-Ssa was, as it were, a great focus of light, the rays of which grew more and more feeble in proportion as they became removed from their center.

One day we had an opportunity of talking with a Thibetian Lama for some time, and the things he told us about religion astounded us greatly. A brief explanation of the Christian doctrine, which we gave to him, seemed scarcely to surprise him; he even maintained that our views differed little from those of the Grand Lamas of Thibet. "You must not confound," said he, "religious truths with the superstitions of the vulgar. The Tartars, poor, simple people, prostrate themselves before whatever they see; everything with them is Borhan. Lamas, prayer-books, temples, Lamaseries, stones, heaps of bones,—'tis all the same to them; down they go on their knees, crying, Borhan! Borhan!" "But the Lamas themselves admit innumerable Borhans?" "Let me explain," said our friend, smilingly; "there is but one sole Sovereign of the universe, the Creator of all things, alike without beginning and without end. In Dchagar (India) he bears the name of Buddha, in Thibet, that of Samtche Mitcheba (all Powerful Eternal); the Dcha-Mi (Chinese) call him Fo, and the Sok-Po-Mi (Tartars), Borhan." "You say that Buddha is sole; in that case who are the Talé-Lama of Lha-Ssa, the Bandchan of Djachi-Loumbo, the Tsong-Kaba of the Sifan, the Kaldan of Tolon-Noor, the Guison-Tamba of the Great Kouren, the Hobilgan of Blue Town, the Hotoktou of Peking, the

Chaberon of the Tartar and Thibetian Lamaseries generally?" "They all are equally Buddha." "Is Buddha visible?" " No, he is without a body; he is a spiritual substance." " So, Buddha is sole, and yet there exist innumerable Buddhas: the Talé-Lama, and so on. Buddha is incorporeal; he cannot be seen, and yet the Talé-Lama, the Guison-Tamba, and the rest are visible, and have bodies like our own. How do you explain all this?" "The doctrine, I tell you, is true," said the Lama, raising his arm, and assuming a remarkable accent of authority; " it is the doctrine of the West, but it is of unfathomable profundity. It cannot be sounded to the bottom."

These words of the Thibetian Lama astonished us strangely; the Unity of God, the mystery of the Incarnation, the dogma of the Real Presence seemed to us enveloped in his creed; yet with ideas so sound in appearance, he admitted the metempsychosis, and a sort of pantheism of which he could give no account.

These new indications respecting the religion of Buddha gave us hopes that we should really find among the Lamas of Thibet a symbolism more refined and superior to the common belief, and confirmed us in the resolution we had adopted, of keeping on our course westward.

Previous to quitting the inn we called in the landlord to settle our bill. We had calculated that the entertainment, during four days, of three men and our animals, would cost us at least two ounces of silver; we were therefore agreeably surprised to hear the landlord say, " Sirs Lamas, there is no occasion for going into any accounts; put 300 sapeks into the till, and that will do very well. My house," he added, " is recently established, and I want to give it a good character. You are come from a distant land, and I would enable you to say to your countrymen that my establishment is worthy of their confidence." We replied that we would everywhere mention his disinterestedness; and that our countrymen, whenever they had occasion to visit the Blue Town, would certainly not fail to put-up at the " Hotel of the Three Perfections."

Tchagan-Kouren.

CHAPTER VI.

A Tartar-eater—Loss of Arsalan—Great Caravan of Camels—Night Arrival at Tchagan-Kouren—We are refused Admission into the Inns—We take up our abode with a Shepherd—Overflow of the Yellow River—Aspect of Tchagan-Kouren—Departure across the Marshes—Hiring a Bark—Arrival on the Banks of the Yellow River—Encampment under the Portico of a Pagoda—Embarkation of the Camels—Passage of the Yellow River—Laborious Journey across the Inundated Country—Encampment on the Banks of the River.

WE quitted the Blue Town on the fourth day of the ninth moon. We had already been traveling more than a month. It was with the utmost difficulty that our little caravan could get out of the town. The streets were encumbered with men, cars, animals, stalls in which the traders displayed their goods; we could only advance step by step, and at times we were obliged to come to a halt, and wait for some minutes until the way became a little cleared. It was near noon before we reached the last houses of the town, outside the western gate. There, upon a level road, our camels were at length able to proceed at their ease in all the fulness of their long step. A chain of rugged rocks rising on our right sheltered us so completely from the north wind, that we did not at all feel the rigor of the weather. The country through which we were now traveling was still a portion of Western Toumet. We observed in all directions the same indications of prosperity and comfort which had so much gratified us east of the town. Everywhere around substantial villages presented proofs of successful agriculture and trade. Although we could not set up our tent in the cultivated fields by which we were now surrounded, yet, so far as circumstances permitted, we adhered to our Tartar habits. Instead of entering an inn to take our morning meal, we seated ourselves under a rock or tree, and there breakfasted upon some rolls fried in oil, of which we had bought a supply at the Blue Town. The passers-by laughed at this rustic proceeding, but they were not surprised at it. Tartars, unused to the manners of civilized nations, are entitled to take their repast by the roadside even in places where inns abound.

During the day this mode of traveling was pleasant and convenient enough; but, as it would not have been prudent to remain out all night, at sunset we sought an inn: the preservation of our animals of itself sufficed to render this proceeding necessary. There was nothing for them to eat on the wayside, and had we not resorted in the evening to places where we could purchase forage for them, they would, of course, have speedily died.

On the second evening after our departure from Blue Town, we encountered at an inn a very singular personage. We had just tied our animals to a manger under a shed in the great court, when a traveler made his appearance, leading by a halter a lean, rawboned horse. The traveler was short, but then his rotundity was prodigious. He wore on his head a great straw hat, the flapping brim of which rested on his shoulders; a long saber suspended from his girdle presented an amusing contrast with the peaceful joyousness of his physiognomy. "Superintendent of the soupkettle," cried he, as he entered, "is there room for me in your tavern?" "I have but one travelers' room," answered the innkeeper, "and three Mongols who have just come occupy it; you can ask them if they will make room for you." The traveler waddled towards us. "Peace and happiness unto you, Sirs Lamas; do you need the whole of your room, or can you accommodate me?" "Why not? We are all travelers, and should serve one another." "Words of excellence! You are Tartars; I am Chinese, yet, comprehending the claims of hospitality, you act upon the truth, that all men are brothers." Hereupon, fastening his horse to a manger, he joined us, and, having deposited his traveling-bag upon the kang, stretched himself at full length, with the air of a man greatly fatigued. "Whither are you bound?" asked we; "are you going to buy up salt or catsup for some Chinese company?" "No; I represent a great commercial house at Peking, and I am collecting some debts from the Tartars. Where are you going?" "We shall to-day pass the Yellow River to Tchagan-Kouren, and then journey westward through the country of the Ortous." "You are not Mongols, apparently?" "No; we are from the West." "Well, it seems we are both of one trade; you, like myself, are Tartar-eaters." "Tartar-eaters! What do you mean?" "Why, we eat the Tartars. You eat them by prayers; I by commerce. And why not? The Mongols are poor simpletons, and we may as well get their money as anybody else." "You are mistaken. Since we entered Tartary we have spent a great deal, but we have never taken a single sapek from the Tartars." "Oh, nonsense!" "What! do you suppose our camels and our baggage came to us from the Mongols?" "Why, I thought you came here to recite your prayers." We entered into some explanation of the difference between our principles and those of the Lamas, for whom the traveler had mistaken us, and he was altogether amazed at our disinterestedness. "Things are quite the other way here," said he. "You won't get a Lama to say prayers for nothing; and certainly, as for me, I should never set foot in Tartary but for the sake of money." "But how is it you manage to make such good meals of the Tartars?" "Oh, we devour them; we pick them clean. You've observed the silly race, no doubt; whatever they see when they come into our towns they want, and when we know who they are, and where we can find them, we let them have goods upon credit, of course at a considerable advance upon the price, and upon interest at thirty or forty per cent, which is quite right and necessary. In China the Emperor's laws do not allow this; it is only done with the Tartars. Well, they don't pay the money, and the interest goes on until there is a good sum owing worth the coming for. When we come for it, they've no money, so we merely take all the cattle and sheep and horses we can get hold of for the interest, and leave the capital debt and future interest to be paid next time, and so it goes on from one generation to another. Oh! a Tartar debt is a complete gold mine."

Day had not broken when the Yao-Tchang-Ti (exactor of debts) was on foot. "Sirs Lamas," said he, "I am going to saddle my horse, and proceed on my way,—I propose to travel to-day with you." "'Tis a singular mode of traveling with people, to start before they're up," said we. "Oh, your camels go faster than my horse; you'll soon overtake me, and we shall enter Tchagan-Kouren (White Enclosure) together." He rode off, and at daybreak we followed him. This was a black day with us, for in it we had to mourn a loss. After traveling several hours, we perceived that Arsalan was not with the caravan. We halted, and Samdadchiemba, mounted on his little mule, turned back in search of the dog. He went through several villages which we had passed in the course of the morning, but his search was fruitless; he returned without having either seen or heard of Arsalan. "The dog was Chinese," said Samdadchiemba; "he was not used to a nomadic life, and getting tired of wandering about over the desert, he has taken service in the cultivated district. What is to be done? Shall we wait for him?" "No, it is late, and we are far from White Enclosure." "Well, if there is no dog, there is no dog; and we must do without him." This sentimental effusion of Samdadchiemba gravely delivered, we proceeded on our way.

At first, the loss of Arsalan grieved us somewhat. We were accustomed to see him running to and fro in the prairie, rolling in the long grass, chasing the gray squirrels, and scaring the eagles from their seat on the plain. His incessant evolutions served to break the monotony of the country through which we were passing, and to abridge, in some degree, the tedious length of the way. His office of porter gave him especial title to our regret. Yet, after the first impulses of sorrow, reflection told us that the loss was not altogether so serious as it had at first appeared. Each day's experience of the nomadic life had served more and more to dispel our original apprehension of robbers. Moreover, Arsalan, under any circumstances, would have been a very ineffective guard; for his incessant galloping about during the day sent him at night into a sleep which nothing could disturb. This was so much the case, that every morning, make what noise we might in taking down our tent, loading the camels, and so on, there would Arsalan remain, stretched on the grass, sleeping a leaden sleep; and when the caravan was about to start, we had always to arouse him with a sound kick or two. Upon one occasion, a strange dog made his way into our tent, without the smallest opposition on the part of Arsalan, and had full time to devour our mess of oatmeal and a candle, the wick of which he left contumeliously on the outside of the tent. A consideration of economy completed our restoration to tranquillity of mind: each day we had had to provide Arsalan with a ration of meal, at least quite equal in quantity to that which each of us consumed; and we were not rich enough to have constantly seated at our table a guest with such excellent appetite, and whose services were wholly inadequate to compensate for the expense he occasioned.

We had been informed that we should reach White Enclosure the same day, but the sun had set, and as yet we saw no signs of the town before us. By and by, what seemed clouds of dust made their appearance in the distance, approaching us. By degrees they developed themselves in the form of camels, laden with western merchandise for sale in Peking. When we met the first camel-driver we asked him how far it was from White Enclosure. "You see here," said he with a grin, "one end of our caravan; the other extremity is still within the town." "Thanks," cried we; "in that case we shall soon be there." "Well, you've not more than fifteen lis to go." "Fifteen lis! why you've just told us that the other end of your caravan is still in the town." "So it is, but our caravan consists of at least ten thousand camels." "If that be the case," said we, "there is no time to be lost: a good journey to you, and peace," and on we went.

The cameleers had stamped upon their features, almost blackened with the sun, a character of uncouth misanthropy. Enveloped from head to foot in goat-skins, they were placed between the humps of their camels, just like bales of merchandise; they scarcely condescended to turn even their heads round to look at us. Five months journeying across the desert seemed almost to have brutefied them. All the camels of this immense caravan wore suspended from their necks Thibetian bells, the silvery sound of which produced a musical harmony which contrasted very agreeably with the sullen taciturn aspect of the drivers. In our progress, however, we contrived to make them break silence from time to time; the roguish Dchiahour attracted their atten-

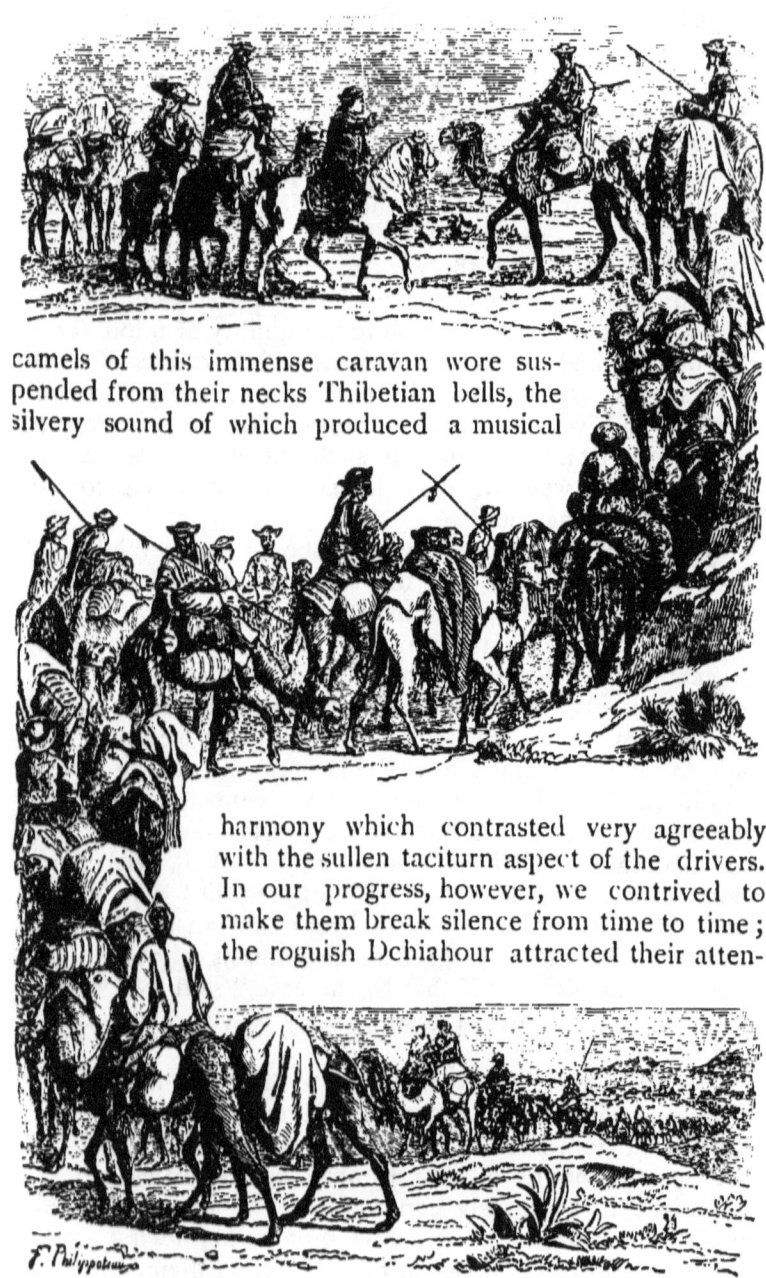

tion to us in a very marked manner. Some of the camels, more timid than others, took fright at the little mule, which they doubtless imagined to be a wild beast. In their endeavor to escape in an opposite direction they drew after them the camels next following them in the procession, so that, by this operation, the caravan assumed the form of an immense bow. This abrupt evolution aroused the cameleers from their sullen torpidity; they grumbled bitterly, and directed fierce glances against us, as they exerted themselves to restore the procession to its proper line. Samdadchiemba, on the contrary, shouted with laughter; it was in vain that we told him to ride somewhat apart in order not to alarm the camels; he turned a deaf ear to all we said. The discomfiture of the procession was quite a delightful entertainment for him, and he made his little mule caracole about in the hope of an encore.

The first cameleer had not deceived us. We journeyed on between the apparently interminable file of the caravan, and a chain of rugged rocks, until night had absolutely set in, and even then we did not see the town. The last camel had passed on, and we seemed alone in the desert, when a man came riding by on a donkey. "Elder brother," said we, "is White Enclosure still distant?" "No, brothers," he replied, "it is just before you, there, where you see the lights. You have not more than five lis to go." Five lis! It was a long way in the night, and upon a strange road, but we were fain to resign ourselves. The night grew darker and darker. There was no moon, no stars even, to guide us on our way. We seemed advancing amid chaos and abysses. We resolved to alight, in the hope of seeing our way somewhat more clearly: the result was precisely the reverse; we would advance a few steps gropingly and slowly; then, all of a sudden, we threw back our heads in fear of dashing them against rocks or walls that seemed to rise from an abyss. We speedily got covered with perspiration, and were only happy to mount our camels once more, and rely on their clearer sight and surer feet. Fortunately the baggage was well secured; what misery would it have been had that fallen off amid all this darkness, as it had frequently done before! We arrived at last in Tchagan-Kouren, but the difficulty now was to find an inn. Every house was shut up, and there was not a living creature in the streets, except a number of great dogs that ran barking after us.

At length, after wandering haphazard through several streets, we heard the strokes of a hammer upon an anvil. We proceeded towards the sound, and before long, a great light, a thick smoke, and sparks glittering in the air, announced that we had come upon a blacksmith's shop. We presented ourselves at the door, and humbly entreated our brothers, the smiths, to tell us where we should find an inn. After a few jests upon Tartars and camels, the company assented to our request, and a boy, lighting a torch, came out to act as our guide to an inn.

After knocking and calling for a long time at the door of the first inn we came to, the landlord opened it, and was inquiring who we were, when, unluckily for us, one of our camels, worried by a dog, took it into its head to send forth a succession of those horrible cries for which the animal is remarkable. The innkeeper at once shut his door in our faces. At all the inns where we successively applied, we were received in much the same manner. No sooner were the camels noticed than the answer was, No room; in point of fact, no innkeeper, if he can avoid it, will receive camels into his stables at all: their size occupies great space, and their appearance almost invariably creates alarm among the other animals; so that Chinese travelers generally make it a condition with the landlord before they enter an inn, that no Tartar caravan shall be admitted. Our guide finding all our efforts futile, got tired of accompanying us, wished us good night, and returned to his forge.

We were exhausted with weariness, hunger, and thirst, yet there seemed no remedy for the evil, when all at once we heard the bleating of sheep. Following the sound, we came to a mud enclosure, the door of which was at once opened upon our knocking. "Brother," said we, "is this an inn?" "No, it is a sheep-house. Who are you?" "We are travelers, who have arrived here, weary and hungry; but no one will receive us." As we were speaking, an old man came to the door, holding in his hand a lighted torch. As soon as he saw our camels and our costume, "Mendou! Mendou!" he exclaimed, "Sirs Lamas, enter; there is room for your camels in the court, and my house is large enough for you; you shall stay and rest here for several days." We entered joyfully, fastened our camels to the manger, and seated ourselves round the hearth, where already tea was prepared for us. "Brother," said we to the old man, "we need not ask whether it is to Mongols that we owe this hospitality." "Yes, Sirs Lamas," said he, "we are all Mongols here. We have for some time past quitted the tent, to reside here; so that we may better carry on our trade in sheep. Alas! we are insensibly becoming Chinese!" "Your manner of life," returned we, "may have changed, but it is certain that your hearts have remained Tartar. Nowhere else in all Tchagan-Kouren, has the door of kindness been opened to us."

Observing our fatigue, the head of the family unrolled some skins in a corner of the room, and we gladly laid ourselves down to repose. We should have slept on till the morning, but Samdadchiemba aroused us to partake of the supper which our hosts had hospitably prepared—two large cups of tea, cakes baked in the ashes, and some chops of boiled mutton, arranged on a stool by way of a table. The meal seemed after our long fasting, perfectly magnificent; we partook of it heartily, and then having exchanged pinches of snuff with the family, resumed our slumber.

Next morning we communicated the plan of our journey to our Mongol hosts. No sooner had we mentioned that we intended to pass the Yellow River, and thence traverse the country of the Ortous, than the whole family burst out with exclamations. "It is quite impossible," said the old man, "to cross the Yellow River. Eight days ago the river overflowed its banks, and the plains on both sides are completely inundated." This intelligence filled us with the utmost consternation. We had been quite prepared to pass the Yellow River under circumstances of danger arising from the wretchedness of the ferry boats and the difficulty of managing our camels in them, and we knew, of course, that the Hoang-Ho was subject to periodical overflows; but these occur ordinarily in the rainy season, towards the sixth or seventh month, whereas we were now in the dry season, and, moreover, in a peculiarly dry season.

We proceeded forthwith towards the river to investigate the matter for ourselves, and found that the Tartar had only told us the exact truth. The Yellow River had become, as it were, a vast sea, the limits of which were scarcely visible. Here and there you could see the higher grounds rising above the water, like islands, while the houses and villages looked as though they were floating upon the waves. We consulted several persons as to the course we should adopt. Some said that further progress was impracticable, for that, even where the inundation had subsided, it had left the earth so soft and slippery that the camels could not walk upon it, while elsewhere we should have to dread at every step some deep pool, in which we should inevitably be drowned. Other opinions were more favorable, suggesting that the boats which were stationed at intervals for the purpose would easily and cheaply convey us and our baggage in three days to the river, while the camels could follow us through the water, and that once at the river side, the great ferry-boat would carry us all over the bed of the stream without any difficulty.

What were we to do? To turn back was out of the question. We had vowed that, God aiding, we would go to Lha-Ssa whatever obstacles impeded. To turn the river by coasting it northwards would materially augment the length of our journey, and, moreover, compel us to traverse the great desert of Gobi. To remain at Tchagan-Kouren, and patiently await for a month the complete retirement of the waters and the restoration of solidity in the roads, was, in one point of view, the most prudent course, but there was a grave inconvenience about it. We and our five animals could not live for a month in an inn without occasioning a most alarming atrophy in our already meager purse. The only course remaining was to place ourselves exclusively under the protection of Providence, and to go on, regardless of mud or marsh. This resolution was adopted, and we returned home to make the necessary preparations.

Tchagan-Kouren is a large, fine town of recent construction. It is not marked on the map of China compiled by M. Andriveau-Goujon, doubtless because it did not exist at the time when the Fathers Jesuits residing at Peking were directed by the Emperor Khang-Hi to draw maps of the empire. Nowhere in China, Mantchouria, or in Thibet, have we seen a town like White Enclosure. The streets are wide, clean, and clear; the houses regular in their arrangement, and of very fair architecture. There are several squares, decorated with trees, a feature which struck us all the more that we had not observed it anywhere else in this part of the world. There are plenty of shops, commodiously arranged, and well supplied with Chinese, and even with European goods. The trade of Tchagan-Kouren, however, is greatly checked by the proximity of the Blue Town, to which, as a place of commerce, the Mongols have been much longer accustomed.

Our worthy Tartar host, in his hospitality, sought to divert us from our project, but unsuccessfully; and he even got rallied by Samdadchiemba for his kindness. "It's quite clear," said our guide, "that you've become a mere Kitat (Chinese), and think that a man must not set out upon a journey unless the earth is perfectly dry and the sky perfectly cloudless. I have no doubt you go out to lead your sheep with an umbrella in one hand and a fan in the other." It was ultimately arranged that we should take our departure at daybreak next morning.

Meantime we went out into the town to make the necessary supply of provisions. To guard against the possibility of being inundation-bound for several days, we bought a quantity of small loaves fried in mutton fat, and for our animals we procured a quantity of the most portable forage we could find.

Next morning we departed full of confidence in the goodness of God. Our Tartar host, who insisted upon escorting us out of the town, led us to an elevation whence we could see in the distance a long line of thick vapor which seemed journeying from west to east; it marked the course of the Yellow River. "Where you see that vapor," said the old man, "you will find a great dike, which serves to keep the river in bounds, except upon any extraordinary rise of the waters. That dike is now dry; when you come to it, proceed along it until you reach the little pagoda you see yonder, on your right; there you will find a boat that will convey you across the river. Keep that pagoda in sight, and you can't lose your way." We cordially thanked the old man for the kindness he had shown us and proceeded on our journey.

We were soon up to the knees of the camels in a thick slimy compost of mud and water, covering other somewhat firmer mud, over which the poor animals slowly slid on their painful way; their heads turning alternately right and left, their limbs trembling, and the sweat exuding from each pore. Every moment we expected them to fall beneath us. It was near noon ere we arrrived at a little village, not more than a couple of miles from the place where we had left the old man. Here a few wretched people, whose rags scarce covered their gaunt frames, came round us, and accompanied us to the edge of a broad piece of water, portion of a lake, which they told us, and which, it was quite clear, we must pass before we could reach the dike indicated by the Tartar. Some boatmen proposed to carry us over this lake to the dike. We asked them how many sapeks they would charge for the service:—"Oh, very little; next to nothing. You see we will take in our boats you, and the baggage, and the mule, and the horse; one of our people will lead the camels through the lake; they are too big to come into the boat. When one comes to reckon on all this load, and all the trouble and fatigue, the price seems absolutely less than nothing." "True, there will be some trouble in the affair, no one denies it; but let us have a distinct understanding. How many sapeks do you ask?" "Oh, scarcely any. We are all brothers; and you, brothers, need all our assistance in traveling. We know that; we feel it in our hearts. If we could only afford it, we should have pleasure in carrying you over for nothing; but look at our clothes. We poor fellows are very poor. Our boat is all we have to depend upon. It is necessary that we should gain a livelihood by that; five lis sail, three men, a horse, a mule, and luggage; but come, as you are spiritual persons, we will only charge you 2,000 sapeks." The price was preposterous; we made no answer. We took our animals by the bridle and turned back, pretending that we would not continue our journey. Scarcely had we advanced twenty paces before the ferryman ran after us. "Sirs Lamas, are not you going to cross the water in my boat?" "Why," said we dryly, "doubtless you are too rich to take any trouble in the matter. If you really wanted to let your boat, would you ask 2,000 sapeks?" "2,000 sapeks is the price I ask; but what will you give?" "If you like to take 500 sapeks, let us set out at once; it is already late." "Return, Sirs Lamas; get into the boat;" and he caught hold, as he spoke, of the halters of our beasts. We considered that the price was at last fixed; but we had scarcely arrived on the border of the lake, when the ferryman exclaimed to one of his comrades,—" Come, our fortune deserts us to-day; we must bear much fatigue for little remuneration. We shall have to row five lis, and after all we shall have only 1,500 sapeks to divide between eight of us." " 1,500 sapeks!" exclaimed we; "you are mocking us; we will leave you;" and we turned back for the second time. Some mediators, inevitable persons in all Chinese matters, presented themselves, and undertook to settle the fare. It was at length decided that we should pay 800 sapeks; the sum was enormous, but we had no other means of pursuing our way. The boatmen knew this, and took accordingly the utmost advantage of our position.

The embarkation was effected with extraordinary celerity, and we soon quitted the shore. Whilst we advanced by means of the oars, on the surface of the lake, a man mounted on a camel and leading two others after him, followed a path traced out by a small boat rowed by a waterman. The latter was obliged every now and then to sound the depth of the water, and the camel-driver needed to be very attentive in directing his course in the straight trail left by the boat, lest he should be swallowed up in the holes beneath the water. The camels advanced slowly, stretching out their long necks, and at times leaving only their heads and the extremity of their humps visible above the lake. We were in continual alarm; for these animals not being able to swim, there only needed a false step to precipitate them to the bottom. Thanks to the protection of God, all arrived safe at the dike which had been pointed out to us. The boatmen, after assisting us to replace, in a hasty manner, our baggage on the camels, indicated the point whither we must direct our steps. " Do you see, to the right, that small Miao? (pagoda). A little from the Miao, do you observe those wooden huts and those black nets hanging from long poles? There you will find the ferry-boat to cross the river. Follow this dike, and go in peace."

After having proceeded with difficulty for half an hour, we reached the ferry-boat. The boatmen immediately came to us. " Sirs Lamas," said they, " you intend, doubtless, to cross the Hoang-Ho, but you see this evening the thing is impracticable—the sun is just setting." "You are right; we will cross to-morrow at daybreak: meanwhile, let us settle the price, so that to-morrow we may lose no time in deliberation." The watermen would have preferred waiting till the morrow to discuss this important point, expecting we should offer a much larger sum, when just about to embark. At first their demands were preposterous: happily, there were two boats which competed together, otherwise we should have been ruined. The price was ultimately fixed at 1,000 sapeks. The passage was not

Navigation of the Yellow River.

long, it is true, for the river had nearly resumed its bed; but the waters were very rapid, and, moreover, the camels had to ride. The amount enormous in itself, appeared, upon the whole, moderate, considering the difficulty and trouble of the passage. This business arranged, we considered how we should pass the night. We could not think of seeking an asylum in the fishermen's cabins; even if they had been sufficiently large, we should have had a considerable objection to place our effects in the hands of these folks. We were sufficiently acquainted with the Chinese not to trust to their honesty. We looked out for a place whereon to set up our tent; but we could find nowhere a spot sufficiently dry: mud or stagnant water covered the ground in all directions. About a hundred yards from the shore was a small Miao, or temple of idols; a narrow, high path led to it. We proceeded thither to see if we could find there a place of repose. It turned out as we wished. A portico, supported by three stone pillars, stood before the entrance door, which was secured by a large padlock. This portico, made of granite, was raised a few feet from the ground, and you ascended it by five steps. We determined to pass the night here.

Samdadchiemba asked us if it would not be a monstrous superstition to sleep on the steps of a Miao. When we had relieved his scruples, he made sundry philosophical reflections. "Behold," said he, "a Miao which has been built by the people of the country, in honor of the god of the river. Yet, when it rained in Thibet, the Pou-sa had no power to preserve itself from inundation. Nevertheless, this Miao serves at present to shelter two missionaries of Jehovah—the only real use it has ever served." Our Dchiahour, who at first had scrupled to lodge under the portico of this idolatrous temple, soon thought the idea magnificent, and laughed hugely.

After having arranged our luggage in this singular encampment, we proceeded to tell our beads on the shores of the Hoang-Ho. The moon was brilliant, and lit up this immense river, which rolled over an even and smooth bed its yellow and tumultuous waters. The Hoang-Ho is beyond a doubt one of the finest rivers in the world; it rises in the mountains of Thibet, and crosses the Koukou-Noor, entering China by the province of Kan-Sou. Thence it follows the sandy regions at the feet of the Alécha mountains, encircles the country of the Ortous; and after having watered China first from north to south, and then from west to east, it falls into the Yellow Sea. The waters of the Hoang-Ho, pure and clear at their source, only take [1] the yellow hue after having passed the sands of the Alécha and the Ortous. They are almost, throughout, level with the lands through which they flow, and it is this circumstance which occasions those inundations so disastrous to the Chinese. As for the Tartar nomads when the waters rise, all they have to do is to strike their tents, and drive their herds elsewhere.[1]

[1] The bed of the Yellow River has undergone numerous and notable variations. In ancient times, its mouth was situated in the Gulf of Pe-Tchi-Li, in latitude 39.

Though the Yellow River had cost us so much trouble, we derived much satisfaction from taking a walk at night upon its solitary banks, and listening to the solemn murmur of its majestic waters. We were contemplating this grand work of nature, when Samdadchiemba recalled us to the prose of life, by announcing that the oatmeal was ready. Our repast was as brief as it was plain. We then stretched ourselves on our goat-skins, in the portico, so that the three described the three sides of a triangle, in the center of which we piled our baggage; for we had no faith at all that the sanctity of the place would deter robbers, if robbers there were in the vicinity.

As we have mentioned, the little Miao was dedicated to the divinity of the Yellow River. The idol, seated on a pedestal of gray brick, was hideous, as all those idols are that you ordinarily see in Chinese pagodas. From a broad, flat, red face, rose two great staring eyes, like eggs stuck into orbits, the smaller end projecting. Thick eyebrows, instead of describing a horizontal line, began at the bottom of each ear, and met in the middle of the forehead, so as to form an obtuse angle. The idol had on its head a marine shell, and brandished, with a menacing air, a sword like a scythe. This Pou-sa had, right and left, two attendants, each putting out its tongue, and apparently making faces at it.

Just as we were lying down, a man approached us, holding in one hand a small paper lantern. He opened the grating which led to the interior of the Miao, prostrated himself thrice, burned incense in the censers, and lighted a small lamp at the feet of the idol. This personage was not a bonze. His hair, hanging in a tress, and his blue garments, showed him to be a layman. When he had finished his idolatrous ceremonies, he came to us. "I will leave the door open," said he; "you'll sleep more comfortably inside than in the portico." "Thanks," replied we; "shut the door, however; for we shall do very well where we are.

At present it is in the 34th parallel, twenty-five leagues from the primitive point. The Chinese government is compelled annually to expend enormous sums in keeping the river within its bed and preventing inundations. In 1779, the embankment for this purpose cost no less a sum than £1,600,000. Yet, despite these precautions, inundations are of frequent occurrence; for the bed of the Yellow River, in the provinces of Ho-Nan and Kiang-Sou, is higher for 200 leagues than the plain through which it passes. This bed, continuing to rise, with the quantity of mud deposited, there is inevitably impending, at no remote period, an awful catastrophe, involving in death and desolation all the adjacent district.

Why have you been burning incense? Who is the idol of this place?" "It is the spirit of the Hoang-Ho, who inhabits this Miao. I have burned incense before him, in order that our fishing may be productive, and that our boats may float without danger." "The words you utter," cried Samdadchiemba, insolently, "are mere *hou-choue* (stuff and nonsense). How did it happen, that the other day when the inundation took place, the Miao was flooded, and your Pou-sa was covered with mud?" To this sudden apostrophe the pagan churchwarden made no answer, but took to his heels. We were much surprised at this proceeding; but the explanation came next morning.

We stretched ourselves on our goat-skins once more, and endeavored to sleep, but sleep came slowly and but for a brief period. Placed between marshes and the river, we felt throughout the night a piercing cold, which seemed to transfix us to the very marrow. The sky was pure and serene, and in the morning we saw that the marshes around were covered with a thick sheet of ice. We made our preparations for departure, but upon collecting the various articles, a handkerchief was missing. We remembered that we had imprudently hung it upon the grating at the entrance of the Miao, so that it was half in and half out of the building. No person had been near the place, except the man who had come to pay his devotions to the idol. We could, therefore, without much rashness, attribute the robbery to him, and this explained why he had made his exit so rapidly, without replying to Samdadchiemba. We could easily have found the man, for he was one of the fishermen engaged upon the station, but it would have been a fruitless labor. Our only effectual course would have been to seize the thief in the fact.

Next morning, we placed our baggage upon the camels, and proceeded to the riverside, fully persuaded that we had a miserable day before us. The camels having a horror of the water, it is sometimes impossible to make them get into a boat. You may pull their noses, or nearly kill them with blows, yet not make them advance a step; they would die sooner. The boat before us seemed especially to present almost insurmountable obstacles. It was not flat and large, like those which generally serve as ferry-boats. Its sides were very high, so that the animals were obliged to leap

over them at the risk and peril of breaking their legs. If
you wanted to move a carriage into it, you had first of all
to pull the vehicle to pieces.

The boatmen had already taken hold of our baggage, for
the purpose of conveying it into their abominable vehicle,
but we stopped them. "Wait a moment; we must first
try and get the camels in. If they won't enter the boat,
there is no use in placing the baggage in it." "Whence
came your camels, that they can't get into people's boats?"
"It matters little whence they came; what we tell you is
that the tall white camel has never hitherto consented to
cross any river, even in a flat boat." "Tall camel or short,
flat boat or high boat, into the boat the camel shall go,"
and so, saying, the ferryman ran and fetched an immense
cudgel. "Catch hold of the string in the camel's nose,"
cried he to a companion. "We'll see if we can't make the
brute get into the boat." The man in the boat hauled at
the string; the man behind beat the animal vehemently on
the legs with his cudgel, but all to no purpose; the poor
camel sent forth piercing cries, and stretched out its long
neck. The blood flowed from its nostrils, the sweat from
every pore; but not an inch forward would the creature
move; yet one step would have placed it in the boat, the
sides of which were touched by its fore legs.

We could not endure the painful spectacle. "No more
of this," we cried to the ferryman; "it is useless to beat
the animal. You might break its legs or kill it before it
would consent to enter your boat." The two men at once
left off, for they were tired, the one of pulling, the other of
beating. What were we to do? We had almost made up
our minds to ascend the banks of the river until we found
some flat boat, when the ferryman all at once jumped up,
radiant with an idea. "We will make another attempt,"
cried he, "and if that fails I give the matter up. Take the
string gently," he added, to a companion, "and keep the
camel's feet as close as ever you can to the side of the
boat." Then, going back for some paces, he dashed forward with a spring and threw himself with all his weight
upon the animal's rear. The shock, so violent and unexpected, occasioned the camel somewhat to bend its fore
legs. A second shock immediately succeeded the first, and
the animal, in order to prevent itself from falling into the

water, had no remedy but to raise its feet and place them within the boat. This effected, the rest was easy. A few pinches of the nose and a few blows sufficed to impel the hind legs after the fore, and the white camel was at last in the boat, to the extreme satisfaction of all present. The other animals were embarked after the same fashion, and we proceeded on our watery way.

First, however, the ferryman deemed it necessary that the animals should kneel, so that no movement of theirs on the river might occasion an overturn. His proceeding to this effect was exceedingly comic. He first went to one camel and then to the other, pulling now this down, then that. When he approached the larger animal, the creature, remembering the man's treatment, discharged in his face a quantity of the grass ruminating within its jaws, a compliment which the boatman returned by spitting in the animal's face. And the absurdity was, that the work made no progress. One camel was no sooner induced to kneel down than the other got up, and so the men went backwards and forwards, gradually covered by the angry creatures with the green substance, half masticated and particularly inodorous, which each animal in turns spat against him. At length, when Samdadchiemba had sufficiently entertained himself with the scene, he went to the camels, and, exercising his recognized authority over them, made them kneel in the manner desired.

We at length floated upon the waters of the Yellow River; but though there were four boatmen, their united strength could scarcely make head against the force of the current. We had effected about half our voyage, when a camel suddenly rose, and shook the boat so violently that it was nearly upset. The boatmen, after ejaculating a tremendous oath, told us to look after our camels and prevent them from getting up, unless we wanted the whole party to be engulfed. The danger was indeed formidable. The camel, infirm upon its legs, and yielding to every movement of the boat, menaced us with a catastrophe. Samdadchiemba, however, managed to get quickly beside the animal, and at once induced it to kneel, so that we were let off with our fright, and in due course reached the other side of the river.

At the moment of disembarkation, the horse, impatient to be once more on land, leaped out of the boat, but striking, on its way, against the anchor, fell on its side in the mud. The ground not being yet dry, we were fain to take off our shoes, and to carry the baggage on our shoulders to an adjacent eminence; there we asked the boatmen if we should be any great length of time in traversing the marsh and mud that lay stretched out before us. The chief boatman raised his head, and after looking for a while towards the sun, said : " It will soon be noon ; by the evening you will reach the banks of the Little River ; to-morrow you will find the ground dry." It was under these melancholy auspices that we proceeded upon our journey, through one of the most detestable districts to be found in the whole world.

We had been told in what direction we were to proceed ; but the inundation had obliterated every trace of path and even of road, and we could only regulate our course by the nature of the ground, keeping as clear as we could of the deeper quagmires, sometimes making a long circuit in order to reach what seemed firmer ground, and then, finding the supposed solid turf to be nothing more than a piece of water, green with stagnant matter and aquatic plants, having to turn back, and, as it were, grope one's way in another direction, fearful, at every step, of being plunged into some gulf of liquid mud.

By and by our animals, alarmed and wearied, could hardly proceed, and we were compelled to beat them severely and to exhaust our voices with bawling at them before they would move at all. The tall grass and plants of the marshes twisted about their legs, and it was only by leaps and at the risk of throwing off both baggage and riders that they could extricate themselves. Thrice did the youngest camel lose its balance and fall ; but on each occasion, the spot on which it fell was providentially dry ; had it stumbled in the mud, it would inevitably have been stifled.

On our way, we met three Chinese travelers, who, by the aid of long staves, were making their laborious way through the marshes, carrying their shoes and clothes over their shoulders. We asked them in what direction we were likely to find a better road : " You would have been wiser," said they, " had you remained at Tchagan-Kouren ; foot passengers can scarcely make their way through these marshes : how do you suppose you can get on with your camels ? "

and with this consolatory assurance, they quitted us, giving us a look of compassion, certain as they were that we should never get through the mud.

The sun was just setting, when we perceived a Mongol habitation; we made our way direct to it, without heeding the difficulties of the road. In fact experience had already taught us that selection was quite out of the question, and that one way was as good as another in this universal slough. Making circuits merely lengthened the journey. The Tartars were frightened at our appearance, covered as we were with mud and perspiration; they immediately gave us some tea, and generously offered us the hospitality of their dwelling. The small mud house in which they lived, though built upon an eminence, had been half carried away by the inundation. We could not conceive what had induced them to fix their abode in this horrible district, but they told us that they were employed to tend the herds belonging to some Chinese of Tchagan-Kouren. After resting for a while, we requested information as to the best route to pursue, and we were told that the river was only five lis off, that its banks were dry, and that we should find there boats to carry us to the other side. "When you have crossed the Paga-Gol" (Little River), said our hosts, "you may proceed in peace; you will meet with no more water to interrupt you." We thanked these good Tartars for their kindness, and resumed our journey.

After half an hour's march, we discovered before us a large extent of water, studded with fishing-vessels. The title, Little River, may, for anything we know, be appropriate enough under ordinary circumstances, but at the time of our visit, the Paga-Gol was a broad sea. We pitched our tent on the bank which, by reason of its elevation, was perfectly dry, and the remarkable excellence of the pasturage determined us upon remaining in this place several days, in order to give rest to our animals, which, since their departure from Tchagan-Kouren had undergone enormous fatigue: we ourselves, too, felt the necessity of some relaxation, after the sufferings which these horrible marshes had inflicted upon us.

Waterfowl and Birds of Passage.

CHAPTER VII.

Mercurial Preparation for the Destruction of Lice—Dirtiness of the Mongols—Lama Notions about the Metempsychosis—Washing—Regulations of Nomadic Life—Aquatic and Passage Birds—The Yuen-Yang—The Dragon's Foot—Fishermen of the Paga-Gol—Fishing Party—Fisherman Bit by a Dog—Kou-Kouo, or, St. Ignatius's Bean—Preparations for Departure—Passage of the Paga-Gol—Dangers of the Voyage—Devotion of Samdadchiemba—The Prime Minister of the King of the Ortous—Encampment.

Upon taking possession of our post our first business was to excavate a ditch round the tent, in order that, should rain occur, the water might be carried into a pond below. The excavated earth served to make a mound round the tent; and, within, the pack-saddles and furniture of the camels formed very comfortable bedsteads for us. Having mode our new habitation as neat as possible, the next business was to make our persons neat also.

We had now been traveling for nearly six weeks, and still wore the same clothing we had assumed on our departure. The incessant pricklings with which we were harassed, sufficiently indicated that our attire was peopled with the filthy vermin to which the Chinese and Tartars are familiarly accustomed, but which with Europeans are objects of horror and disgust,—lice, which of all our miseries on our long journey have been the greatest. Hunger and thirst, fierce winds and piercing cold, wild beasts, robbers, avalanches, menaced death and actual discomfort, all had been as nothing compared with the incessant misery occasioned by these dreadful vermin.

Before quitting Tchagen-Kouren we had bought in a chemist's shop a few sapeks' worth of mercury. We now made with it a prompt and specific remedy against the lice. We had formerly got this receipt from some Chinese, and as it may be useful to others, we think it right to describe it here. You take half-an-ounce of mercury, which you mix with old tea-leaves, previously reduced to paste by mastication. To render this softer, you generally add saliva, water would not have the same effect. You must afterwards bruise and stir it awhile, so that the mercury may be divided into little balls as fine as dust. You infuse this composition into a string of cotton, loosely twisted, which you hang round the neck; the lice are sure to bite at the bait, and they thereupon as surely swell, become red, and die forthwith. In China and in Tartary you have to renew this sanitary necklace once a month, for otherwise, in these dirty countries you could not possibly keep clear from vermin, which swarm in every Chinese house and in every Mongol tent.

The Tartars are acquainted with the cheap and efficacious anti-louse mixture I have described, but they make no use of it. Accustomed from their infancy to live amid vermin, they at last take no heed whatever of them, except, indeed, when the number becomes so excessive as to involve the danger of their being absolutely eaten up. Upon such a juncture they strip off their clothes, and have a grand battue, all the members of the family and any friends who may have dropped in, taking part in the sport. Even Lamas, who may be present, share in the hunt, with this distinction, that they do not kill the game, but merely catch it and throw it away; the reason being, that according to the doctrine of metempsychosis, to kill any living being whatever, is to incur the danger of homicide, since the smallest insect before you may be the transmigration of a man. Such is the general opinion; but we have met with

Lamas whose views on this subject were more enlightened. They admitted that persons belonging to the sacerdotal class should abstain from killing animals; but not, said they, in fear of committing a murder by killing a man transmigrated into an animal, but because to kill is essentially antagonistic with the gentleness which should characterize a man of prayer, who is ever in communication with the Deity.

There are some Lamas who carry this scruple to a point approaching the puerile, so that as they ride along, they are constantly maneuvering their horses in and out, here and there, in order to avoid trampling upon some insect or other that presents itself in their path. Yet, say they, the holiest among them occasion inadvertently, the death, every day, of a great many living creatures. It is to expiate these involuntary murders that they undergo fasting and penitence, that they recite certain prayers, and that they make prostrations.

We who had no such scruples, and whose conscience stood upon a solid basis as to the transmigration of souls, concocted, as effectively as possible, our anti-louse preparation, doubling the dose of mercury in our anxiety to kill the greatest practicable number of the vermin that had been so long tormenting us by day and by night.

It would have been to little purpose merely to kill the present vermin; it was necessary to withhold any sort of shelter or encouragement from their too probable successors, and the first point, with this view, was to wash all our underclothing, which, for some time past, had not been subjected to any such operation. For nearly two months since our departure, we had been wholly dependent, in all respects, upon ourselves, and this necessity had compelled us to learn a little of various professions with which we had been previously unacquainted; becoming our own tailors and shoe menders, for example, when clothes or shoes required repairs. The course of nomadic life now practically introduced us also to the occupation of washermen. After boiling some ashes and soaking our linen in the lye, we next proceeded to wash it in an adjacent pond. One great stone on which to place the linen when washed, and another wherewith to beat it while washing, were our only implements of trade; but we got on very well, for the softness of the pond water gave every facility for cleansing the articles. Before long, we had the delight of seeing our linen once more clean; and when, having dried it on the grass, we folded and took it home to our tent, we were quite radiant with satisfaction.

The quiet and ease which we enjoyed in this encampment, rapidly remedied the fatigue we had undergone in the marshes. The weather was magnificent; all that we could have possibly desired. By day, a gentle, soothing heat; by night, a sky pure and serene; plenty of fuel; excellent and abundant pasturage; nitrous water, which our camels delighted in; in a word, everything to renovate the health and revive the spirits. Our rule of daily life may appear odd enough to some, and perhaps not altogether in harmony with the regulations of monastic houses, but it was in exact adaptation to the circumstances and wants of our little community.

Every morning, with the first dawn, before the earliest rays of the sun struck upon our tent, we rose spontaneously, requiring neither call-bell nor valet to rouse us. Our brief toilet made, we rolled up our goat-skins and placed them in a corner; then we swept out the tent, and put the cooking utensils in order, for we were desirous of having everything about us as clean and comfortable as possible. All things go by comparison in this world. The interior of our tent, which would have made a European laugh, filled with admiration the Tartars who from time to time paid us a visit. The cleanliness of our wooden cups, our kettle always well polished, our clothes not altogether as yet incrusted with grease; all this contrasted favorably with the dirt and disorder of Tartar habitations.

Having arranged our apartment, we said prayers together, and then dispersed each apart in the desert to engage in meditation upon some pious thought. Oh! little did we need, amid the profound silence of those vast solitudes, a printed book to suggest a subject for prayer! The void and vanity of all things here below, the majesty of God, the inexhaustible measures of his Providence, the shortness of life, the essentiality of laboring with a view to the world to come, and a thousand other salutary reflections, came of themselves, without any effort on our parts, to occupy the mind with gentle musings. In the desert the heart of man is free; he is subject to no species of tyranny. Far away from us were all those hollow theories and systems, those utopias of imaginary happiness which men are constantly aiming at, and which as constantly evade their grasp; those inexhaustible combinations of selfishness and self-sufficiency, those burning passions which in Europe are ever contending, ever fermenting in men's minds and hardening their hearts. Amid these silent prairies there was nothing to disturb our tranquil thoughts, or to prevent us from reducing to their true value the futilities of this world, from appreciating at their lofty worth the things of God and of eternity.

The exercise which followed these meditations was, it must be admitted, far from mystic in its character; but it was necessary, and not wholly without entertainment in its course. Each of us hung a bag from his shoulders and went in different directions to seek argols for fuel. Those who have never led a nomadic life will, of course, find it difficult to understand how this occupation could possibly develop any enjoyment. Yet, when one is lucky enough to find, half concealed among the grass, an argol, recommendable for its size and dryness, there comes over the heart a gentle joy, one of those sudden emotions which create a transient happiness. The pleasure at finding a fine argol is cognate with that which the hunter feels when he discovers the track of game, with which the boy regards, his eyes sparkling, the linnet's nest he has long sought; with which the fisherman sees quivering at the end of his line a large fish; nay, if we may compare small things with great, one might even compare this pleasure with the enthusiasm of a Leverrier when he has discovered a new planet.

Our sack, once filled with argols, we returned, and piled the contents with pride at the entrance of the tent; then we struck a light and set the fire in movement; and while the tea was boiling in the pot, pounded the meal and put some cakes to bake in the ashes. The repast, it is observable, was simple and modest, but it was always extremely delicious, first, because we had prepared it ourselves, and secondly, because our appetites provided most efficient seasoning.

After breakfast, while Samdadchiemba was collecting round the tent the animals which had dispersed in search of pasturage, we recited a portion of our breviary. Towards noon we indulged in a brief repose, a few minutes of gentle but sound sleep, never interrupted by nightmare or by unpleasant dreams. This repose was all the more necessary that the evenings were prolonged far into the night. It was always with difficulty that we tore ourselves from our walks by moonlight on the banks of the river. During the day all was silent and tranquil around us; but so soon as the shades of night began to overspread the desert, the scene became animated and noisy. Aquatic birds, arriving in immense flocks, diffused themselves over the various pools, and soon thousands of shrill cries filled the air with wild harmony. The cries of anger, the accents of passion, proceeding from those myriads of migratory birds, as they disputed among themselves possession of the tufts of marsh grass in which they desired to pass the night, gave one quite the idea of a numerous people in all the fury of civil war, fighting and clamoring, in agitation and violence, for some supposed advantage, brief as this eastern night.

Tartary is populated with nomadic birds. Look up when you may, you will see them floating high in air, the vast battalions forming, in their systematically capricious flight, a thousand fantastic outlines, dissipating as soon as formed, forming again as soon as dissipated, like the creations of a Kaleidoscope. Oh! how exactly are these migrant birds in their place, amid the deserts of Tartary, where man himself is never fixed in one spot, but is constantly on the move. It was very pleasant to listen to the distant hum of these winged bands, wandering about like ourselves. As we reflected upon their long peregrinations, and glanced in thought over the countries which their rapid flight must have comprehended, the recollections of our native land came vividly before us. "Who knows," we would say to each other, "who knows but that among these birds there are some who have traversed—who have, perhaps, alighted for awhile in our dear France: who have sought transient repose and refreshment in the plains of Languedoc, or on the heights of the Jura. After visiting our own country, they have doubtless pursued their route towards the north of Europe, and have come hither through the snows of Siberia, and of Upper Tartary. Oh! if these birds could understand our words, or if we could speak their tongue, how many questions should we not put to them!" Alas!

we did not then know that for two years more we should be deprived of all communication with our native land. The migratory birds which visit Tartary are for the most part known in Europe; such as wild geese, wild ducks, teal, storks, bustards, and so on. There is one bird which may deserve particular mention : the Youen-Yang, an aquatic bird frequenting ponds and marshes; it is of the size and form of the wild duck, but its beak, instead of being flat, is round, its red head is sprinkled with white, its tail is black, and the rest of its plumage a fine purple; its cry is exceedingly loud and mournful, not the song of a bird, but a sort of clear, prolonged sigh, resembling the plaintive tones of a man under suffering. These birds always go in pairs; they frequent, in an especial manner, desert and marshy places. You see them incessantly skimming over the surface of the waters without the couple ever separating from each other; if one flies away, the other immediately follows; and that which dies first does not leave its companion long in widowhood, for it is soon consumed by sorrow and lonesomeness. Youen is the name of the male, Yang that of the female; Youen-Yang their common denomination.

We remarked in Tartary another species of migratory bird, which offers various peculiarities singular in themselvee, and perhaps unknown to naturalists. It is about the size of a quail; its eyes, of a brilliant black, are encircled by a magnificent ring of azure; its body is of ash color, speckled with black; its legs, instead of feathers, are covered with a sort of long, rough hair, like that of the musk-deer; its feet are totally different from those of any other bird; they exactly resemble the paws of the green lizard, and are covered with scales so hard as to resist the edge of the sharpest knife. This singular creature, therefore, partakes at once of the bird, of the quadruped, and of the reptile. The Chinese call it Loung-Kio (Dragon's Foot). These birds make their periodical appearance in vast numbers from the north, especially after a great fall of snow. They fly with astonishing swiftness, and the movements of their wings makes a loud, rattling noise, like that of heavy hail.

While we had the charge, in Northern Mongolia, of the little christendom of the Valley of Black Waters, one of our Christians, a skilful huntsman, brought us two of these birds which he had caught alive. They were excessively ferocious; no sooner was your hand extended to touch them, than the hair on their legs bristled; and if you had the temerity to stroke them, you instantly were assailed with vehement strokes of the bill. The nature of these Dragon's Feet was evidently so wild as to preclude the possibility of preserving them alive : they would touch nothing we offered them. Perceiving, therefore, that they must soon die of starvation, we determined to kill and eat them; their flesh was of agreeable, pheasant-like savor, but terribly tough.

The Tartars might easily take any number of these migratory birds, especially of the wild geese and ducks, the crowds of which are perfectly prodigious : and take them, moreover, without the expenditure of a single ounce of powder, by merely laying traps for them on the banks of the pools, or by surprising them in the night amongst the aquatic plants; but as we have before observed, the flesh of wild creatures is not at all to the taste of the Tartars; there is nothing to their palates at all comparable with a joint of mutton, very fat and half boiled.

The Mongols are equally disinclined to fishing; and accordingly, the highly productive lakes and ponds which one meets with so frequently in Tartary, have become the property of Chinese speculators, who, with the characteristic knavery of their nation, having first obtained from the Tartar kings permission to fish in their states, have gradually converted this toleration into a monopoly most rigorously enforced. The Paga-Gol (Little River), near which we were now encamped, has several Chinese fishing stations upon its banks. This Paga-Gol is formed by the junction of two rivers, which, taking their source from the two sides of a hill, flow in opposite directions; the one, running towards the north, falls into the Yellow River; the other proceeding southwards, swells the current of another stream, which itself also falls into the Hoang-Ho; but at the time of the great inundations, the two rivers, in common with the hill which separates their course, all alike disappear. The overflowing of the Hoang-Ho reunites the two currents, and that which then presents itself is a large expanse of water, the breadth of which extends to nearly two miles. At this period, the fish which abound in the Yellow River repair in shoals to this new basin, wherein the waters remain collected until the commencement of the winter; and during the autumn, this little sea is covered in all directions with the boats of Chinese fishermen, whose habitations for the fishing season are miserable cabins constructed on either bank.

During the first night of our encampment in this locality, we were kept awake by a strange noise, constantly recurring in the distance, as it seemed to us, the muffled and irregular roll of drums; with daybreak the noise continued, but more intermittent and less loud; it apparently came from the water. We went out and proceeded towards the bank of the lake, where a fisherman, who was boiling his tea in a little kettle, supported by three stones, explained the mystery; he told us that during the night, all the fishermen seated in their barks, keep moving over the water, in all directions, beating wooden drums for the purpose of alarming the fish, and driving them towards the places where the nets are spread. The poor man whom we interrogated had himself passed the whole night in this painful toil. His red, swollen eyes and his drawn face clearly indicated that it was long since he had enjoyed adequate rest. "Just now," he said, "we have a great deal of work upon our hands; there is no time to be lost if we wish to make any money of the business. The fishing season is very short; at the outside not more than three months; and a few days hence we shall be obliged to withdraw. The Paga-Gol will be frozen, and not a fish will be obtainable. You see, Sirs Lamas, we have no time to lose. I have passed all the night hunting the fish about; when I have drunk some tea and eaten a few spoonfuls of oatmeal, I shall get into my boat, and visit the nets I have laid out there westward; then I shall deposit the fish I have taken in the osier reservoirs you see yonder; then I shall examine my nets, and mend them if they need mending; then I shall take a brief repose, and after that, when the old grandfather (the sun) goes down, I shall once more cast my nets; then I shall row over the water, now here, now there, beating my drum, and so it goes on." These details interested us, and as our occupations at the moment were not very urgent, we asked the fisherman if he would allow us to accompany him when he went to raise his nets. "Since personages like you," answered he, "do not disdain to get into my poor boat and to view my unskilful and disagreeable fishing, I accept the benefit you propose." Hereupon we sat down in a corner of his rustic hearth to wait until he had taken his repast. The meal of the fisherman was as short as the preparations for it had been hasty. When the tea was sufficiently boiled, he poured out a basin full of it; threw into this a handful of oatmeal, which he partially kneaded with his forefinger; and then, after having pressed it a little, and rolled it into a sort of cake, he swallowed it without any other preparation. After having three or four times repeated the same operation, the dinner was at an

Fishing Party.

end. This manner of living had nothing in it to excite our curiosity; having adopted the nomad way of living, a sufficiently long experience had made it familiar to us.

We entered his small boat and proceeded to enjoy the pleasure of fishing. After having relished for some moments the delight of a quiet sail on the tranquil water, smooth and unbroken as glass, through troops of cormorants and wild geese, which were disporting on the surface of the expanse, and which, half running, half flying, made a free passage for us as we advanced, we reached the place where the nets lay. At intervals we saw pieces of wood floating on the water, to which the nets were attached which rested at the botfom. When we drew them up we saw the fish glitter as they struggled in the meshes. These fish were generally large, but the fisherman only kept the largest; those that were under half a pound he threw back into the water.

After having examined a few of the nets, he stopped to see if the haul had been productive. Already the two wells, constructed at the extremities of the boat, were nearly full. "Sirs Lamas," said the fisherman, "do you eat fish? I will sell you some if you please." At this proposition, the two poor French missionaries looked at each other without saying a word. In that look you might see that they were by no means averse to trying the flavor of the fish of the Yellow River, but that they dared not, a sufficient reason keeping them in suspense. "How do you sell your fish?" "Not dear, eighty sapeks a pound." "Eighty sapeks! why that is dearer than mutton." "You speak the words of truth; but what is mutton compared with the fish of the Hoang-Ho?" "No matter; it is too dear for us. We have still far to go; our purse is low, we must economize." The fisherman did not insist; he took his oar, and directed the boat towards those nets which had not yet been drawn up from the water. "For what reason," asked we, "do you throw back so much fish? Is it because the quality is inferior?" "Oh, no; all the fish in the Yellow River are excellent, these are too small, that is all." "Ah, just so; next year they will be bigger. It is a matter of calculation; you refrain now, so that in the end you may get more by them." The fisherman laughed. "It is not that," he said; "we do not hope to re-capture these fish. Every year the basin is filled with fresh fish, brought hither by the overflowings of the Hoang-Ho; there come great and small; we take the first; and the others we throw back, because they do not sell well. The fish here are very abundant. We are able to select the best . . . Sirs Lamas, if you like to have these little fish, I will not throw them back." The offer was accepted, and the small fry, as they came, were placed in a little basket. When the fishing was over, we found ourselves possessors of a very respectable supply of fish. Before leaving the boat, we washed an old basket, and having deposited our fish in it, we marched in triumph to the tent. "Where have you been?" exclaimed Samdadchiemba, as soon as he saw us; "the tea is now boiled, and it soon gets cold: I have boiled it up again; it has again got cold." "Pour out some of your tea," answered we. "We will not have oatmeal to-day, but some fresh fish. Place some loaves under the ashes to bake." Our prolonged absence had put Samdadchiemba in an ill humor. His forehead was more contracted than usual, and his small black eyes flashed with displeasure. But when he beheld in the basket the fish which were still in motion, his face relaxed into a smile, and his countenance insensibly grew more cheerful. He opened smilingly the bag of flour, the strings of which were never untied except on rare occasions. Whilst he was busily occupied with the pastry, we took some of the fish, and proceeded to the shore of a lake at a short distance from the tent. We had scarcely got there, when Samdadchiemba ran to us with all his might. He drew aside the four corners of the cloth which contained the fish. "What are you going to do?" said he, with an anxious air. "We are going to cut open and scale this fish." "Oh, that is not well; my spiritual fathers, wait a little; you must not transgress thus." "What are you talking about? Who is committing a sin?" "Why, look at these fish; they are still moving. You must let them die in peace, before you open them: is it not a sin to kill a living creature?" "Go make your bread and let us alone. Are we always to be pestered with your notions of metempsychosis? Do you still think that men are transformed into beasts, and beasts into men?" The lips of our Dchiahour opened for a long laugh. "Bah!" said he, striking his forehead, "what a thick head I have; I did not think of that; I had forgotten the doctrine," and he returned not a little ashamed at having come to give us such ridiculous advice.

The fish were fried in mutton fat, and we found them exquisite.

In Tartary and in the north of China, the fishing continues to the commencement of winter, when the ponds and rivers are frozen. At that time they expose to the air, in the night, the fish they have kept alive in the reservoirs; these immediately freeze, and may be laid up without trouble. It is in this state that they are sold to the fishmongers. During the long winters of the northern part of the empire, the wealthy Chinese can always, by this means, procure fresh fish; but great care must be taken not to make too large a provision of them to be consumed during the time of the great frosts, for on the first thaw the fish become putrid.

During our few days' rest, we considered the means of crossing the Paga-Gol. A Chinese family having obtained from the King of the Ortous the privilege of conveying travelers across, we were obliged to address ourselves to the master of the boat. He had undertaken to conduct us to the other side, but we had not yet agreed about the fare; he required upwards of 1,000 sapeks. The sum appeared to us exorbitant, and we waited.

On the third day of our halt, we perceived a fisherman coming towards our tent, dragging himself along with great difficulty by the aid of a long staff. His pale and extremely meager face, showed that he was a man in suffering. As soon as he had seated himself beside our hearth, "Brother," said we, "it seems that your days are not happy." "Ah," said he, "my misfortune is great, but what am I to do? I must submit to the irrevocable laws of heaven. It is now a fortnight since, as I was going to visit a Mongol tent, I was bitten in the leg by a mad dog; there has been formed a wound which grows larger and mortifies day by day. They told me that you were from the Western Heaven, and I am come to you. The men of the Western Heaven, say the Tartar Lamas, have an unlimited power. With a single word they are able to cure the most grievous disorders." "They have deceived you, when they said we had such great powers:" and hereupon we took occasion to elucidate to this man the great truths of the faith. But he was a Chinese, and, like all his nation, but little heedful of religious matters. Our words only glanced over his heart; his hurt absorbed all his thoughts. We resolved to treat his case with the Kou-Kouo, or bean of St. Ignatius. This vegetable, of a brown or ashy color, and of a substance which resembles horn, extremely hard, and of intolerable bitterness, is a native of the Philippine Isles. The manner of using the Kou-Kouo is to bruise it in cold water, to which it communicates its bitterness. This water, taken inwardly, modifies the heat of the blood, and extinguishes internal inflammation. It is an excellent specific for all sorts of wounds and contusions, and enjoying a high character in the Chinese Materia Medica, is sold in all chemists' shops. The veterinary doctors also apply it with great success to the internal diseases of cattle and sheep. In the north of China we have often witnessed the salutary effects of the Kou-Kouo.

We infused the powder of one of these beans in some cold water, with which we washed the poor man's wound, and we supplied some clean linen, in place of the disgustingly dirty rags which previously served for a bandage. When we had done all we could for the sufferer, we observed that he still seemed very embarrassed in his manner. His face was red with blushes, he held down his eyes, and he began several sentences which he could not complete. "Brother," said we, "you have something on your mind." "Holy personages, you see how poor I am! you have tended my wound, and you have given me a great mug of healing water to take; I know not what I can offer in exchange for all this." "If this be the subject of your uneasiness," said we, "be at once reassured. In doing what we could for your leg, we only fulfilled a duty commanded by our religion. The remedies we have prepared, we freely give you." Our words evidently relieved the poor fisherman from a very grave embarrassment. He immediately prostrated himself before us, and touched the ground thrice with his forehead, in token of his gratitude. Before withdrawing, he asked us whether we intended to remain where we were for any length of time. We told him that we should gladly depart the next day, but that we had not as yet agreed with the ferryman as to the fare. "I have a boat," said the fisherman, "and since you have tended my wound, I will endeavor to-morrow, to convey you over the water. If my boat belonged entirely to myself, I would at once undertake the matter; but as I have two partners, I must first get their consent. Moreover, we must procure some particulars as to our course; we fishermen are not acquainted with the depth of water at all the points of the passage. There are dangerous places here and there, which we must ascertain the exact nature and locality of beforehand, so that we may not incur some misfortune. Don't say anything more about the matter to the ferry people. I will come back in the course of the evening, and we will talk over the subject."

These words gave us hopes of being able to continue our journey, without too heavy an outlay for the river passage. As he had promised, the fisherman returned in the evening. "My partners," said he, "were not at first willing to undertake this job, because it would lose them a day's fishing. I promised that you would give them 400 sapeks, and so the affair was arranged. To-morrow we will make inquiries as to the best course to follow on the river. Next morning, before sunrise, fold your tent, load your camels, and come down to the river side. If you see any of the ferry people, don't tell them you are going to give us 400 sapeks. As they have the sole right of carrying passengers for hire, they might prosecute us for carrying you, if they knew you had paid us anything."

At the appointed hour, we proceeded to the fisherman's hut. In a minute the baggage was packed in the boat, and the two missionaries seated themselves beside it, attended by the boatman whose wound they had cured. It was agreed that a young companion of his should ride the horse across the shallows, leading the mule, while Samdadchiemba, in like manner, was to conduct the camels over. When all was ready we started, the boat following one course, the horses and camels another, for the latter were obliged to make long circuits in order to avoid the deeper parts of the river.

The navigation was at first very pleasant. We floated tranquilly over the broad surface of the waters, in a small skiff, propelled by a single man with two light sculls. The pleasure of this water party, amid the deserts of Mongolia, was not, however, of long duration. The poetry of the thing, soon at an end, was succeeded by some very doleful prose. We were advancing gently over the smooth water, vaguely listening to the measured dips of the sculls, when, all of a sudden, we were aroused by a clamor behind, of which the shrieks of the camels constituted a prominent share. We stopped, and, looking round, perceived that horse, mule, and camels were struggling in the water, without making any onward progress. In the general confusion we distinguished Samdadchiemba flourishing his arms, as if to recall us. Our boatman was not at all disposed to accept the invitation, reluctant as he was to quit the easy current he had found; but as we insisted, he turned back, and rowed towards the other party.

Samdadchiemba was purple with rage. As soon as we came up to him, he furiously assailed the boatman with invectives: "Did you want to drown us," bawled he, "that you gave us for a guide a fellow that doesn't know a yard of the way. Here are we amid gulfs, of which none of us know the depth or extent." The animals, in fact, would neither advance nor recede; beat them as you might, there they remained immovable. The boatman hurled maledictions at his partner: "If you did not know the way, what did you come for? The only thing to be done now is to go back to the hut, and tell your cousin to get on the horse; he'll be a better guide than you."

To return for a better guide was clearly the safest course, but this was no easy matter; the animals had got so frightened at finding themselves surrounded with such a body of water, that they would not stir. The young guide was at his wits' end; it was in vain that he beat the horse, and pulled the bridle this way and that; the horse struggled and splashed up the water, and that was all; not an inch would it move, one way or the other. The young man, no better horseman than guide, at last lost his balance and fell into the water; he disappeared for a moment, to our increased consternation, and then rose at a little distance, just where he could stand and have his head above water. Samdadchiemba grew furious, but at last, seeing no other alternative, he quietly took off all his clothes as he sat on the camel, threw them into the boat, and slipped down the camel's side into the stream. "Take that man into your boat," cried he to our boatman; "I'll have nothing more to do with him. I'll go back and find some one who can guide us properly." He then made his way back through the water, which sometimes rose up to his neck, leading the animals, whose confidence returned when they saw themselves preceded by the Dchiahour.

Our hearts were filled with gratitude at observing the devotion and courage of this young neophyte, who for our sakes, had not hesitated to plunge into the water which, at that season, was bitterly cold. We anxiously followed him with our eyes until we saw him close upon the shore. "You may now," said the boatman, "be quite at your ease; he will find in my hut a man who will guide him, so as to avoid the least danger."

We proceeded on our way, but the navigation was by no means so agreeable as before; the boatman could not find again the clear path on the waters which he was pursuing when we returned to aid Samdadchiemba; and hampered with aquatic plants, the vessel made but very slow progress. We tried to mend matters, by turning to the right and then to the left, but the difficulty only grew greater; the water was so shallow that the boat, in its labored advance, turned up the mud. We were compelled ourselves to take the sculls, while the boatman, getting into the water and passing across his shoulders a rope, the other end of which was tied to the boat, tried to pull us along. We applied our united efforts to the task of moving the vessel, but all in vain; it scarcely advanced a foot. The boatman at last resumed his seat and folded his arms in utter despair: "Since we cannot get on by ourselves," said he, "we must wait here until the passage-boat comes up, and then follow in its course." We waited.

The boatman was evidently altogether disconcerted; he loudly reproached himself for having undertaken this laborious business; while we, on our parts, were angry with ourselves for having permitted a consideration of economy to deter us from proceeding with the ferry-boat. We should have got into the water and waded to the shore, but, besides the difficulty connected with the baggage, the undertaking was dangerous in itself. The ground was so irregular that, while at one moment you passed through water so shallow that it would scarcely float the boat, in the next moment you came to a hole, deep enough to drown you three times over.

It was near noon when we saw three passage-boats passing us, which belonged to the family who enjoyed the monopoly of the ferry. After having, with infinite labor, extricated ourselves from the mud and attained the channel indicated by these boats, we were quietly following their course when they stopped, evidently awaiting us. We recognized the person with whom we had tried to bargain for our passage over, and he recognized us, as we could easily perceive by the angry glances which he directed against us. "You tortoise-egg," cried he to our boatman, "what have these western men given you for the passage? They must have handed over a good bagful of sapeks to have induced you to trespass upon my rights! You and I will have a little talk about the matter, by and by; be sure of that." "Don't answer him," whispered the boatman to us; then raising his voice and assuming an air of virtuous indignation, he cried to the ferryman: "What do you mean? You don't know what you're talking about. Consult the dictates of reason, instead of getting into a fury about nothing. These Lamas have not given me a sapek; they have cured my leg with one of their western specifics, and do you mean to say that in gratitude for such a benefit I am not to carry them over the Paga-Gol? My conduct is perfectly right, and in conformity with religion." The ferryman grumbling between his teeth, pretended to accept the statement thus made.

This little altercation was succeeded by profound silence on both sides. While the flotilla was peaceably advancing, pursuing the thread of a narrow current, just wide enough to admit the passage of a boat, we saw galloping towards us, along the shallows, a horseman whose rapid progress dashed aside the water in all directions. As soon as he came within call he stopped short: "Make haste," cried he, " make haste; lose no time, row with all your might! The Prime Minister of the King of the Ortous is yonder on the prairie with his suite, waiting the arrival of your boat. Row quickly." He who spoke was a Tartar Mandarin, his rank being indicated by the blue button which surmounted his hair cap. After issuing his orders he turned round, whipped his horse, and galloped back the same way he had come. When he was out of sight, the murmurs which his presence had restrained burst out. "Here's a day's labor marked out! A fine thing, truly, to be employed by a Mongol Toudzelaktsi (Minister of State), who'll make us row all day, and then not give us a single sapek for our pains." "As to that, it need not so much matter; but the chances are that this Tcheou-ta-dze will break every bone in our bodies into the bargain." "Well, row away, it can't be helped; after all, we shall have the honor of ferrying over a Toudzelaktsi." This little piece of insolence excited a laugh, but the prevalent expression was that of furious invective against the Mongol authorities.

Our boatman remained silent; at last he said to us: "This is a most unfortunate day for me. I shall be obliged to carry some of this Toudzelaktsi's suite perhaps to Tchagan-Kouren itself. I am by myself, I am ill, and my boat ought this evening to be engaged in fishing." We were truly afflicted at this unlucky turn of affairs, feeling as we did that we were the involuntary occasion of the poor fisherman's misfortune. We knew very well that it was no trifling matter to be called into the service, in this way, of a Chinese or Tartar Mandarin, for whom everything must be done at once, unhesitatingly and cheerfully. No matter what may be the difficulties in the way, that which the Mandarin desires must be done. Knowing the consequences of the meeting to our poor boatman, we determined to see what we could do to relieve him from the dilemma. "Brother," said we, "do not be uneasy; the Mandarin who awaits the passage-boats is a Tartar, the minister of the king of this country. We will endeavor to manage matters for you. Go very slowly, stop now and then; while we are in your boat no one, attendants, Mandarins, not even the Toudzelaktsi himself will venture to say a word to you." We stopped short in our course, and meanwhile the three passage-boats reached the landing-place where the Mongol authorities were waiting for them. Soon two Mandarins, with the blue button, galloped towards us: "What are you stopping there for?" cried they. "Why do you not come on?" We interposed: "Brother Mongols," said we, "request your master to content himself with the three boats already at the shore. This man is ill, and has been rowing a long time; it would be cruel to prevent him from resting himself awhile." "Be it as you desire, Sirs Lamas," replied the horsemen, and they galloped back to the Toudzelaktsi.

We then resumed our course, but very slowly, in order to give time for every person to embark before we reached the shore. By and by, we saw the three ferry-boats returning, filled with Mandarins and their attendants; the horses were fording the river in another direction, under the guidance of one of the boatmen. As the party approached, our boatman grew more and more afraid; he did not venture to raise his eyes, and he scarcely breathed. At last the boats were level with each other; "Sirs Lamas," cried a voice, "is peace with you?" The red button in the cap of the speaker, and the richness of his embroidered dress, indicated that it was the prime minister who addressed to us this Tartar compliment. "Toudzelaktsi of the Ortous," replied we, "our progress is slow, but it is favorable; may peace also attend you." After a few other civilities, required by Tartar forms, we proceeded on our way. When we had attained a safe distance from the Mandarins, our boatman was perfectly relieved; we had extricated him from a most serious difficulty. The ferry-boats, it was probable, would be engaged at least three days in their gratuitous labor, for the Toudzelaktsi not choosing to travel across the marshes, the boats would have to convey him down the Yellow River all the way to Tchagan-Kouren.

After a long, laborious, and dangerous passage, we reached the other side of the waters. Samdadchiemba had arrived long before us, and was awaiting us on the margin of the stream. He was still naked, as to clothes, but then he was covered well nigh up to the shoulders with a thick layer of mud, which gave him a negro aspect. In consequence of the extreme shallowness of the water, the boat could not get within thirty feet of the shore. The boatmen who preceded us had been obliged to carry the Mandarins and their attendants on their shoulders to the boats. We did not choose to adopt the same process, but rather to make use of the animals for our disembarkation. Samdadchiemba accordingly brought them close to the boat; M. Gabet got on the horse, M. Huc on the mule, and so we reached the shore, without having occasion to employ any person's shoulders.

The sun was just about to set. We would willingly have encamped at once, for we were exhausted with hunger and fatigue, but we could not possibly do so, for we had, they told us, fully two lis to journey before we should get out of the mud. We loaded our camels, therefore, and proceeded onward, completing the miserable day in pain and suffering. Night had closed in before we came to a place where we could set up our tent; we had no strength left for preparing the usual meal, so drinking some cold water, and eating a few handfuls of millet, we lay down, after a brief prayer, and fell into a deep slumber.

Election of a Living Buddha.

CHAPTER VIII.

Glance at the Country of the Ortous—Cultivated Lands—Sterile, sandy steppes of the Ortous—Form of the Tartar-Mongol Government—Nobility—Slavery—A small Lamasery—Election and Enthronization of a Living Buddha—Discipline of the Lamaseries—Lama Studies—Violent Storm—Shelter in some Artificial Grottoes—Tartar concealed in a Cavern—Tartaro-Chinese Anecdote—Ceremonies of Tartar Marriages—Polygamy—Divorce—Character and Costume of the Mongol Women.

THE sun was already very high when we rose. On leaving the tent we looked round us, in order to get acquainted with this new country, which the darkness of the preceding evening had not allowed us to examine. It appeared to us dismal and arid; but we were happy, on any terms, to lose sight of bogs and swamps. We had left behind us the Yellow River, with its overflowing waters, and entered the sandy steppes of Ortous.

The land of Ortous is divided into seven banners; it extends a hundred leagues from east to west, and seventy from south to north. It is surrounded by the Yellow River on the west, east, and north, and by the Great Wall on the south. This country has been subjected, at all periods, to the influence of the political revolutions, by which the Chinese empire has been agitated. The Chinese and Tartar conquerors have taken possession of it in turns, and made it the theater of sanguinary wars. During the tenth, eleventh, and twelfth centuries, it remained under the scepter of the kings of Hia, who derived their origin from the Thou-Pa Tartars of the land of Si-Fan. The capital of their kingdom, called Hia-Tcheou, was situated at the foot of the Alécha mountains between the Hoang-Ho and the Great Wall. At present, this town is called Ning-Hia, and belongs to the province Kan-Sou. In 1227 the kingdom of Hia, and afterwards Ortous, were involved in the common desolation by the victories of Tchingghis-Khan, founder of the Tartar dynasty of the Youen.

After the expulsion of the Tartar Mongols by the Ming, the Ortous fell under the power of the Khan of the Tchakar. When the latter submitted to the Mantchou conquerors in 1635, the Ortous followed his example, and were reunited to the empire as a tributary people.

The Emperor Khang-Hi resided for some time among the Ortous in 1696, when he was on his expedition against the Eleuts; and this is what he wrote of this people in a letter to the prince, his son, who had remained at Peking: —"Till now, I never had at all an accurate idea respecting the Ortous: they are a very civilized nation, and have lost nothing of the old manners of the true Mongols. All their princes live in perfect union among themselves, and do not know the difference between *mine* and *thine*. No one ever heard of a thief amongst them, although they take not the slightest precautions for guarding their camels and horses. If by chance one of these animals goes astray, it is taken care of by him who finds it, till he has discovered its owner, to whom he restores it, without the least payment. The Ortous are extremely skilful in breeding cattle; most of their horses are tame and tractable. The Tchakars, north of the Ortous, enjoy the reputation of training them with more care and success; nevertheless, I believe that the Ortous excel them in this point. Notwithstanding these advantages, they are not at all so rich as the other Mongols."

This quotation, which we take from the Abbé Grosier, is

in every point conformable with what we ourselves were able to observe among the Ortous; so that, since the time of the Emperor Khang-Hi, this people has not at all changed in its manners.

The aspect of the country through which we traveled on the first day of our journey seemed affected by the vicinity of the Chinese fishermen, who reside on the banks of the Yellow River. We saw here and there cultivated grounds, but there can be nothing more wretched and bare looking than this cultivation, except, perhaps, the cultivator himself. These miserable agriculturists are a mixed people, half Chinese, half Tartars, but possessing neither the industry of the former, nor the frank and simple manners of the latter. They live in houses, or rather in dirty sheds built of branches intertwined, rudely covered with mud and cow's excrement. Thirst obliging us to enter one of these habitations to ask for some water, we were able to convince ourselves that the interior did not in any way contradict the misery which appeared outside. Men and animals live together higgledy-piggledy in these abodes, which are far inferior to those of the Mongols, where, at least, the air is not infected by the presence of cattle and sheep.

The sandy soil, which is cultivated by these poor people, beyond a little buckwheat and millet, produces only hemp, but this is very large and abundant. Though, when we were there, the crop was already gathered in, we could nevertheless judge of the beauty of its stem from what remained in the fields. The farmers of Ortous do not pull up the hemp when it is ripe, as is done in China; they cut it off above the ground, so high as to leave a stump of about an inch in diameter. It was accordingly great toil for our camels to traverse those vast fields of hemp; the stumps, occurring at every step beneath their large feet, compelled them to execute all sorts of fantastic movements, which would have excited our mirth, had we not been fearful of seeing them wounded. However, that which so impeded our camels proved of great use to ourselves. When we had set up our tent, these stumps furnished us with a ready and abundant fuel.

We soon entered once more the Land of Grass, if, indeed, one can give this name to such a barren, arid country, as that of the Ortous. Wherever you turn you find only a soil, bare and without verdure; rocky ravines, marly hills, and plains covered with a fine, moving sand, blown by the impetuous winds in every direction; for pasture, you will only find a few thorny bushes and poor fern, dusty and fetid. At intervals only, this horrible soil produces some thin, sharp grass, so firm in the earth, that the animals can only get it up by digging the sand with their muzzles. The numerous swamps, which had been so heavy a desolation to us on the borders of the Yellow River, became matter of regret in the country of the Ortous, so very rare here is water; not a single rivulet is there, not a spring, where the traveler can quench his thirst; at distances only are there ponds and cisterns, filled with a fetid, muddy water.

The Lamas, with whom we had been in communication at Blue Town, had warned us of all the miseries we should have to endure in the country of the Ortous, especially on account of the scarcity of water. By their advice we had bought two wooden pails, which proved indeed of the greatest service to us. Whenever we were lucky enough to find on our way pools or wells dug by the Tartars, we filled our pails, without considering too nicely the quality of the water, which we used with the greatest economy, as if it had been some rare and precious beverage. In spite of all these precautions, it happened more than once that we were obliged to pass whole days without getting a single drop of water wherewith to moisten our lips. But our personal privations were trifling compared with the pain we felt at seeing our animals wanting water almost every day in a country where they had nothing to eat beyond a few plants nearly dried up, and, as it were, calcined by nitre, and where they accordingly fell away visibly. After some days' traveling, the horse assumed a truly wretched appearance; it bent down its head, and seemed, at every step, as though it would sink down with weakness; the camels painfully balanced themselves on their long legs, and their emaciated humps hung over their backs like empty bags.

The steppes of the Ortous, though so destitute of water and good pasture, have not been quite abandoned by wild animals. You often find there gray squirrels, agile yellow goats, and beautifully plumaged pheasants. Hares are in abundance, and are so far from shy, that they did not even take the trouble to move at our approach; they merely rose

The Steppes of Ortous.

on their hind legs, pricked up their ears, and looked at us as we passed with the utmost indifference. The fact is, these animals feel perfectly secure, for, with the exception of a few Mongols who follow the chase, nobody ever molests them.

The herds of the Tartars of the Ortous are not very numerous, and are quite different from those which feed on the rich pastures of the Tchakar, or of Gechekten. The cattle and horses appeared very miserable; the goats, sheep, and camels, however, looked very well, which is undoubtedly the consequence of their predilection for plants impregnated with saltpeter, whereas cattle and horses prefer fresh pastures, and pure and abundant water.

The Mongols of Ortous are very much affected by the wretchedness of the soil upon which they live. In the course of our journey we saw no indication that they had become much richer than they were in the time of the Emperor Khang-Hi. Most of them live in tents made of some rags of felt, or of goat-skins framed on a wretched woodwork. Everything about these tents is so old and dirty, so tattered with time and storms, that you would with difficulty suppose they could serve as abodes for human beings. Whenever we happened to pitch our tent near these poor habitations, we were sure to be visited by a crowd of wretches who prostrated themselves at our feet, rolled on the earth, and gave us the most magnificent titles, in order to extract something from our charity. We were not rich, but we could not abstain from bestowing upon them a part of the modicum which the goodness of Providence had bestowed upon us. We gave them some leaves of tea, a handful of oatmeal, some broiled millet, sometimes some mutton fat. Alas! we would fain have given more, but we were obliged to give according to our means. The missionaries are themselves poor men, who only live upon the alms distributed among them every year by their brothers in Europe.

Any one not acquainted with the laws by which the Tartars are ruled, would not readily understand why men condemn themselves to spend their lives in the wretched country of the Ortous, whilst Mongolia presents, in every direction, immense uninhabited plains, where water and pasture are to be found in abundance. Although the Tartars are nomads, and incessantly wandering about from one place to another, they are, nevertheless, not at liberty to live in any other country than their own. They are bound to remain in their own kingdom, under the dominion of their own sovereign, for slavery is still maintained among the Mongol tribes with the utmost rigor. In order to attain an accurate idea of the degree of liberty these people enjoy in their desert regions, it is expedient to enter into some details as to the form of their government.

Mongolia is divided into several sovereignties, whose chiefs are subject to the Emperor of China, himself a Tartar, but of the Mantchou race; these chiefs bear titles corresponding to those of kings, dukes, earls, barons, etc. They govern their states according to their own pleasure, none having any right to meddle with their affairs. They acknowledge as sovereign only the Emperor of China. Whenever there arise differences among them, they appeal to Peking. Instead of leveling lances at each other, as used to be done in the middle ages of Europe, among its little sovereigns, so warlike and so turbulent, they always submit with respect to the decision of the Court of Peking, whatever it may be. Though the Mongol sovereigns think it their duty to prostrate themselves, once a year, before the Son of Heaven, Lord of the Earth, they nevertheless do not concede to the Grand-Khan the right of dethroning the reigning families in the Tartar principalities. He may, they say, cashier a king for grave misconduct, but he is bound to fill up the vacant place with one of the superseded prince's sons. The sovereignty belongs, they contend, to such and such a family, by a right which is inalienable, and of which it were a crime to dispossess the owner.

A few years ago, the King of Barains[1] was accused at Peking of having conspired a rebellion against the Emperor; he was tried by the Supreme Tribunal without being heard, and condemned to be "shortened at both ends," the meaning of the decree being, that his head and feet should be cut off. The king made enormous presents to the officials who were sent to superintend the execution of the imperial edict, and they contented themselves with cutting off his braid of hair, and the soles of his boots. They reported at Peking that the order had been executed, and no more was said about the matter. The king however, descended from his throne, and was succeeded by his son.

Although it is a sort of customary right that power shall always remain in the same family, it cannot be said that there is anything precisely fixed in this respect. There can be nothing more vague and indefinite than the relations between the Tartar sovereigns and the Grand-Khan or Emperor of China, whose omnipotent will is above all laws and all customs. In practice, the Emperor has the right to do whatever he chooses to do, and the right is never disputed by any person. If doubtful or disputed cases arise, they are decided by force.

In Tartary, all the families that are in any way related to the sovereign, form a nobility, or a patrician cast, who are proprietors of the whole soil. These nobles, called Taitsi, are distinguished by a blue button surmounting the cap. It is from among them that the sovereigns of the different states select their ministers, who are generally three in number, and called Toutzelaktsi—that is to say, a man who assists or lends his aid. This rank gives them the right of wearing the red button. Below the Toutzelaktsi are the Touchimel, subaltern officers, who are charged with the details of government. Lastly, a certain number of secretaries

---

[1] Barains is a principality situated north of Peking. It is one of the most celebrated in Mongol Tartary.

or interpreters, who must be versed in the Mongol, Mantchou, and Chinese languages, complete the hierarchy.

In the country of the Khalkhas, to the north of the desert of Gobi, there is a district entirely occupied by Taitsi, who are supposed to be descendants of the Mongol dynasty, that was founded by Tchinggiskhan, and which occupied the imperial throne from 1260 to 1341. After the revolution, which restored the national independence of the Chinese, these people sought refuge among the Khalkhas, obtained, without difficulty, a portion of their immense territory, and adopted the nomad life, which their ancestors had led prior to the conquest of China. These Taitsi live in the greatest independence, liable to no duty, paying no tribute to anyone, and recognizing no sovereign. Their wealth consists in tents and cattle. The country of the Taitsi is, of all the Mongol regions, that wherein the patriarchal manners are found to be most accurately preserved, such as the Bible describes them in the lives of Abraham, Jacob, and the other pastors of Mesopotamia.

The Tartars who do not belong to the royal family, are all slaves, living in absolute subjection to their masters. Besides the rents they pay, they are bound to keep their master's flocks and herds, but they are not forbidden to breed also cattle on their own account. It would be a fallacy to imagine that slavery in Tartary is oppressive and cruel, as amongst some nations; the noble families scarcely differ from the slave families. In examining the relations between them, it would be difficult to distinguish the master from the slave: they live both alike in tents, and both alike occupy their lives in pasturing their flocks. You will never find among them luxury and opulence insolently staring in the face of poverty. When the slave enters his master's tent, the latter never fails to offer him tea and milk; they smoke together, and exchange their pipes. Around the tents the young slaves and the young noblemen romp and wrestle together without distinction; the stronger throws the weaker; that is all. You often find families of slaves becoming proprietors of numerous flocks, and spending their days in abundance. We met many who were richer than their masters, a circumstance giving no umbrage to the latter. What a difference between this slavery and that of Rome, for instance, where the Roman citizen, when he made up the inventory of his house, classed his slaves as furniture. With these haughty and cruel masters the slave did not merit even the name of man; he was called, without ceremony, a domestic thing, *res domestica*. Slavery, with the Mongol Tartars, is even less oppressive, less insulting to humanity, than the bondage of the middle ages. The Mongol masters never give to their slaves those humiliating nicknames which were formerly used to designate serfs; they call them *brothers;* never villeins, never scum, never *gent taillable et corvéable à merci.*

The Tartar nobles have the right of life and death over their slaves. They may administer justice themselves upon their bondsmen, even to sentence of death; but this privilege is never exercised in an arbitrary way. In case a slave has been put to death, a superior tribunal investigates the action of the master, and if it be found that he has abused his right, the innocent blood is revenged. The Lamas who belong to slave families become free, in some degree, as soon as they enter the sacerdotal tribe; they are liable neither to rents nor enforced labor; they are at liberty to quit their country, and ramble through the world at their pleasure, without anybody having the right to stay them.

Although the relations between master and slave are generally full of humanity and good-will, there are, nevertheless Tartar sovereigns who abuse their right, and oppress their people and exact exorbitant tributes. We know one who makes use of a system of oppression that is truly revolting. He selects from among his flocks the oldest and sickliest cattle, camels, sheep and goats, and gives them in charge to the rich slaves in his states, who cannot, of course, object to pasture the cattle of their sovereign master; but are fain to consider it rather an honor. After a few years, the king applies for his cattle, by this time all dead or dying of illness or old age, and selects from the flocks of his slaves the youngest and strongest; often even, not content with this, he demands double or treble the number. "Nothing," says he, "is more just; for in two or three years my beasts must have multiplied, and therefore a great number of lambs, colts, calves and young camels belong to me."

Slavery, however mitigated and softened, can never be in harmony with the dignity of man. It has been abolished in Europe, and we hope will be abolished one day among the Mongol people. But this great revolution will, as everywhere else, be operated by the influence of Christianity. It will not be theory-mongers who will liberate these nomad people. The work will be the work of the priests of Jesus Christ, of the preachers of the Holy Gospel, that Divine Charter, wherein are set forth the true rights of man. So soon as the missionaries shall have taught the Mongols to say, "Our Father who art in Heaven," slavery will fall in Tartary, and the tree of liberty will grow beside the cross.

After some days' march across the sands of the Ortous, we noticed on our way a small Lamasery, richly built in a picturesque and wild situation. We passed on without stopping. We had advanced a gunshot from the place, when we heard behind us the galloping of a horse. On looking round we saw a Lama following us at full speed. "Brothers," he said, "you have passed our *Soumé* (Lamasery) without stopping. Are you in such haste that you cannot repose for a day and offer your adorations to our saint?" "Yes, we are rather in a hurry; our journey is not of a few days; we are going to the West." "I knew very well by your physiognomies that you were not Mongols, and that you came from the West; but as you are going so far, you had better prostrate yourselves before our saint; that will bring you good luck." "We never prostrate ourselves before men; the true creed of the West forbids that." "Our saint is not a mere man; you do not imagine, perhaps, that in our little Lamasery we have the happiness to possess a Chaberon, a living Buddha. It is two years since he deigned to descend from the holy mountains of Thibet; he is now seven years old. In one of his former lives he was Grand Lama of a splendid Lamasery in this vale, which was destroyed, according to the prayer-books, in the time of the wars of Tching-Kis. The saint having reappeared a few years since, we have constructed in haste a small Lamasery. Come, brothers, our saint will hold his right hand over your heads, and luck will accompany your steps!" "The men who know the Holy Doctrine of the West do not believe in all these transmigrations of the Chaberons. We adore only the Creator of Heaven and earth; his name is Jehovah. We believe that the child you have made superior of your Lamasery is destitute of all power. Men have nothing to hope or to fear from him." When the Lama heard these words, which he certainly never expected, he was quite stupefied. By degrees his face became animated, and at last exhibited indignation and anger. He looked at us several times, then, pulling the bridle of his horse, he turned short round and left us hastily, muttering between his teeth some words which we could not exactly hear, but which we were aware did not constitute a benediction.

The Tartars believe with firm and absolute faith in all these various transmigrations. They would never allow themselves to entertain the slightest doubt as to the authenticity of their Chaberons. These living Buddhas are in large numbers, and are always placed at the head of the most important Lamaseries. Sometimes they modestly begin their career in a small temple, and have only a few disciples; but very soon their reputation increases around, and the small Lamasery becomes a place of pilgrimage and devotion. The neighboring Lamas, speculating upon the rising fashion, surround it with their cells; the Lamasery acquires development from year to year, and becomes at last famous in the land.

The election and enthronization of the living Buddhas are conducted in so singular a manner as to be well worth relating. When a Grand Lama has gone, that is to say, is dead, the circumstance is no occasion of mourning in the Lamasery. There are no tears, no lamentations, for everybody knows the Chaberon will very soon reappear. This apparent death is but the beginning of a new existence, as it were, one ring more added to the unlimited, uninterrupted chain of successive lives—a regular palingenesis. While the saint is in a state of chrysalis, his disciples are in the greatest anxiety; for it is their most important affair to discover the place where their master will resume life. A rainbow appearing in the air is considered a signal sent to them by their old Great Lama to aid them in their research. Every one thereupon says his prayers, and while the Lamasery which has lost its Buddha redoubles its fastings and prayers, a troop of elect proceeds to consult the Tchurtchun or augur, famous for the knowledge of things hidden from the common herd. He is informed that on such a day of such a moon the rainbow of the Chaberon has manifested itself on the sky; it made its appearance in such a place; it was more or less luminous, and it was visible so long;

then it disappeared amid such and such circumstances. When the Tchurtchun has received all the necessary indications, he recites some prayers, opens his books of divination, and pronounces at last his oracle, while the Tartars who have come to consult him, listen, kneeling, and full of unction. " Your Great Lama," says he, " has reappeared in Thibet, at such a distance from your Lamasery. You will find him in such a family." When these poor Mongols have heard this oracle, they return full of joy to announce the glad tidings to their Lamasery.

It often happens that the disciples of the defunct have no occasion to trouble themselves at all in order to discover the new birth-place of their Great Lama. He himself takes the trouble to initiate them into the secret of his transformation. As soon as he has effected his metamorphosis in Thibet, he reveals himself at an age when common children cannot yet articulate a single word. " It is I," he says with the accent of authority; "it is I who am the Great Lama, the living Buddha of such a temple; conduct me to my ancient Lamasery. I am its immortal superior." The wonderful baby having thus spoken, it is speedily communicated to the Lamas of the Soumé indicated, that their Chaberon is born in such a place, and they are summoned to attend and invite him home.

In whatever manner the Tartars discover the residence of their Great Lama, whether by the appearance of the rainbow, or by the spontaneous revelation of the Chaberon himself, they are always full of intense joy on the occasion. Soon all is movement in the tents, and the thousand preparations for a long journey are made with enthusiasm, for it is almost always in Thibet that they have to seek their living Buddha, who seldom fails to play them the trick of transmigrating in some remote and almost inaccessible country. Everyone contributes his share to the organization of the holy journey. If the king of the country does not place himself at the head of the caravan, he sends either his own son or one of the most illustrious members of the royal family. The great Mandarins, or ministers of the king, consider it their duty and an honor to join the party. When everything is at last prepared, an auspicious day is chosen, and the caravan starts.

Sometimes these poor Mongols, after having endured incredible fatigues in horrible deserts, fall into the hands of the brigands of the Blue Sea, who strip them from head to foot. If they do not die of hunger and cold in those dreadful solitudes—if they succeed in returning to the place whence they came—they commence the preparations for a new journey. There is nothing capable of discouraging them. At last, when, by dint of energy and perseverance, they have contrived to reach the eternal sanctuary, they prostrate themselves before the child who has been indicated to them. The young Chaberon, however, is not saluted and proclaimed Great Lama without a previous examination. There is held a solemn sitting, at which the new living Buddha is examined publicly, with a scrupulous attention. He is asked the name of the Lamasery of which he assumes to be the Great Lama; at what distance it is; what is the number of the Lamas residing in it. He is interrogated respecting the habits and customs of the defunct Great Lama, and the principal circumstances attending his death. After all these questions, there are placed before him different prayer-books, articles of furniture, teapots, cups, etc., and amongst all these things he has to point out those which belonged to his former life.

Generally this child, at most but five or six years old, comes forth victorious out of all these trials. He answers accurately all the questions that are put to him, and makes without any embarrassment the inventory of his goods. "Here," he says, "are the prayer-books I used; there is the japanned porringer out of which I drank my tea." And so on.

No doubt the Mongols are often dupes of the fraud of those who have an interest in making a Great Lama out of this puppet. Yet we believe that often all this proceeds on both sides with honesty and good faith. From the information we obtained from persons worthy of the greatest credit, it appears certain that all that is said of the Chaberons must not be ranged amongst illusion and deception. A purely human philosophy will, undoubtedly, reject such things, or put them, without hesitating, down to the account of Lama imposture. We Catholic missionaries believe that the great liar who once deceived our first parents in the earthly Paradise still pursues his system of falsehood in the world. He who had the power to hold up in the air Simon

Magus may well at this day speak to mankind by the mouth of an infant, in order to maintain the faith of his adorers.

When the titles of the living Buddha have been confirmed, he is conducted in triumph to the Lamasery, of which he is to be the Grand Lama. Upon the road he takes, all is excitement, all is movement. The Tartars assemble in large crowds to prostrate themselves on his way, and to present to him their offerings. As soon as he is arrived at his Lamasery, he is placed upon the altar; and then, kings, princes, mandarins, Lamas, Tartars, from the richest to the poorest, come and bend the head before this child, which has been brought from the depths of Thibet, at enormous expense, and whose demoniac possessions excite everybody's respect, admiration, and enthusiasm.

There is no Tartar kingdom which does not possess, in one of its Lamaseries of the first class, a living Buddha. Besides this superior, there is always another Grand Lama, who is selected from the members of the royal family. The Thibetian Lama resides in the Lamasery, like a living idol, receiving every day the adorations of the devout, upon whom in return he bestows his blessing. Everything which relates to prayers and liturgical ceremonies, is placed under his immediate superintendence. The Mongol Grand Lama is charged with the administration, good order, and executive of the Lamasery; he governs whilst his colleague is content to reign. The famous maxim, *Le roi règne et ne gouverne pas*, is not, therefore, the grand discovery in politics that some people imagine. People pretend to invent a new system, and merely plunder, without saying a word about it, the old constitution of the Tartar Lamaseries.

Below these two sovereigns, are several subaltern officers, who direct the details of the administration, the revenues, the sales, the purchases, and the discipline. The scribes keep the registers, and draw up the regulations and orders which the governor Lama promulgates for the good keeping and order of the Lamasery. These scribes are generally well versed in the Mongol, Thibetian, and sometimes in the Chinese and Mantchou languages. Before they are admitted to this employment, they are obliged to undergo a very rigorous examination, in presence of all the Lamas and of the principal civil authorities of the country.

After this staff of superiors and officers, the inhabitants

of the Lamasery are divided in Lama-masters and Lama-disciples or Chabis; each Lama has under his direction one or more Chabis, who live in his small house, and execute all the details of the household. If the master possesses cattle, they take charge of them, milk the cows, and prepare the butter and cream. In return for these services, the master directs his disciples in the study of the prayers, and initiates them into the liturgy. Every morning the Chabi must be up before his master; his first task is to sweep the chamber, to light a fire and to make the tea; after that he takes his prayer-book, presents it respectfully to his master, and prostrates himself thrice before him, without saying a single word. This sign of respect is equivalent to a request that the lesson he has to learn in the course of the day may be marked. The master opens the book, and reads some pages, according to the capacity of his scholar, who then makes three more prostrations in sign of thanks, and returns to his affairs.

The Chabi studies his prayer-book, when he is disposed to do so, there being no fixed period for that: he may spend his time, sleeping or romping with the other young pupils, without the slightest interference on the part of his master. When the hour for retiring to bed has arrived, he recites the lesson assigned him in the morning, in a monotonous manner; if the recitation is good, he is looked upon as having done his duty, the silence of his master being the only praise he is entitled to obtain; if, on the contrary he is not able to give a good account of his lesson, the severest punishment makes him sensible of his fault. It often happens, that under such circumstances, the master, laying aside his usual gravity, rushes upon his scholar, and overwhelms him at once with blows and terrible maledictions. Some of the pupils, who are over maltreated, run away and seek adventures far from their Lamasery; but in general they patiently submit to the punishment inflicted on them, even that of passing the night in the open air, without any clothes and in full winter. We often had opportunities of talking with Chabis, and when we asked them whether there was no means of learning the prayers without being beaten, they ingenuously and with an accent manifesting entire conviction, replied, that it was impossible. " The prayers one knows best," they said, " are always those for which one has got most blows. The Lamas who cannot recite prayers, or cure maladies, or tell fortunes, or predict the future, are those who have not been beaten well by their masters."

Besides these studies, which are conducted at home, and under the immediate superintendence of the master, the Chabis may attend, in the Lamasery, public lectures, wherein the books which relate to religion and to medicine are expounded. But these commentaries are mostly vague, unsatisfactory, and quite inadequate to form learned Lamas; there are few of them who can give an exact account of the books they study; to justify their omission in this respect, they never fail to allege the profundity of the doctrine. As to the great majority of the Lamas, they think it more convenient and expeditious to recite the prayers in a merely mechanical way, without giving themselves any trouble about the ideas they contain. When we come to speak of the Lamaseries of Thibet, where the instruction is more complete than in those of Tartary, we shall enter into some details upon Lama studies.

The Thibetian books alone being reputed canonical, and admitted as such by the Buddhist Reformation, the Mongol Lamas pass their lives in studying a foreign idiom, without troubling themselves at all about their own language. There are many of them well versed in the Thibetian literature, who do not even know their own Mongol alphabet. There are indeed a few Lamaseries where the study of the Tartarian idiom receives some slight attention, and where they sometimes recite Mongol prayers, but these are always a translation of Thibetian books. A Lama who can read Thibetian and Mongol is reputed quite a *savant;* he is thought a being raised above mankind, if he has some knowledge of Chinese and Mantchou literature.

As we advanced in the Ortous, the country seemed more and more desert and dismal. To make matters still worse, a terrible storm, solemnly closing in the autumn season, brought upon us the cold of winter.

One day, we were proceeding with difficulty through the arid sandy desert; the perspiration ran down our foreheads, for the heat was stifling; we felt overpowered by the closeness of the atmosphere, and our camels, with outstretched necks and mouths half open, vainly sought in the air a breath of cooling freshness. Towards noon, dark clouds began to gather in the horizon; fearful of being surprised by the storm, we determined to pitch our tent. But where? We looked round on all sides; we ascended to the tops of the hillocks and anxiously sought with our eyes for some Tartar habitation, which might provide us with fuel, but in vain; we had before us on all sides nothing but a mournful solitude. From time to time, we saw the foxes retiring to their holes, and herds of yellow goats running to take repose in the defiles of the mountains. Meantime, the clouds continued to rise and the wind began to blow violently. In the irregularity of its gusts it seemed now to bring us the tempest, now to drive it from us. While we were thus suspended between hope and fear, loud claps of thunder, and repeated flashes of lightning, that seemed to enkindle the sky, gave us notice that we had no other resource than to place ourselves entirely in the hands of Providence. The icy north wind blowing fiercely, we directed our steps to a defile, which opened near us; but before we had time to reach it the storm exploded. At first, rain fell in torrents, then hail, and at last snow half melted. In an instant we were wet through to the skin, and felt the cold seizing upon our limbs. We immediately alighted, hoping that walking would warm us a little, but we had hardly advanced ten steps amidst the deluge of sand, when our legs sank as in mortar. When we found it impossible to go any further we sought shelter by the side of our camels, and crouched down, pressing our arms closely against our sides, in order to attain, if possible, a little warmth.

While the storm continued to hurl against us its fury, we awaited with resignation the fate which Providence destined for us. It was impossible to pitch the tent; it was beyond human power to spread cloth saturated with rain, and half frozen by the north wind. Besides it would have been difficult to find a site for it, since the water streamed in every direction. Amid circumstances so dreadful, we looked at each other in sadness and in silence; we felt the natural warmth of our body diminishing every minute, and our blood beginning to freeze. We offered, therefore, the sacrifice of our lives to God, for we were convinced that we should die of cold during the night.

One of us, however, collecting all his strength and all his

Caves of the Ortous,

energy, climbed up an eminence, which commanded a view of the contiguous defile, and discovered a footpath, leading by a thousand sinuosities into the depths of the immense ravine; he pursued its direction, and after a few steps in the hollow, perceived in the sides of the mountain large openings, like doors. At this sight recovering at once his courage and his strength, he ascended once more the eminence in order to communicate the good news to his companions. "We are saved," he cried; "there are caves in this defile; let us hasten to take refuge in them." These words immediately aroused the little caravan; we left our animals upon the hill, and speedily descended into the ravine. A footpath led to the opening; we advanced our heads, and discovered in the interior of the mountain, not simple caves formed by nature, but fine, spacious apartments excavated by the hand of man. Our first exclamation was an expression of thankfulness for the goodness of Providence. We selected the cleanest and largest of these caverns, and in an instant passed from the utmost misery to the height of felicity. It was like a sudden and unhoped-for transition from death to life.

On viewing these subterranean dwellings, constructed with so much elegance and solidity, we were of opinion that some Chinese families had repaired to this country to cultivate the soil; but that, repelled by its barrenness, they had given up their enterprise. Traces of cultivation, which we perceived here and there, confirmed our conjecture. When the Chinese establish themselves anywhere in Tartary, if they find mountains, the earth of which is hard and solid, they excavate caverns in their sides. These habitations are cheaper than houses, and less exposed to the irregularity of the seasons. They are generally very well laid out; on each side of the door there are windows, giving sufficient light to the interior; the walls, the ceiling, the furnaces, the kang, everything inside is so coated with plaster, so firm and shining, that it has the appearance of stucco. These caves have the advantage of being very warm in winter and very cool in summer; the want of sufficient air, however, sometimes makes a sojourn in them dangerous to the health. Those dwellings were no novelty to us, for they abound in our mission of Si-Wan. However, we had never seen any so well constructed as these of the Ortous.

We took possession of one of those subterranean abodes, and commenced proceedings by making a large fire in the furnaces, with plentiful bundles of hemp-stems, which we found in one of the caves. Never, on our journey, had we at our disposal such excellent fuel. Our clothes dried very soon, and we were so happy at being in this fine hotel of Providence, that we spent the greater part of the night enjoying the delightful sensation of warmth, while Samdadchiemba was never tired of broiling little cakes in mutton fat. It was altogether quite a festival with us, and our flour felt somewhat the effects of it.

The animals were not less happy than we. We found for them stables out in the mountain, and, which was better still, excellent forage. One cave was filled with millet stems and oat-straw. But for this horrible storm, which had nearly killed us, our animals would never have got so grand a treat. After having for a long time enjoyed the poetry of our miraculous position, we yielded to the necessity of taking repose, and laid down upon a well-warmed kang, which made us forget the terrible cold we had endured during the tempest.

Next morning, while Samdadchiemba was using the rest of the hemp stems, and drying our baggage, we went out for a nearer inspection of these numerous subterrenes. We had scarcely gone ten steps, when we beheld, to our great astonishment, whirls of smoke issuing from the door and windows of a cave adjoining our own. As we fancied we were alone in the desert, the sight of this smoke excited a surprise, mingled with fear. We directed our steps to the opening of the cavern, and, on reaching the threshold of the door, perceived within a large fire of hemp stems, whose undulating flame reached the ceiling, so that the place looked like an oven. On further investigation we observed a human form moving amidst the thick smoke; we soon heard the Tartar salute, Mendou! uttered by a sonorous voice; "Come and sit beside this fire." We did not like to advance. This cave of Cacus, that loud voice, presented to our minds something fantastic. Finding that we remained silent and motionless, the inhabitant of this sort of vent-hole of Erebus, rose and came to the threshold. He was neither a devil nor a ghost, but simply a Mongol Tartar, who, the night before, having been surprised by the storm, had fled to this cave, where he had passed the night. After a few words about the rain, wind and hail, we invited him to breakfast with us, and brought him to our dwelling. While Samdadchiemba, aided by our guest, made the tea, we went out again to pursue our researches.

We walked amid these deserted and silent abodes with a curiosity not free from terror. All were constructed upon much the same model, and still preserved their pristine integrity. Chinese characters engraved on the walls, and pieces of porcelain vases, confirmed our impression that these caves had been inhabited not long since by Chinese. Some old woman's shoes, which we discovered in a corner, removed any remaining doubt. We could not shake off a feeling of sadness and melancholy, when we thought of those numerous families, who, after having lived a long time in the entrails of this large mountain, had gone elsewhere to seek a more hospitable soil. As we entered the caves, we alarmed flocks of sparrows, which had not yet left these former dwellings of man, but had, on the contrary, boldly taken possession of these grand nests. The millet and oats strewn around profusely, induced them to remain. "Undoubtedly," said we, "they too will fly away when they no longer find here any more grains, when they find that the old inhabitants of these caves return no more, and they will seek hospitality under the roofs of houses."

The sparrow is a regular cosmopolite; we have found it wherever we have found man; ever with the same vivid, petulant, quarrelsome character; ever with the same sharp, angry cry. It is, however, to be remarked that in Tartary, China, and Thibet it is, perhaps, more insolent than in Europe; because there, nobody makes war upon it, and its nest and brood are piously respected, You see it boldly enter the house, live there on familiar terms, and peck up at its leisure the remnants of man's food. The Chinese call it Kio nio-eul (bird of the family).

After having inspected about thirty of these caves, which did not present anything remarkable, we returned to our own. At breakfast, the conversation naturally turned upon the Chinese who had excavated these dwellings. We asked the Tartar if he had seen them. "What!" said he, "have I seen the Kitats who inhabited this defile? Why, I knew all of them; it is not more than two years since they left the country. For that matter," he added, "they had no right to remain here; as they were rascals, it was quite proper to turn them out." "Rascals, say you? why, what mischief could they do in this wretched ravine?" "Oh, the Kitats are sly, cheating fellows. At first, they seemed very good; but that did not last long. It is more than twenty years ago that a few of their families sought our hospitality: as they were poor, they got permission to cultivate some land in the vicinity, on condition, that every year after harvest they should furnish some oatmeal, to the Taitsi of the country. By degrees, other families arrived, who also excavated caverns wherein to dwell; and soon this defile was full of them. In the beginning, these Kitats showed a gentle, quiet character; we lived together like brothers. Tell me, Sirs Lamas, is it not well to live together like brothers? Are not all men brothers?" "Yes, that is true; you speak the words of justice; but why did these Kitats go hence?" "Peace did not last long; they soon showed themselves wicked and false. Instead of being content with what had been given them, they extended their cultivation at their pleasure, and took possession of a large territory, without asking any one's leave. When they were rich they would not pay the oatmeal they had agreed to pay as tribute. Every year, when we claimed the rent, we were received with insults and maledictions. But the worst thing was, that these rascally Kitats turned thieves, and took possession of all the goats and sheep that lost their way in the sinuosities of the ravine. At last, a Taitsi of great courage and capacity, called together the Mongols of the neighborbood, and said,—'The Kitats take away our land, they steal our beasts, and curse us; as they do not act or speak as brothers, we must expel them.' Everybody was pleased with these words of the old Taitsi. After a deliberation, it was decided that the principal men of the country should go to the king, and supplicate an order condemning the Kitats to be expelled. I was one of the deputation. The king reproached us for having permitted foreigners to cultivate our lands; we prostrated ourselves before him, observing profound silence. However, the king, who always acts with justice, had the order written, and sealed with his red seal. The ordonnance said, that the king would not permit the Kitats to live any longer in the country; and that they must leave it before the first day of the eighth moon. Three Taitsi rode off to present the ordonnance to the Kitats. They made no answer to the three deputies, but said amongst themselves, 'The king desires us to go; very well.'

"Afterwards we learned that they had assembled and had resolved to disobey the orders of the king and to remain in the country, in spite of him. The first day of the eighth moon arrived, and they still occupied calmly their habitations, without making any preparations for departure. In the morning, before daybreak, all the Tartars mounted their horses, armed themselves with their lances, and drove their flocks and herds upon the cultivated lands of the Kitats, on which the crop was still standing: when the sun rose, nothing of that crop was left. All had been devoured by the animals, or trodden down. The Kitats yelled and cursed us, but the thing was done. Seeing that their position was desperate, they collected, the same day, their furniture and agricultural implements, and went off to settle in the eastern parts of the Ortous, at some distance from the Yellow River, near the Paga-Gol. As you came through Tchagan-Kouren, you must have met on your route, west of the Paga-Gol, Kitats cultivating some pieces of land; well, it was they who inhabited this defile, and excavated all these caves."

Having finished his narrative, the Tartar went out for a moment and brought back a small packet, which he had left in the cavern, where he had passed the night. "Sirs Lamas," he said on his return, "I must depart; but will you not come and repose for a few days in my dwelling? My tent is not far hence: it is behind that sandy mountain which you perceive there towards the north. It is at the utmost not more than thirty lis off." "We are much obliged to you," answered we. "The hospitality of the Mongols of Ortous is known everywhere, but we have a long journey before us; we cannot stop on our way." "What are a few days, sooner or later, in a long journey? Your beasts cannot alway be on their feet; they need a little rest. You yourselves have had much to endure from the weather of yesterday. Come with me; all will then be well. In four days we shall have a festival. My eldest son is going to establish a family. Come to the nuptials of my son; your presence will bring him good fortune." The Tartar, seeing us inflexible, mounted his horse, and after having ascended the pathway which led to the defile, disappeared across the heath and sand of the desert.

Under other circumstances, we should have accepted with pleasure the offer thus made; but we desired to make the shortest possible stay amongst the Ortous. We were anxious to leave behind us that miserable country, where our animals were wasting away daily, and where we had ourselves met with such fatigue and misery. Besides, a Mongol wedding was no new thing to us. Since we had entered Tartary, we had witnessed, more than once, ceremonies of that kind.

The Mongols marry very young, and always under the influence of the absolute authority of the parents. This affair, so grave and important, is initiated, discussed and concluded, without the two persons most interested in it, taking the least part in it. Whatever promises of marriage may take place in youth, or at more advanced age, it is the parents who always settle the contract, without even speaking to their children about it. The two future consorts do not know, perhaps never saw each other. It is only when they are married that they have the opportunity to inquire whether there is sympathy between their characters or not.

The daughter never brings any marriage portion. On the contrary, the young man has to make presents to the family of his bride: and the value of these presents is seldom left to the generosity of the husband's parents. Everything is arranged beforehand and set forth in a public document, with the minutest details. In fact, the matter is less a marriage present than the price of an object, sold by one party and bought by the other. The thing is indeed very clearly expressed in their language; they say, " I have bought for my son the daughter of so and so." "We have sold our daughter to such and such a family." The marriage contract is thus simply a contract of sale. There are mediators, who bargain and haggle, up and down, till at last they come to an agreement. When it is settled how many horses, oxen, sheep, pieces of linen, pounds of butter, what quantity of brandy and wheat-flour shall be given to the family of the bride, the contract is at length drawn up before witnesses, and the daughter becomes the property of the purchaser. She remains, however, with her family till the time of the nuptial ceremonies.

When the marriage has been concluded between the mediators, the father of the bridegroom, accompanied by his nearest relations, carries the news to the family of the bride. On entering, they prostrate themselves before the little domestic altar, and offer to the idol of Buddha a boiled sheep's head, milk, and a sash of white silk. Then they partake of a repast provided by the parents of the bridegroom. During the repast, all the relations of the bride receive a piece of money, which they deposit in a vase filled with wine made of fermented milk. The father of the bride drinks the wine, and keeps the money. This ceremony is called Tahil-Tébihou, " striking the bargain."

The day indicated by the Lamas as auspicious for the marriage having arrived, the bridegroom sends early in the morning a deputation to fetch the girl who has been betrothed to him, or rather whom he has bought. When the envoys draw near, the relations and friends of the bride

place themselves in a circle before the door, as if to oppose
the departure of the bride, and then begins a feigned fight,
which of course terminates with the bride being carried off.
She is placed on a horse, and having been thrice led round
her paternal house, she is then taken at full gallop to the
tent which has been prepared for the purpose, near the
dwelling of her father-in-law. Meantime, all the Tartars of
the neighborhood, the relations and friends of both families,
repair to the wedding-feast, and offer their presents to the
new married pair. The extent of these presents, which
consists of beasts and eatables, is left to the generosity of
the guests. They are destined for the father of the bridegroom and often fully indemnify him for his expenses in the
purchase of the bride. As the offered animals come up
they are taken into folds ready constructed for them. At
the weddings of rich Tartars, these large folds receive great
herds of oxen, horses and sheep. Generally the guests are
generous enough, for they know that thay will be paid in
return, upon a similar occasion.

When the bride has finished dressing, she is introduced to
her father-in-law; and while the assembled Lamas recite the
prayers prescribed by the ritual, she first prostrates herself
before the image of Buddha, then before the hearth, and
lastly before the father, mother, and other near relatives of
the bridegroom, who, on his part, performs the same ceremonies towards the family of his bride, assembled in an adjacent tent. Then comes the wedding-feast, which sometimes continues for seven or eight days. An excessive pro-
fusion of fat meat, infinite tobacco, and large jars of brandy,
constitute the splendor and magnificence of these repasts.
Sometimes music is added to the entertainment, and they
invite Toolholos, or Tartar singers, to give more solemnity to
the festival.

The plurality of wives is admitted in Tartary, being opposed
neither to the laws, nor to the religion, nor to the manners
of the country. The first wife is always the mistress of the
household, and the most respected in the family. The other
wives bear the name of little spouses (paga ème), and owe
obedience and respect to the first.

Polygamy, abolished by the Gospel, and contrary in itself
to the happiness and concord of families, may, perhaps, be
regarded as a blessing to the Tartars. Considering the

present state of society with them, it is, as it were, a barrier opposed to libertinism and corruption of morals. Celibacy being imposed on the Lamas, and the class of those who shave the head and live in lamaseries being so numerous, it is easy to conceive what disorders would arise from this multiplication of young women without support and abandoned to themselves, if girls could not be placed in families in the quality of second wives.

Divorce is very frequent among the Tartars. It takes place without any participation of the civil or ecclesiastical authorities. The husband, who repudiates his wife, has not even occasion for a pretext to justify his conduct. He sends her back, without any formality, to her parents, and contents himself with a message that he does not require her any longer. This proceeding is in accordance with Tartar manners, and does not offend any one. The husband thinks himself entitled to the privilege, in consideration of the oxen, sheep and horses he was obliged to give as nuptial presents. The parents of the repudiated wife do not complain at having their daughter back; she resumes her place in the family till another husband presents himself, in which case, they even rejoice over the profit they make by thus selling the same merchandise twice over.

In Tartary, the women lead an independent life enough. They are far from being oppressed and kept in servitude, as with other Asiatic nations. They may come and go at their pleasure, ride out on horseback, and pay each other visits from tent to tent. Instead of the soft, languishing physiognomy of the Chinese women, the Tartar woman presents in her bearing and manners a power and force well in accordance with her active life and nomad habits, and her attire augments the effect of her masculine, haughty mein.

Large leather boots, and a long green or violet robe fastened round the waist by a black or blue girdle, constitute her dress, except that sometimes she wears over the great robe a small coat, resembling in form our waistcoats, but very large, and coming down to the hips. The hair of the Tartar women is divided in two tresses, tied up in taffetas, and hanging down upon the bosom; their luxury consists in ornamenting the girdle and hair with spangles of gold and silver, pearls, coral, and a thousand other toys, the form and quality of which it would be difficult for us to define, as we had neither opportunity, nor taste, nor patience to pay serious attention to these futilities.

Barbarous Lamanesque Ceremony.

CHAPTER IX.

Departure of the Caravan—Encampment in a fertile Valley—Intensity of the Cold—Meeting with numerous Pilgrims—Barbarous and Diabolical Ceremonies of Lamaism—Project for the Lamasery of Rache-Tchurin—Dispersion and rallying of the little Caravan—Anger of Samdadchiemba—Aspect of the Lamasery of Rache-Tchurin—Different Kinds of Pilgrimages around the Lamaseries—Turning Prayers—Quarrel between two Lamas—Similarity of the Soil—Description of the Tabsoun-Noor or Salt Sea—Remarks on the Camels of Tartary.

THE Tartar who had just taken his leave had informed us, that at a short distance from the caverns we should find in a vale the finest pasturage in the whole country of the Ortous. We resolved to depart. It was near noon already when we started. The sky was clear, the sun brilliant; but the temperature, still affected by the storm of the preceding day, was cold and sharp. After having traveled for nearly two hours over a sandy soil, deeply furrowed by the streams of rain, we entered, on a sudden, a valley whose smiling, fertile aspect singularly contrasted with all that we had hitherto seen among the Ortous. In the center flowed an abundant rivulet, whose sources were lost in the sand; and on both sides, the hills, which rose like an amphitheater, were covered with pasturage and clumps of shrubs.

Though it was still early, we gave up all idea of continuing our journey that day. The place was too beautiful to be passed by: besides, the north wind had risen, and the air became intolerably cold. We pitched our tent, therefore, in a corner, sheltered by the hills. From the interior of the tent, our view extended, without obstruction, down the valley, and we were thus enabled to watch our animals without moving.

After sunset, the violence of the wind increased, and the cold became more and more intense. We thought it advisable to take some measures of security. Whilst Samdadchiemba piled up large stones to consolidate the borders of the tent, we went about the adjacent hills, and made, by aid of a hatchet, an abundant provision of fuel. As soon as we had taken our tea and our daily broth, we went to sleep. But sleep did not last long; the cold became so severe that it soon roused us. "We can't remain so," said the Dchiahour; "if we don't want to die of cold on our goatskins, we must get up and make a large fire." Samdadchiemba's words were full of sense; it was not advisable to sleep at such a time, and accordingly we rose, and added to our usual dress the great sheepskin robes that we had bought at Blue Town.

Our fire of roots and green branches was hardly lighted, when we felt our eyes as it were calcined by the biting acid influence of a thick smoke, which filled the tent. We opened the door; but as this gave admission to the wind, without getting rid of the smoke, we were soon obliged to shut it again. Samdadchiemba was not in any way molested by the thick smoke, which stifled us and drew burning tears from our eyes. He laughed without pity at seeing us crouched by the fire, our heads bending over our knees, and our faces buried in both hands. "My spiritual fathers," he said, "your eyes are large and bright, but they cannot endure a little smoke; mine are small and ugly, but never mind, they perform their service very well." The jests of our camel driver were not much adapted to cheer us up; we suffered dreadfully. Yet, amid our tribulations, we saw occasion to feel our happiness to be very great. We could not reflect without gratitude upon the goodness of Providence, which had led us to caves, whose great value we now fully appreciated. If we had not been able to dry our clothes, if we had been surprised by the cold in the piteous state in which the storm had left us, we certainly could not have lived long; we should have been frozen with our clothes in one immovable block.

We did not think it prudent to proceed amid such severe cold, and to leave an encampment, where at least our animals got sufficient herbage to browse upon, and where fuel was abundant. Towards noon, the weather having grown milder, we went out to cut wood on the hills. On our way we observed that our animals had left the pasturage and collected on the banks of the rivulet. We at once conceived that they were tormented by thirst, and that the stream being frozen, they could not quench it. We bent our steps to them, and found, in fact, the camels eagerly licking the surface of the ice, while the horse and the mule were kicking upon it with their hard hoofs. The hatchet we had brought with us to cut wood, served to break the ice, and to dig a small pond, where our animals could quench their thirst.

Towards evening, the cold having resumed its intensity, we adopted a plan for enabling us to obtain a better sleep than we had in the preceding night. Until morning, the time was divided into three watches, and each of us was charged, in turn, with keeping up a large fire in the tent, while the others slept. Thus we did not feel much of the cold, and slept in peace, without fear of setting our linen house on fire.

After two days of horrible cold the wind abated, and we resolved to proceed on our way. It was only with great difficulty that we got down our tent. The first nail that we tried to draw out, broke like glass under the hammer. The sandy, humid soil on which we had made our encampment, was so frozen that the nails stuck in it as if they had been incrusted in stone. To uproot them, we were obliged to wet them several times with boiling water.

At the time of our departure, the temperature was so

mild that we were fain to take off our skin coats, and to pack them up until further occasion. Nothing is more frequent in Tartary than these sudden changes of temperature. Sometimes the mildest weather is abruptly followed by the most horrible frost. All that is needed for this is the falling of snow, and the subsequent rise of the north wind. Any one not inured to these sudden changes of the atmosphere, and not provided, in traveling, with well-furred robes, is often exposed to dreadful accidents. In the north of Mongolia especially, it is not unusual to find travelers frozen to death amidst the desert.

On the fifteenth day of the new moon, we came upon numerous caravans, following, like ourselves, the direction from east to west. The road was filled with men, women, and children, riding on camels or oxen. They were all repairing, they said, to the Lamasery of Rache-Tchurin. When they had asked whether our journey had the same object, they were surprised at receiving an answer in the negative. These numerous pilgrims, the astonishment they showed upon hearing that we were not going to the Lamasery of Rache-Tchurin, excited our curiosity. At the turn of a defile, we overtook an old Lama, who, laden with a heavy pack, seemed to make his way with great labor and pain. "Brother," said we, "you are old; your black hairs are not so numerous as the gray. Doubtless your fatigue must be extreme. Place your burden upon one of our camels; that will relieve you a little." Upon hearing these words the old man prostrated himself before us, in order to express his gratitude. We made a camel kneel, and Samdadchiemba added to our baggage that of the Lama. So soon as the pilgrim was relieved from the weight which had oppressed him, his walk became more elastic, and an expression of satisfaction was diffused over his countenance. "Brother," said we, "we are from the West, and the affairs of your country not being well known to us, we are astonished at finding so many pilgrims here in the desert." "We are all going to Rache-Tchurin," replied he, in accents full of emotion. "Doubtless," said we, "some grand solemnity calls you together?" "Yes to-morrow will be a great day: a Lama Boktè will manifest his power: Kill himself, yet not die." We at once understood what solemnity it was that thus attracted the Ortous-Tartars. A

Lama was to cut himself open, take out his entrails and place them before him, and then resume his previous condition. This spectacle, so cruel and disgusting, is very common in the Lamaseries of Tartary. The Boktè who is to manifest his power, as the Mongols phrase it, prepares himself for the formidable operation by many days fasting and prayer, pending which, he must abstain from all communication whatever with mankind, and observe the most absolute silence. When the appointed day is come, the multitude of pilgrims assemble in the great court of the Lamasery, where an altar is raised in front of the Temple-gate. At length the Boktè appears. He advances gravely, amid the acclamations of the crowd, seats himself upon the altar, and takes from his girdle a large knife which he places upon his knees. At his feet, numerous Lamas, ranged in a circle, commence the terrible invocations of this frightful ceremony. As the recitation of the prayers proceeds, you see the Boktè trembling in every limb, and gradually working himself up into phrenetic convulsions. The Lamas themselves become excited: their voices are raised; their song observes no order, and at last becomes a mere confusion of yelling and outcry. Then the Boktè suddenly throws aside the scarf which envelopes him, unfastens his girdle, and seizing the sacred knife, slits open his stomach, in one long cut. While the blood flows in every direction, the multitude prostrate themselves before the terrible spectacle, and the enthusiast is interrogated about all sorts of hidden things, as to future events, as to the destiny of certain personages. The replies of the Boktè to all these questions are regarded, by everybody, as oracles.

When the devout curiosity of the numerous pilgrims is satisfied, the Lamas resume, but now calmly and gravely, the recitation of their prayers. The Boktè takes, in his right hand, blood from his wound, raises it to his mouth, breathes thrice upon it, and then throws it into the air, with loud cries. He next passes his hand rapidly over his wound, closes it, and everything after a while resumes its pristine condition, no trace remaining of the diabolical operation, except extreme prostration. The Boktè once more rolls his scarf round him, recites in a low voice, a short prayer; then all is over, and the multitude disperse, with the exception of a few of the especially devout, who remain to contemplate and to adore the blood-stained altar which the Saint has quitted.

These horrible ceremonies are of frequent occurrence in the great Lamaseries of Tartary and Thibet, and we do not believe that there is any trick or deception about them; for from all we have seen and heard, among idolatrous nations, we are persuaded that the devil has a great deal to do with the matter; and moreover, our impression that there is no trick in the operation is fortified by the opinion of the most intelligent and most upright Buddhists whom we have met in the numerous Lamaseries we visited.

It is not every Lama that can perform miraculous operations. Those who have the fearful power to cut themselves open, for example, are never found in the higher ranks of the Lama hierarchy. They are generally lay Lamas of indifferent character, and little esteemed by their comrades. The regular Lamas generally make no scruple to avow their horror of the spectacle. In their eyes, all these operations are wicked and diabolical. Good Lamas, they say, are incapable of performing such acts, and should not even desire to attain the impious talent.

Though these demoniac operations are, in general, decried in well-regulated Lamaseries, yet the superiors do not prohibit them. On the contrary, there are certain days in the year set apart for the disgusting spectacle. Interest is, doubtless, the only motive which could induce the Grand Lamas to favor actions which in their conscience they reprove. The fact is, that these diabolical displays are an infallible means of collecting together a swarm of stupid and ignorant devotees, who communicate renown to the Lamasery, and enrich it with the numerous offerings which the Tartars never fail to bring with them on such occasions.

Cutting open the abdomen is one of the most famous *sië-fa* (supernaturalisms) possessed by the Lamas. There are others of the same class, less imposing, but more common; these are practised in people's houses, privately, and not at the great solemnities of the Lamaseries. For example, they heat irons red-hot, and then lick them with impunity; they make incisions in various parts of the body, which an instant afterwards leave no trace behind, etc. All these operations have to be preceded by the recitation of some prayer.

We knew a Lama who, according to every one's belief, could fill a vase with water, by the mere agency of a prayer; but we could never induce him to try the experiment in our presence. He told us that as we held not the same faith with him, the experiment, in our company, would not be merely fruitless, but would expose him to serious danger. One day, however, he recited to us the prayer of his sié-fa. It was brief, but we readily recognized in it a direct appeal to the assistance of the demon. "I know thee, thou knowest me;" thus it ran: "Come old friend, do what I ask of thee. Bring water, and fill the vase I hold out to thee. To fill a vase with water, what is that to thy vast power! I know thou chargest dear for a vase of water; but never mind: do what I ask of thee, and fill the vase I present to thee. Some time hence we'll come to a reckoning: on the appointed day thou shalt receive thy due." It sometimes happens that the appeal remains without effect: in such cases, praying is discontinued, and the being invoked is assailed with insults and imprecations.

The famous sié-fa that was now attracting so large a number of pilgrims to the Lamasery of Rache-Tchurin, inspired us with the idea of repairing thither also, and of neutralizing, by our prayers, the satanic invocations of the Lamas. Who knows, said we to each other, who knows but that God even now has designs of mercy towards the Mongols of the Ortous land; perhaps the sight of their Lama's power, fettered and overcome by the presence of the priests of Jesus Christ, will strike upon the hearts of these people, and make them renounce the lying creed of Buddha, and embrace the faith of Christianity! To encourage each other in this design, we dwelt upon the history of Simon Magus, arrested in his flight by the prayer of St. Peter, and precipitated from the air to the feet of his admirers. Of course, poor missionaries, such as we, had not the insane pretension to compare ourselves with the prince of the Apostles; but we knew that the protection of God, which is sometimes granted in virtue of the merit and sanctity of him who seeks it, is also often accorded to the omnipotent efficacy in prayer itself.

We resolved, therefore, to go to Rache-Tchurin, to mingle with the crowd, and, at the moment when the diabolical invocations should commence, to place ourselves, fearlessly, and with an air of authority before the Boktè, and to solemnly forbid him, in the name of Jesus Christ, to make a display of his detestable power. We did not disguise from ourselves the possible results of this proceeding; we knew that it would assuredly excite the fury and hatred of the adorers of Buddha; and that perhaps a violent death would be an instant reward for the endeavor to convert these Tartars; "But what matter!" exclaimed we; "let us do courageously our work as missionaries; let us employ fearlessly the power that we have received from on high, and leave to Providence the care of a future which does not appertain to us."

Such were our intentions and our hopes; but the views of God are not always in conformity with the designs of man, even when these appear most in harmony with the plan of His Providence. That very day there happened to us an accident which, carrying us far away from Rache-Tchurin, involved us in the most distressing perplexities.

In the evening, the old Lama who was traveling with us asked us to make the camel kneel, so that he might take his pack from its back. "Brother," said we, "are we not going to journey together to the Lamasery of Rache-Tchurin?" "No; I must follow the path which you see meandering towards the north, along those hills. Behind that sand-hill is a trading place, where, upon festival days, a few Chinese merchants set up their tents and sell goods. As I want to make a few purchases, I cannot continue to walk in your shadow." "Can we buy flour at the Chinese encampment?" "Millet, oatmeal, flour, beef, mutton, tea-bricks, everything is sold there." Not having been able to purchase provisions since our departure from Tchagan-Kouren, we considered this a favorable opportunity for supplying our deficiency in this respect. In order not to fatigue our beasts of burden with a long circuit across stony hills, M. Gabet took the flour-sacks upon his camels, separated from the caravan, and went off at a gallop towards the Chinese post. According to the indications furnished by the old Lama, he was to meet us again in a valley at no great distance from the Lamasery.

After traveling for nearly an hour along a rugged road, continually intersected by pits and quagmires, the Missionary Purveyor reached the small heath, on which he found a number of Chinese encamped, some of their tents serving as shops, and the rest as dwellings. The encampment presented the appearance of a small town full of trade and activity, the customers being the Lamas of Rache-Tchurin and the Mongol pilgrims. M. Gabet speedily effected his purchases; and having filled his sacks with flour, and hung two magnificent sheeps' livers over one of the camel's humps, rode off to the place where it had been arranged the caravan should await him. He soon reached the spot, but he found no person there, and no trace of man or beast having recently passed was visible on the sand. Imagining that perhaps some derangement of the camels' loads had delayed our progress, he turned into the road, which it had been agreed we should follow; but it was to no purpose that he hastened along it, that he galloped here and there, that he ascended every hill he came to,—he could see nothing; and the cries he uttered to attract our attention remained unanswered. He visited several points where various roads met, but he found merely another confusion of the steps of horses, camels, oxen, sheep, tending in every direction, and crossing and recrossing each other, so that he was left, at last, without even a conjecture.

By and by he recalled to mind that our aim, as last resolved, had been the Lamasery of Rache-Tchurin; he turned round, and perceiving the Lamasery in the distance, hurried thither as fast as he could go. When he reached the structure, which stood in the form of an amphitheater upon the slope of a hill, he looked everywhere for us, and asked everybody about us, for here, at least, there was no lack of persons from whom to seek information, and our little caravan was composed in a manner likely to attract the attention of those who saw it at all: two laden camels, a white horse, and, above all, a black mule, that every one we passed stopped to remark, on account of its extreme diminutiveness, and the splendid tint of its skin. M. Gabet inquired and inquired, but to no purpose; no one had seen our caravan. He ascended to the summit of the hill, whence the eye extended over a large expanse, but he could see nothing at all like us.

The sun set, yet the caravan did not appear. M. Gabet, beginning to fear that some serious accident had befallen it, once more set off, and searched in every direction, up hill and down dale, but he could see nothing of us, and learn nothing of us, from the travelers whom he met.

The night advanced, and soon the Lamasery of Rache-Tchurin disappeared in the darkness. M. Gabet found himself alone in the desert, without path and without shelter, fearing alike to advance or to recede, lest he should fall into some abyss. He was fain, therefore, to stop where he was, in a narrow, sandy defile, and to pass the night there. By way of supper, he had to content himself with an *Impression de Voyage*. Not that provisions were wanting, by any means, but fire was, and water. Besides, the feeling of hunger was superseded by the anxieties which afflicted his heart as to the caravan. He knelt on the sand, said his evening prayer, and then lay down his head upon one of the flour-sacks beside the camel, keeping its bridle round his arm lest the animal should stray during the night. It is needless to add that his sleep was neither sound nor continuous; the cold, bare ground is not a very eligible bed, especially for a man preyed upon by dark anxieties.

With the earliest dawn, M. Gabet mounted his camel, and though well-nigh exhausted with hunger and fatigue, proceeded anew in search of his companions.

The caravan was not lost, though it was terribly astray. After M. Gabet had quitted us, in order to visit the Chinese post, we at first exactly followed the right path; but before long we entered upon a vast steppe, all trace of road insensibly faded away amidst sand so fine that the slightest wind made it undulate like sea-waves, there was no vestige upon it of the travelers who had preceded us. By and by the road disappeared altogether, and we found ourselves environed with yellow hills, which presented not the slightest suggestion even of vegetation. M. Huc, fearing to lose himself amid these sands, stopped the cameleer. "Samdadchiemba," said he, "do not let us proceed at random. You see yonder, in the valley, the Tartar horseman driving a herd of oxen; go and ask him the way to Rache-Tchurin." Samdadchiemba raised his head, looked for a moment, closing one eye, at the sun, which was veiled with some passing clouds. "My spiritual father," said he, "I am accustomed to wander about the desert; my opinion is, that we are quite in the right road: let us continue our course westward, and we cannot go astray." "Well, well, since you think you know the desert, keep on." "Oh, yes; don't be afraid. You see that long, white line on the mountain yonder? that's the road, after its issue from the sands."

On Samdadchiemba's assurance, we continued to advance in the same direction. We soon came to a road, as he had promised, but it was a road disused, upon which we could see no person to confirm or contradict the assertion of Samdadchiemba, who persisted that we were on the way to Rache-Tchurin. The sun set, and the twilight gradually gave place to the darkness of night, without our discovering the least indication of the Lamasery, or, which surprised us still more, of M. Gabet, who, according to the information of the old Lama, ought to have rejoined us long ago. Samdadchiemba was silent, for he now saw that we had lost our way.

It was important to encamp before the night had altogether closed in. Perceiving a well at the end of a hollow, we set up our tent beside it. By the time our linen-house was in order, and the baggage piled, the night had completely set in; yet M. Gabet had not appeared. "Get on a camel," said M. Huc to Samdadchiemba, "and look about for M. Gabet." The Dchiahour made no reply; he was thoroughly disconcerted and depressed. Driving a stake into the ground, he fastened one of the camels to it, and mounting upon the other, departed mournfully in quest of our friend. He had scarcely got out of sight, when the camel that was left behind, finding itself alone, sent forth the most frightful cries; by and by it became furious; it turned round and round the stake, backed to the very limit of the rope and of its long neck, made longer by painful extension, and applied every effort to get rid of the wooden curl that was passed through its nose: the spectacle of its struggle was really frightful. At last it succeeded in breaking the cord, and then dashed off boundingly into the desert. The horse and mule had also disappeared; they were hungry and thirsty; and about the tent there was not a blade of grass, not a drop of water. The well beside which we had encamped was perfectly dry; in fact, it was nothing more than an old cistern which had probably been for years useless.

Thus our little caravan, which for nearly two months had journeyed, without once separating, through the desert plains of Tartary, was now utterly dispersed; man and beast—all had disappeared. There remained only M. Huc, solitary in his little linen-house, and a prey to the most corroding anxieties. For a whole day he had neither eaten nor drunk; but under such circumstances you do not ordinarily feel either hunger or thirst; the mind is too full to give any place to the suggestions of the body; you seem environed with a thousand fearful phantoms: and great indeed were your desolation, but that you have for your safety and your consolation, prayer, the sole lever that can raise from off your heart the weight of somber apprehensions that would otherwise crush it.

The hours passed on, and no one returned. As, in the obscurity of night, persons might pass quite close to the tent, and yet not see it, M. Huc, from time to time, ascended the adjacent hills and rocks, and, in his loudest tones, called out the names of his lost companions, but no one replied; all still was silence and solitude. It was near midnight, when at length the plaintive cries of a camel, apparently remonstrating against being driven so fast, were heard in the distance. Samdadchiemba soon came up. He had met several Tartar horsemen who had no tidings, indeed, of M. Gabet, but from whom he learned that we had gone altogether astray; that the road we were pursuing led to a Mongol encampment, in precisely the contrary direction to Rache-Tchurin. "By daybreak," said Samdadchiemba, "we must raise the tent, and find the right path; we shall there, no doubt, meet the elder spiritual father." "Samdadchiemba, your advice is a bubble; the tent and the baggage must remain here, for the excellent reason that they cannot be moved without animals." "Animals!" exclaimed the Dchiahour, "where, then, is the camel I fastened to the stake?" "It broke the rope and ran away; the horse and the mule have run away too, and I have not the least idea where any of them are to be sought." "This is a pretty business," grumbled the cameleer; "however, when day breaks we must see what can be done. Meanwhile let us make a little tea." "Make tea, by all means, if you can make tea without water, but water there is none; the well is perfectly dry." This announcement completed the discomfiture of poor Samdadchiemba; he sank back quite exhausted upon the baggage, and his weariness soon threw him into deep slumber.

With the first streaks of dawn, M. Huc ascended the adjacent hill in the hope of discovering something or somebody. He perceived, in a distant valley, two animals, one black, one white; he hastened to them, and found our horse and mule browsing on some thin, dusty grass, beside a cistern of soft water. When he led the animals back to the tent, the sun was about to rise, but Samdadchiemba still slumbered, lying in exactly the same position which he had assumed when he went to sleep. "Samdadchiemba," cried M. Huc, "won't you have some tea this morning?" At the word *tea*, our cameleer jumped up as though he had been electrified; he looked round, his eyes heavy with sleep. "Did not the spiritual father mention tea? Where is the tea? Did I dream I was going to have some tea?" "I don't know whether you dreamed it, but tea you may have, if you wish, as there is soft water in the valley yonder, where, just now, I found the horse and the mule. Do you go and fetch some water, while I light the fire." Samdadchiemba joyfully adopted the proposition, and putting the buckets over his shoulders, hastened to the cistern.

When tea was ready, Samdadchiemba became quite comfortable; he was absorbed with his beloved beverage, and seemed to have altogether forgotten the disruption of the caravan. It was necessary, however, to recall the circumstance to him, in order that he might go in search of the camel that had run away.

Nearly one half the day elapsed, yet his companions did not rejoin M. Huc. From time to time there passed Tartar horsemen or pilgrims returning from the festival of Rache-Tchurin. Of these M. Huc inquired whether they had not seen, in the vicinity of the Lamasery, a Lama dressed in a yellow robe and a red jacket, and mounted on a red camel. "The Lama," said he, "is very tall, with a great gray beard, a long pointed nose, and a red face." To this description, there was a general answer in the negative: "Had we seen such a personage," said the travelers, "we should certainly have remarked him."

At length, M. Gabet appeared on the slope of a hill; from its summit he had recognized our blue tent pitched in the valley, and he galloped towards his recovered companion as fast as his camel could go. After a brief, animated conversation, wherein both spoke and neither answered, we burst into a hearty laugh at the misadventure thus happily terminated. The reorganization of the caravan was completed before sunset, by Samdadchiemba's return with the missing camel, which, after a long round, he had found fastened to a tent; the Tartar, who owned the tent, having seen the animal running away, had caught it and secured it until some one should claim it.

Though the day was far advanced, we determined to remove, for the place where we had encamped was miserable beyond all expression. Not a blade of grass was to be seen, and the water I had discovered was at so great a distance, that it involved quite a journey to fetch it. "Besides," said we, "if we can only, before night, manage to get within sight of the right road, it will be a great point gained." Our departure thus determined, we sat down to tea. The conversation naturally turned upon the vexatious mischance which had given us so much fatigue and trouble. Already more than once, on our journey, the intractable, obstinate temperament of Samdadchiemba had been the occasion of our losing our way. Mounted on his little mule, as we have described, it was he who led the caravan, preceding the beasts of burden. Upon his assumption that he thoroughly understood the four cardinal points, and that he was perfectly conversant with the deserts of Mongolia, he would never condescend to inquire the route from persons whom he met, and we not unfrequently suffered from his self opinion. We were resolved, therefore, to convert the accident which had just befallen us, into the basis of a warning to our guide. "Samdadchiemba," said we, "listen with attention to the important advice we are about to impart. Though in your youth you may have traveled a good deal in Mongolia, it does not follow that you are master of all the routes; distrust, therefore, your own conjectures, and be more willing to consult the Tartars whom we meet. If yesterday, for example, you had asked the way, if you had not persisted in your practise of being guided wholly by the course of the sun, we should not have endured so much misery." Samdadchiemba made no reply.

We then got up to make the preparations for departure. When we had put in order the different articles that had been confusedly thrown about the tent, we remarked that the Dchiahour was not occupied, as usual, in saddling the camels. We went to see what he was about, and to our great surprise found him tranquilly seated upon a large stone behind the tent. "Well!" exclaimed we, "has it not been determined that we are to encamp elsewhere this evening? What are you seated on that stone for?" Samdadchiemba made no reply; he did not even raise his eyes, but kept them fixedly directed towards the ground. "Samdadchiemba, what is the matter with you? Why don't you saddle the camels?" "If you wish to go," replied he dryly, "you can go; as for me, I remain here. I cannot any longer accompany you. I am, it seems, a wicked man, devoid of conscience; what occasion can you have for such a person?" We were greatly surprised to hear this from a young neophyte who had seemed so attached to us. We, however, thought it best to attempt no persuasion, lest we should aggravate the sullen pride of his character, and render him still more indocile for the future. We accordingly proceeded to do the necessary work ourselves.

We had already folded the tent and packed it on a camel, not a word being spoken by any of the party. Samdadchiemba remained seated on the stone, covering his face with his hands, and probably watching through his fingers how we got on with the labor which he was accustomed to fulfil. When he saw that we were doing very well without him, he rose, without uttering a word, loaded the other camel, saddled his own mule, mounted it, and led the way as usual. M. Gabet and M. Huc exchanged smiles, but they said nothing, for they feared that any observations at that moment might irritate a temperament which evidently required the greatest care in its management.

We halted in a spot beside the road, not very magnificent, certainly, as a station, but at all events, infinitely preferable to the ravine of desolation in which we had experienced such misery. There was this great blessing, that we were once more united; an immense satisfaction in the desert, and which we had never sufficiently appreciated until the occurrence of the mischance that had for a while separated us. We celebrated the occasion by a splendid banquet, of which the flour and sheep's liver, purchased by M. Gabet, formed the basis. This unaccustomed treat relaxed the frowning brow of Samdadchiemba, who applied himself to the culinary arrangements with absolute enthusiasm, and effected, with very limited resources, a supper of several courses.

Next morning, at daybreak, we were in motion. We had not proceeded far when we discovered before us, outlined on the yellow ground of a sandy hill, several large buildings,

Lamasery of Rache-Tchurin.

surrounded with a multitude of white huts. This was the Lamasery of Rache-Tchurin, which, as we approached it, seemed to us a well-built, well-kept place. The three Buddhist temples which rise from the center of the establishment, are of elegant, of majestic construction. The entrance to the principal temple is through a square tower of colossal proportions, at each angle of which is a monstrous dragon, elaborately carved in stone. We traversed the Lamasery from one end to the other, along the chief streets. There was throughout religious and solemn silence. The only persons we saw were a few Lamas enveloped in their large red scarfs, who, after giving us the salutation of the day in a tone scarce above a whisper, gravely continued their melancholy walk.

Towards the western extremity of the Lamasery, Samdadchiemba's little mule shied, and then dashed off at a gallop, followed in its irregular flight, by the two baggage camels. The animals on which we were mounted were equally alarmed. All this disorder was occasioned by a young Lama, who was stretched at full length in the middle of the street, performing a rite in great vogue among the Buddhists, and which consists in making the circuit of a Lamasery, prostrating yourself, with your forehead to the ground, at every single step you make. Sometimes the number of devotees performing together this painful pilgrimage is perfectly prodigious; they follow each other, in Indian file, along a narrow path which encircles the entire Lamasery and its appendant buildings. Any one who deviates in the slightest degree from the prescribed line, is considered to have failed in his devotion, and loses all the fruit he would otherwise have derived from his previous toil. Where the Lamasery is of any extent, the devotees have hard work to get through the ceremony in the course of a long day; so that the pilgrims, who have undertaken this exercise, and have started early in the morning, think themselves lucky if they can complete the operation by nightfall. For the pilgrimage must be performed without intermission, so strictly, that the pilgrims are not allowed to stop for a moment even to take a little nourishment. If, after commencing the rite you do not complete it off-hand, it does not count; you have acquired no merit, and you are not to expect any spiritual profit.

Each prostration must be perfect, so that the body shall be stretched flat along the ground, and the forehead touch the earth, the arms being spread out before you, and the hands joined, as if in prayer. Before rising, the pilgrim describes each time a semicircle on the ground by means of a goat's horn, which he holds in either hand, the line being completed by drawing the arm down to the side. You cannot but feel infinite compassion when you look upon these wretched creatures, their face and clothes all covered with dust or mud. The most inclement weather will not check their intrepid devotion; they continue their prostrations amid snow and rain and the most piercing cold.

There are various modes of performing the pilgrimage round a Lamasery. Some pilgrims do not prostrate themselves at all, but carry, instead, a load of prayer-books, the exact weight of which is prescribed them by the Great Lama, and the burden of which is so oppressive at times that you see old men, and women, and children absolutely staggering under it. When, however, they have successfully completed the circuit, they are deemed to have recited all the prayers contained in the books they have carried. Others content themselves with simply walking the circuit, telling the beads of their long chaplets, or constantly turning a sort of wheel placed on the right hand, and which whirls about with inconceivable rapidity. This instrument is called Tchu-Kor (turning prayer). You see in every brook a number of these Tchu-Kor, which are turned by the current, and in their movement are reputed to be praying, night and day, for the benefit of those who erect them. The Tartars suspend them over the fireplace, and these in their movements are supposed to pray for the peace and prosperity of the whole family, emblemed by the hearth. The movement itself is effected by the thorough draught occasioned by the openings at the top of the tent.

The Buddhists have another mode of simplifying pilgrimages and devotional rites. In all the great Lamaseries you find at short intervals figures in the form of barrels, and turning upon an axle. The material of these figures is a thick board, composed of infinite sheets of paper pasted together, and upon which are written in Thibetian characters the prayers most reputed throughout the country. Those who have not the taste, or the zeal, or the strength to carry huge boards of books on their shoulders, or to prostrate themselves, step after step, in the dust and mire, or to walk round the Lamasery in winter's cold or summer's heat, have recourse to the simple and expeditious medium of the prayer barrel. All they have to do is to set it in motion; it then turns of itself for a long time, the devotees drinking, eating, or sleeping, while the complacent mechanism is turning prayers for them.

One day, on approaching a prayer barrel, we found two

Turning Prayers.

Lamas quarreling furiously, and just on the point of coming to blows, the occasion being the fervor of each for prayer. One of them having set the prayer automaton in motion, had quietly returned to his cell. As he was entering it he turned his head, doubtless to enjoy the spectacle of the fine prayers he had set to work for himself, but to his infinite disgust, he saw a colleague stopping his prayers, and about to turn on the barrel on his own account. Indignant at this pious fraud, he ran back, and stopped his competitor's prayers. Thus it went on for some time, the one turning on, the other stopping the barrel, without a word said on either side. At last, however, their patience exhausted, they came to high words; from words they proceeded to menaces, and it would doubtless have come to a fight, had not an old Lama, attracted by the uproar, interposed words of peace, and himself put the automaton in motion for the joint benefit of both parties.

Besides the pilgrims whose devotion is exercised within

or about the Lamaseries, you find many who have undertaken fearfully long journeys, which they execute with a prostration at every step. Sad and lamentable is it to see these unhappy victims of error enduring, to no purpose, such terrible and painful labors; one's heart is pierced with grief, and one's soul impressed with yearning for the day when these poor Tartars shall consecrate to the service of the true God that religious energy which they daily waste upon a vain and lying creed. We had hoped to profit by the solemnities at Rache-Tchurin to announce the true faith to the Ortous; but such was doubtless not the will of God, since He had permitted us to lose our way on the very day which seemed most favorable for our project. We accordingly passed through the Lamasery of Rache-Tchurin without stopping, eager as we were to arrive at the very source of that immense superstition, of which, as yet, we had only witnessed a few shallow streams.

At a short distance from Rache-Tchurin we reached a road well marked out, and covered with travelers. It was not, however, devotion that had set these people in motion, as it had the pilgrims whom we saw at the Lamasery; mere matter of business was leading them towards the Dabsoun-Noor, (the Salt Lake), celebrated throughout Western Mantchou, and which supplies with salt not only the adjacent Tartars, but also several provinces of the Chinese Empire.

For a day's journey before you reach Dabsoun-Noor the soil changes by degrees its form and aspect; losing its yellow tint, it becomes insensibly white, as though thinly covered with snow. The earth swelling in every direction, forms innumerable hillocks, cone-shaped, and of a regularity so perfect that you might suppose them to have been constructed by the hand of man. Sometimes they are grouped in heaps, one on the other, like pears piled on a plate; they are of all sizes, some but just created, others old, exhausted, and falling to decay. Around these excrescences grow creeping thorns, long-pointed, without flowers or leaves, which, intertwining spirally, surmount them with a sort of net-work cap. These thorns are never found elsewhere than about these hillocks; upon those of more recent growth they are firm, vigorous, and full of shoots. Upon the elder elevations they are dried up, calcined by the niter, brittle, and in shreds.

As you look upon these numerous mounds, covered with a thick efflorescence of niter, it is obvious to your sense that beneath the surface, and at no great depth, some great chemical operation is in progress. Springs, generally so rare in the Ortous country, are here of frequent occurrence, but the water is for the most part excessively salt. Here and there, however, by the very side of a brackish pool, there is a spring of soft, sweet, delicious water; all such are indicated to travelers by a small flag, fluttering from the end of a long pole.

Dabsoun-Noor is not so much a lake as a reservoir of mineral salt, mixed with nitrous efflorescence. The latter, in color pale white, and crumbling between the fingers, is easily distinguishable from the salt, which is of a gray tint, and glitters like crystal when broken. Dabsoun-Noor is about twenty lis in circumference. Around it, at intervals, are the tents occupied by the Mongols who work it, and the Chinese who have thrust themselves in as partners. It were difficult indeed to find any description of industry or commerce within a certain range of their own country in which the Chinese do not contrive to have a hand. The manipulation to which the salt is subjected requires neither great labor nor great science. All the workers do is to pick it up as it comes in the reservoir, to pile it, and, when the heap is of a certain size, to cover it with a thin coating of potter's earth. When the salt has sufficiently purified itself, the Tartars convey it to the nearest Chinese mart and exchange it for tea, tobacco, brandy, and other commodities. In the locality itself salt is of no value: at every step you see lumps of it, sometimes of remarkable purity. We filled a bag with these for our own use and for that of the camels, which are all very fond of salt. We traversed Dabsoun-Noor throughout its breadth from east to west, and we had to take the utmost precaution as we proceeded over its loose, and at times almost moving, soil. The Tartars recommended us not to deviate in the least from the path we should find marked out, and by all means to avoid any places where we should see the water bubbling up, for there, they informed us, were gulfs which they had frequently endeavored to sound, but without result. This statement induced us to believe that there is a noor, or lake, here, but that it is underground, the place called Dabsoun-Noor being merely the covering or roof of the lake, composed of the saline and saltpetrous matter produced by the constant evaporation of the subterranean waters. Foreign matter, brought by the wind, and consolidated by the rain, would in the lapse of time form a crust upon such a roof strong enough to bear the caravans that incessantly traverse Dabsoun-Noor.

This great salt mine seems to pervade with its influence the whole Ortous district, throughout whose extent the water is brackish, the soil arid, and the surface encrusted with saline matter. This absence of rich pasturage and fresh water is very adverse to the growth of cattle; but the camel, whose robust and hardy temperament adapts itself to the most sterile regions, affords compensation to the Tartars of the Ortous. This animal, a perfect treasure to the dwellers in the desert, can remain a fortnight, or even a month, without eating or drinking. However wretched the land may be on which it is put to feed, it can always find wherewith to satisfy its hunger, especially if the soil be impregnated with salt or niter. Things that no other animal will touch, to it are welcome; briers and thorns, dry wood itself, supply it with efficient food.

Though it costs so little to keep, the camel is of an utility inconceivable to those who are not acquainted with the countries in which Providence has placed it. Its ordinary load is from 700 to 800 lbs., and it can carry this load ten leagues a day. Those, indeed, which are employed to carry despatches, are expected to travel eighty leagues per diem, but then they only carry the despatch bearer. In several countries of Tartary the carriages of the kings and princes are drawn by camels, and sometimes they are harnessed to palanquins; but this can only be done in the level country. The fleshy nature of their feet does not permit them to climb mountains, when they have a carriage or litter of any sort to draw after them.

The training of the young camel is a business requiring great care and attention. For the first week of its life it can neither stand nor suck without some helping hand. Its long neck is then of such excessive flexibility and fragility, that it runs the risk of dislocating it, unless some one is at hand to sustain the head while it sucks the teats of its dam.

The camel, born to servitude, seems impressed from its birth with a sense of the yoke it is destined to bear through life. You never see the young camel playing and frolicking about, as you see kids, colts, and other young animals. It is always grave, melancholy, and slow in its movements, which it never hastens, unless under compulsion. In the night, and often in the day also, it sends forth a mournful cry, like that of an infant in pain. It seems to feel that joy or recreation are not within its portion; that its inevitable career is forced labor and long fastings, until death shall relieve it.

The maturation of the camel is a long affair. It cannot carry even a single rider, until its third year; and it is not in full vigor until it is eight years old. Its trainers then begin to try it with loads, gradually heavier and heavier. If it can rise with its burden, this is a proof that it can carry it throughout the journey. When that journey is only of brief duration, they sometimes load the animal in excess, and then they aid it to rise by means of bars and levers. The camel's capacity for labor endures for a long time. Provided that at certain periods of the year it is allowed a short holiday for pasturing at its leisure, it will continue its service for fully fifty years.

Nature has provided the camel with no means of defense against other animals, unless you may so consider its piercing prolonged cry, and its huge, shapeless, ugly frame, which resembles, at a distance, a heap of ruins. It seldom kicks, and when it does, it almost as seldom inflicts any injury. Its soft, fleshy foot cannot wound, or even bruise you; neither can the camel bite an antagonist. In fact, its only practical means of defense against man or beast is a sort of vehement sneeze, wherewith it discharges, from nose and mouth, a mass of filth against the object which it seeks to intimidate or to annoy.

Yet the entire male camels, *bore* as the Tartars call them, (*temen* being the generic appellation of the animal), are very formidable during the twelfth moon, which is their rutting time. At this period, their eyes are inflamed; an oily, fetid humor exhales from their heads; their mouths are constantly foaming; and they eat and drink absolutely nothing whatever. In this state of excitement they rush at whatever presents itself, man or beast, with a fierceness of precipitation which it is impossible to avoid or to resist; and when they have overthrown the object they have pursued they pound it beneath the weight of their bodies. The epoch passed, the camel resumes its ordinary gentleness, and the routine of its laborious career.

The females do not produce young until their sixth or seventh year; the period of gestation is fourteen months. The Tartars geld most of their male camels, which, by this operation, acquire a greater development of strength, height, and size. Their voices become at the same time thinner and lower, in some instances wholly lost; and the hair is shorter and finer than that of the entire camels.

The awkward aspect of the camel, the excessive stench of its breath, its heavy, ungraceful movements, its projecting hare-lips, the callosities which disfigure various parts of its body, all contribute to render its appearance repulsive; yet its extreme gentleness and docility, and the services it renders to man, render it of pre-eminent utility, and make us forget its deformity.

Notwithstanding the apparent softness of its feet, the camel can walk upon the most rugged ground, upon sharp flints, or thorns, or roots of trees, without wounding itself. Yet, if too long a journey is continuously imposed upon it, if after a certain march you do not give it a few days' rest, the outer skin wears off, the flesh is bared, and the blood flows. Under such distressing circumstances, the Tartars make sheep-skin shoes for it, but this assistance is unavailing without rest; for if you attempt to compel the camel to proceed, it lies down, and you are compelled either to remain with or to abandon it.

There is nothing which the camel so dreads as wet, marshy ground. The instant it places its feet upon anything like mud, it slips and slides, and, generally, after staggering about like a drunken man, falls heavily on its sides.

When about to repose, it kneels down, folds its fore legs symmetrically under its body, and stretches out its long neck before it on the ground. In this position, it looks just like a monstrous snail.

Every year, towards the close of spring, the camel sheds its hair, every individual bristle of which disappears before a single sprout of the new stock comes up. For twenty days the animal remains completely bare, as though it had been closely shaved all over, from the top of the head to the extremity of the tail. At this juncture, it is excessively sensitive to cold or wet; and you see it, at the slightest chillness in the air or the least drop of rain, shivering and shaking in every limb, like a man without clothes exposed on the snow. By degrees the new hair shows itself, in the form of fine, soft, curling wool, which gradually becomes a long, thick fur, capable of resisting the extremest inclemency of the weather. The greatest delight of the animal is to walk in the teeth of the north wind, or to stand motionless on the summit of a hill, beaten by the storm and inhaling the icy wind. Some naturalists say that the camel cannot exist in cold countries; these writers must have wholly forgotten the Tartarian camels, which on the contrary, cannot endure the least heat, and which certainly could not exist in Arabia.

The hair of an ordinary camel weighs about ten pounds. It is sometimes finer than silk, and always longer than sheep's wool. The hair growing below the neck and on the legs of the entire camels is rough, bushy, and in color black, whereas that of the ordinary camel is red, gray, and white. The Tartars make no sort of use of it. In the places where the animals pasture, you see great sheets of it, looking like dirty rags, driven about by the wind, until they are collected in sheltered corners, in the hill sides. The utmost use the Tartars make of it is to twist some of it into cord, or into a sort of canvas, of which they construct sacks and carpets.

The milk of the camel is excellent, and supplies large quantities of butter and cheese. The flesh is hard, unsavory, and little esteemed by the Tartars. They use the hump, however, which, cut into slices, and dissolved in tea, serves the purpose of butter. It is known that Heliogabalus had camel's flesh served up at his banquets, and that he was very fond of camel's feet. We cannot speak as to the latter dish, which the Roman Emperor piqued himself upon having invented, but we can distinctly affirm that camel's flesh is detestable.

Mongol Butcher.

CHAPTER X.

Purchase of a Sheep—A Mongol Butcher—Great Feast *à la Tartare*—Tartar Veterinary Surgeons—Strange Cure of a Cow—Depth of the Wells of the Ortous—Manner of Watering the Animals—Encampment of the Hundred Wells—Meeting with the King of the Alechan—Annual Embassies of the Tartar Sovereigns to Peking—Grand Ceremony in the Temple of the Ancestors—The Emperor gives Counterfeit Money to the Mongol Kings—Inspection of our Geographical Map—The Devil's Cistern—Purification of the Water—A Lame Dog—Curious Aspect of the Mountains—Passage of the Yellow River.

THE environs of the Dabsoun-Noor abound in flocks of goats and sheep. These animals like to browse on the furze and thorny bushes, the sole vegetation of these barren steppes; they especially delight in those nitrous efflorescences which are found here on all sides in the utmost abundance. The soil, miserable as it is in other respects, seems very favorable to the growth of these animals, which enter largely into the consumption of the Tartars, constituting indeed the basis of their food. If bought on the spot, they are of very moderate price. As we calculated that a pound of meat would cost us less than a pound of flour, we resolved, as a matter of economy, to buy a sheep. The thing was not difficult to find; but as it would of course oblige us to stop, at least for a day, we waited till we should come to some place, not quite barren, and where our animals could find some pasturage to browse upon.

Two days after crossing Dabsoun-Noor, we entered a long narrow valley, where some Mongol families had stationed themselves. The earth was covered with a close herb, which, in form and character, had much resemblance to thyme. Our beasts, as they proceeded, browsed furtively, right and left, on this plant, and seemed to be very fond of it. This new pasturage gave us the idea of encamping on the spot. Not far from a tent, a Lama was sitting on a hillock, making ropes with camel's hair. "Brother," said we as we approached him, "the flock upon that hill doubtless belongs to you. Will you sell us a sheep?" "Certainly," he answered, "I will let you have an excellent sheep; as to the price, we shall not quarrel about that. We men of prayer are not like merchants." He indicated to us a spot near his own tent, and unloaded our beasts. The entire family of the Lama, when they heard the cries of our camels, hastened to assist us to encamp. We, indeed, were not allowed to do anything to it; for our new friends took delight in making themselves useful, in unsaddling the beasts, pitching the tent, and putting our baggage in order within.

The young Lama, who had received us with so much kindness, after having unsaddled the horse and the mule, perceived that both these beasts were hurt a little on the back. "Brothers," he said, "here is a bad business; and as you are upon a long journey, it must be remedied, or you will not be able to go on." So saying, he took the knife, which hung from his girdle, sharpened it with rapidity upon his boot-tops, took our saddles to pieces, examined the rough parts of the wood, and pared them away on both sides till he had removed the slightest unevenness. He then put together again, with wonderful skill, all the pieces of the saddles, and returned them to us. "That will do," said he; "now you may travel in peace." This operation was effected rapidly and in the readiest manner possible. The Lama was then about to fetch the sheep; but as it was already late, we said it was unnecessary, for that we should remain a whole day in his valley.

Next morning, before we were awake, the Lama opened

the door of our tent, laughing so loud that he aroused us. "Ah," said he, "I see plainly that you do not intend to depart to-day. The sun is already very high, and you sleep still." We rose quickly, and as soon as we were dressed, the Lama spoke of the sheep. "Come to the flock," he said; "you may choose at your pleasure." "No, go by yourself, and select a sheep for us yourself. At present we have an occupation. With us, Lamas of the Western sky, it is a rule to pray as soon as we rise." "Oh, what a fine thing!" said the Lama; "oh, the holy rules of the West!" His admiration, however, did not make him forget his little affair of business. He mounted his horse and rode towards a flock of sheep which we saw undulating upon the slope of a hill.

We had not yet finished our prayers when we heard the Tartar returning at full gallop. He had fastened the sheep to the back of his saddle, like a portmanteau. Hardly arrived at the door of our tent, he dismounted; and in the twinkling of an eye he had put upon its four legs the poor sheep, quite astounded at the ride it had been favored with. "That is the sheep; is it not fine? Does it suit you?" "Admirably. What is the price?" "One ounce; is that too much?" Considering the size of the animal, we thought the price moderate. "You ask an ounce; here is an ingot, which is just of the weight you require. Sit down for a moment; we will fetch our scales, and you shall ascertain whether this piece of silver really weighs an ounce." At these words the Lama drew back, and cried, stretching out both hands towards us: "Above there is a heaven, below there is the earth, and Buddha is the lord of all things. He wills that men behave towards each other like brothers; you are of the West, I am of the East. Is that any reason why the intercourse between us should not be frank and honorable? You have not cheapened my sheep: I take your money without weighing it." "An excellent principle," said we. "As you will not weigh the money, pray sit, nevertheless, for a moment; we will take a cup of tea together and talk over a little matter." "I know what you mean; neither you nor I may cause the transmigration of this living being. We must find a layman who knows how to kill sheep. Is it not so?" and without awaiting an answer, he added, "another thing; from your appearance, one may easily guess that you are no great hands at cutting up sheep and preparing them." "You are not mistaken," we answered, laughing. "Well, keep the sheep tied to your tent; and for the rest, rely upon me; I shall be back in a minute." He mounted his horse, went off at full gallop and disappeared in a bend of the vale.

According to his promise, the Lama soon returned. He went straight to his tent, tied his horse to a post, took off his saddle, bridle and halter, gave it a cut with his whip, and so sent it off to pasture. He went into his tent for a little while, and then appeared with all the members of his family, that is to say, his old mother and two younger brothers. They advanced slowly towards our tent, in truly ridiculous fashion, just as if they were going to remove all their furniture. The Lama carried on his head a large pot, which covered him as with an enormous hat. His mother had on her back a large basket, filled with argols. The two young Mongols followed with a trivet, an iron spoon, and several other minor kitchen implements. At this sight, Samdadchiemba was full of joy, for he saw before him a whole day of poetry.

When the entire *batterie de cuisine* was arranged in open air, the Lama invited us, in his politeness, to go and repose in our tent for awhile. He judged from our air, that we could not, without derogation, be present at the approaching scene of butchering. The suggestion, however, did not meet our views, and we requested that if we could do so without inconveniencing them, we might sit down on the grass at a respectful distance, and with the promise that we would not touch anything. After some objections, perceiving that we were curious to be spectators, they dispensed with the etiquette of the matter.

The Lama seemed anxious; he kept looking towards the north of the valley, as if expecting some one. "All right," he said at last, with an air of satisfaction, "here he comes." "Who comes? Of whom do you speak?" "I forgot to tell you that I had been just now to invite a layman to come, who is very skilful in killing a sheep. There he is." We rose and perceived, indeed, something moving among the heath of the valley. At first we could not clearly distinguish what it was, for though it advanced with some rapidity, the object did not seem to enlarge. At last the most singular person we had ever met with in our lives presented himself to our view. We were obliged to make the utmost efforts to repress the strong impulse to laughter that came upon us. This layman seemed to be about fifty years old, but his height did not exceed three feet. On the top of his head, which terminated like a sugar-loaf, rose a small tuft of badly combed hair; a gray, thin beard descended in disorder down his chin. Finally, two prominences, one on his back, the other on his breast, communicated to this little butcher a perfect resemblance with Æsop, as he appears in various editions of the " Fables de la Fontaine."

The strong, sonorous voice of the layman was in singular contrast with the exiguity of his thin, stunted frame. He did not lose much time in saluting the company. After having darted his small black eyes at the sheep, which was tied to one of the nails of our tent, he said : " Is this the beast you wish to have put in order ? " And while feeling its tail in order to judge its fat, he gave it a turn, and placed it on its back with remarkable dexterity. He next tied together its legs; then while uncovering his right arm by throwing back the sleeve of his leathern coat, he asked whether the operation was to be effected in the tent or outside ? " Outside," said we. " Outside, very well, outside ; " so saying, he drew from a leathern sheath, suspended from his sash, a knife with a large handle, but whose blade by long use had become thin and narrow. After having examined for a moment its point with his thumb, he plunged it to the hilt into the side of the sheep, and drawing it out quite red, the sheep was dead, dead at once, without making any movement ; not a single drop of blood had spouted from the wound. We were greatly astonished at this, and asked the little man how he managed to kill a sheep so very easily and quickly. " We Tartars," he said, " do not kill in the same way as the Kitat ; they cut the throat, we go straight to the heart. By our method, the animal suffers less, and all the blood is, as it should be, retained in the interior."

The transmigration once operated, nobody had any further scruples. Our Dchiahour and the Tartar Lama turned back their sleeves and advanced to assist the little butcher. The sheep was skinned with admirable celerity. Meantime the mother of the Lama had made the two pots boil. She now took the entrails of the sheep, washed them pretty clean, and then, with the blood which she took from the interior of the sheep by means of a large wooden spoon, prepared some puddings, the basis of which was the never-failing oatmeal. "Sirs Lamas," said the little layman, "shall I bone the sheep?" Upon our answering in the affirmative, he had the animal hooked upon the tent, for he was not big enough to perform that operation himself; he then mounted upon a large stone, and passing his knife rapidly along the bones, he detached, in one piece, all the meat, so as to leave dangling from the tent a mere skeleton, clean, cleared, and nicely polished.

While the little layman was, according to his expression, putting in order the flesh of the sheep, the rest of the company had prepared a gala in the Tartar fashion. The young Lama was director of the feast. "Now," he cried, "let us all sit round; the great pot is going to be emptied." Forthwith everyone sat down upon the turf. The old Mongol woman plunged both hands into the pot, which was boiling over, and drew out all the intestines—the liver, the heart, the kidneys, the spleen, and the bowels, stuffed with blood and oatmeal. In this gastronomical preparation, the most remarkable thing was, that all the intestines had been retained in their integrity, so that they presented themselves much as they are seen in the living beast. The old woman served up, or rather threw this splendid dish upon the lawn, which was at once our chair, table, plate, and, in case of need, our napkin. It is unnecessary to add, that we used our fingers instead of forks. Every one seized with his hands a portion of the bowels, twisted it from the mass, and devoured it without seasoning or salt.

The two French missionaries were not able, despite their utmost willingness, to do honor to this Tartar dish. First we burned our fingers when we tried to touch the hot and smoking repast. Although our guests urged that it ought not to be allowed to grow cold, we waited a little, afraid of burning our lips also. At last we tasted these puddings of sheep's blood and oatmeal, but after getting down a few mouthfuls, we were quite satisfied. Never, perhaps, had we eaten anything so utterly tasteless and insipid. Samdadchiemba, having foreseen this, had withdrawn from the common dish the liver and the kidneys, which he placed before us, with some salt, which he had previously crushed between two stones. We were thus enabled to keep pace with the company, who, with a devouring appetite, were swallowing the vast system of entrails.

When the whole had disappeared, the old woman brought up the second service, by placing in the midst of us the large pot in which the puddings had been cooked. Instantly all the members of the banquet invited each other, and every one taking from his bosom his wooden porringer, ladled out bumpers of a smoking, salt liquid, which they dignified with the pompous name of sauce. As we did not wish to appear eccentric, or as if we despised the Tartar *cuisine*, we did like the rest. We plunged our porringer into the pot, but it was only by the most laudable efforts that we could get down this green stuff, which gave us the idea of half masticated grass. The Tartars, on the contrary, found it delicious, and readily reached the bottom of the extempore tureen, not stopping for a moment, till nothing was left—not a drop of sauce, not an inch of pudding.

When the feast was finished, the little layman took leave, receiving as his fee the four feet of the sheep. To this fee, fixed by the old custom of the Mongols, we added, as a supplement, a handful of tea leaves, for we desired that he should long remember and talk to his countrymen of the generosity of the Lamas of the Western sky.

Every one having now thoroughly regaled, our neighbors took their kitchen utensils and returned home, except the young Lama, who said he would not leave us alone. After much talk about the east and west, he took down the skeleton, which was still hanging at the entrance of the tent, and amused himself with reciting, or rather singing, the nomenclature of all the bones, large and small, that compose the frame of the sheep. He perceived that our knowledge on this subject was very limited, and this extremely astonished him; and we had the greatest trouble to make him understand, that in our country ecclesiastical studies had for their object more serious and important matters than the names and number of the bones of a sheep.

Every Mongol knows the number, the name, and the position of the bones which compose the frame of animals; and thus they never break the bones when they are cutting up an ox or a sheep. With the point of their large knife they go straight and at once to the juncture of the bones and separate them with astonishing skill and celerity. These frequent dissections, and especially the habit of being every day amongst their flocks, make the Tartars well acquainted with the diseases of animals, and skilful in their cure. The remedies, which they employ internally, are always simples gathered in the prairie, and the decoction of which they make the sick animals drink. For this purpose, they use a large cow-horn. When they have contrived to insert the small end of this into the mouth of the animal, they pour the physic in at the other extremity, as through a funnel. If the beast persists in not opening its mouth, the liquid is administered through the nostrils. Sometimes the Tartars employ a lavement in their treatment of the diseases of animals; but their instruments are still of primitive simplicity. A cow's horn serves for the pipe, and the pump is a great bladder, worked by squeezing it.

Internal remedies, however, are not very often applied; the Tartars make more frequent use of punctures and incisions in different parts of the body. Some of these operations are extremely ludicrous. One day, when we had pitched our tent beside a Mongol dwelling, a Tartar brought to the chief of the family a cow, which, he said, would not eat, and which was pining away day by day. The chief examined the animal, opened its mouth, and rubbed its fore teeth with his nail. "Fool, blockhead," said he to the man who had come to ask his advice, "why did you not come before? Your cow is on the verge of death; there is scarce a day's life more in her. Yet, there may be tried one means; I will attempt it. If your cow dies, you will say it is your own fault; if it recovers, you will regard it as a great favor from Hormousdha, operated by my skill." He called some of his slaves, and ordered them to keep a firm hold of the beast, while he was operating upon it. Then he entered his tent, whence he soon returned, armed with a nail and a great hammer. We waited with impatience this strange chirurgical operation, which was to be performed with a nail and a hammer. While several Mongols held the cow, in order to prevent its running away, the operator placed the nail under its belly, and then drove it in up to the head with a violent stroke of the hammer. Next, he seized with both hands the tail of the cow, and ordered those who were holding it to let go. Instantly, the animal that had been so very singularly operated upon, dashed off, dragging after it the veterinary Tartar, clinging to its tail. In this fashion, they ran nearly a li. The Tartar then quitted his victim, and came quietly back to us, who were quite amazed at this new method of curing cows. He declared there was no further danger for the beast; for he had ascertained, he said, by the stiffness of the tail, the good effect of the ferruginous medicine he had administered.

The Tartar veterinarians sometimes perform their operations at the belly, as we have just seen; but it is more generally, with the head, ears, temple, upper lip, and about the eyes that they deal. The latter operation is principally had recourse to, in the disease which the Tartars call Hen's dung, to which mules are greatly subject. When this disease breaks out, the animals leave off eating, and fall into extreme weakness, so that they can hardly keep themselves on their legs; fleshly excrescences, similar to the excrements of poultry, grow under the lids, in the corners of the eyes. If these excrescences are removed in time, the mules are saved, and recover by degrees their original vigor; if not, they pine for a few days, and then die.

Although cupping and bleeding have great place in the veterinary art of the Tartars, you must not suppose that they have at their disposal fine collections of instruments, such as those of European operators. Most of them have nothing but their ordinary knife, or the small iron awl, which they keep in their girdle, and which they use daily to clear their pipes and mend their saddles and leathern boots.

The young Lama who had sold us the sheep, spent a great part of the day in telling us anecdotes, more or less piquant and curious, about the veterinary science in which he seemed to be very skilful. Moreover, he gave us important instructions concerning the road we had to pursue. He settled the stages we ought to make, and indicated the places where we should encamp, so as to prevent our dying from thirst. We had still before us in the country of the Ortous, a journey of about fourteen days; in all that time we should find neither rivulet nor spring, nor cistern; but only, at certain distances, wells of an extraordinary depth; some of them distant from each other two days' march, so that we should have to carry with us our provision of water.

Next morning, after having paid our respects to the Tartar family, who had shown us so much kindness, we proceeded on our way. Towards evening, when it was nearly time to pitch our tent, we perceived in the distance a large assemblage of various herds. Thinking that one of the indicated wells lay probably there, we bent our steps in the direction, and soon found that we were correct in our anticipations; the water was before us. The beasts were collected from every quarter, waiting to be watered. We halted accordingly, and set up our encampment. As we gazed upon the assembled flocks, and the well, the covering of which was a large stone, we recalled with pleasure the passage of Genesis, which relates the journey of Jacob in Mesopotamia, to Laban, son of Bathuel the Syrian.

"Then Jacob went on his journey, and came into the land of the people of the east.

"And he looked, and behold a well in the field, and, lo, there were three flocks of sheep lying by it; for out of that well they watered the flocks: and a great stone was upon the well's mouth.

"And thither were all the flocks gathered; and they rolled the stone from the well's mouth, and watered the sheep, and put the stone again upon the well's mouth in its place."[1]

The wooden troughs placed around the well, reminded us of the other passage, where the meeting of Rebecca with the servant of Abraham is related.

"And when she had done giving him drink, she said, I will draw water for thy camels also, until they have done drinking.

"And she hasted, and emptied her pitcher into the trough, and ran again unto the well to draw water, and drew for all his camels."[2]

One cannot travel in Mongolia, amongst a pastoral and nomad population, without one's mind involuntarily going back to the time of the first patriarch, whose pastoral life had so close a relation with the manners and customs which we still find amongst the Mongol tribes. But how sad and painful do these coincidences become, when we reflect that these unfortunate people are still ignorant of the God of Abraham, Isaac, and Jacob.

---

[1] Gen. xxix. 1–3. [2] Gen. xxiv. 19, 20.

We had scarcely pitched our tent, and arranged our modest kitchen, when we saw several Tartar horsemen advancing at full gallop. They were coming to draw water and give it to the numerous flocks that had been long awaiting them. These animals, which had hitherto stood at a distance, seeing the shepherds approach, hastened to the spot, and soon all were grouped round the well, eager to quench their thirst. This large assemblage of animals, so numerous and so various, created an agitation, a tumult to which we were quite unused amid the silent solitude of the desert; and it was perhaps on account of its novelty that this confusion was, to us, full of entertainment. It was amusing to see the half-tamed horses pushing and struggling to arrive first at the well; then, instead of drinking in peace, biting, quarreling, and even leaving the water in order to pursue each other on the plain. The scene was especially entertaining and picturesque, when an enormous camel came forward, spreading alarm round the well, and driving away the vulgar herd by its despotic presence.

There were four Mongol shepherds; while two of them, armed with a long rod, ran about trying to effect a little order among the flocks, the two others drew the water in a manner which greatly excited our surprise. First, the utensil they used by way of pail, appeared to us very remarkable; it was the entire skin of a goat, solidly fastened at the four feet, the only opening being at the neck. A hoop kept this orifice open; a long, strong rope of camel's hair was fastened at one end to the wooden handle that crossed the diameter of the orifice, and at the other end to the saddle of the horse ridden by one of the Tartars, who, when the skin was filled rode off, and thus hauled up the bucket to the edge of the well, where it was received by another man, who emptied its contents into the troughs.

The well was of astonishing depth; the rope used to raise the bucket seemed more than 200 feet long. Instead of running in a pulley, it went right over a large stone, in which a large groove was already made by the constant friction. Although the drawing up of the water was performed with great activity, it was nearly dark before all the flock had been watered; we then brought our five animals to participate in the general banquet, and the Tartars had the complaisance to draw water also for us; otherwise, it is probable we should never have got it, but have been obliged to suffer thirst beside an abundant well.

These Tartars did not seem contented, like those we had met with in the other parts of Mongolia; we saw they were very depressed at being obliged to spend their lives in such a barren country, where pasturage is so very scarce and water still rarer. They talked to us of the Mongol kingdoms through which we had passed, and where it was so easy, so agreeable indeed, to feed animals. "Oh, how happy are the inhabitants of these countries!" said they. "How fortunate were we, could we spend our days amidst those rich pasturages."

Before they returned to their dwelling, which lay behind a high mountain, these Tartars told us that we ought to depart next morning before daybreak, for that we should not find any water until we came to the Hundred Wells, which was distant a hundred and fifty lis (fifteen leagues).

Dawn had not yet appeared when we left. The country was, as before, sandy, barren, and dismal. About noon we halted, in order to take a little food, and to make tea with the water we had brought with us on one of the camels. Night was setting in before we reached the Hundred Wells; our poor animals could hardly move for hunger and fatigue; yet, at all cost, we were obliged to reach the encampment. To remain where we were would have caused infinite wretchedness. At last we came to the wells, and without troubling ourselves to ascertain whether or no there were a hundred of them, as the Tartar name of the place imported, we hastened to pitch our tent. Happily the well was not so deep as that we had seen the night before. Our first care was to draw some water for the horse and the mule; but when we went to lead them to the trough, we did not find them near the tent, where they usually stood to be unsaddled. This misfortune occasioned us an alarm that made us forget the fatigues of the day. We had, it is true, no fear of robbers, for in this respect no country is more safe than the Ortous; but we thought that our animals, thirsty as they were, had run away in search of water. They will go, meditated we, till they have found water; perhaps they will go without stopping to the frontiers of the Ortous to the very banks of the Yellow River.

The night was quite dark; nevertheless, we thought it

proper to go instantly in search of our horses, while Samdadchiemba was preparing supper. We wandered about for a long time in all directions without seeing anything; ever and anon we stopped to listen whether we could distinguish the sound of the bells suspended from the horse's neck; but our efforts were vain; nothing interrupted the dead silence of the desert. We went on, without losing courage, still hoping to find animals so very necessary to us, and the loss of which would have placed us in such difficulties. Sometimes we fancied we heard in the distance the tinkling of the bells. Then we laid flat down, applying our ears to the earth, in order to catch more readily the slightest noise that might occur; but it was all in vain; our search was fruitless.

The fear of losing our way in a dark night in a country, the bearings of which we had not been able to examine, made us think of retracing our steps. Judge of our consternation when, on turning round, we perceived, apparently in the place where we had pitched our tent, a large volume of flame and smoke rising. We did not doubt for an instant that Samdadchiemba also had set out in search of the animals, and that in his absence the tent had caught fire. Oh, how sad and discouraging was that moment. In the middle of the desert, at two thousand lis distance from our christendom, we contemplated without hope those flames consuming our tent, our sole shelter against the inclemency of the weather. "Alas!" we said, "the tent is certainly destroyed, and doubtless all that was in it has also become a prey to the flames."

We mournfully directed our steps to the place of our encampment. Though anxious to ascertain our misfortune, we advanced slowly, for we were, at the same time, afraid to approach the fearful spectacle, destructive of our plans, and plunging us into misery of every description. As we advanced, we heard loud cries; at last we distinguished the voice of Samdadchiemba, apparently calling for assistance. Imagining that we could still save something from the conflagration, we hastened to the spot, calling out, at the pitch of our voices, that we were coming. When we at last arrived at the encampment, we stood for an instant quite stupefied upon seeing Samdadchiemba quietly seated beside an immense fire, and drinking with the greatest satisfaction bumpers of tea. The tent was untouched, and all our animals lying around it: there had been no conflagration at all. The Dchiahour, having found the horse and the mule, had imagined that, having doubtless got to some distance, we should have a difficulty in finding our way back to the encampment, and therefore he had made a large fire to direct our steps, and sent forth vehement cries inviting us to return. We had so fully believed in the reality of our misfortune that, on beholding our tent again, we seemed to pass at once from the extreme of misery to the height of happiness.

As the night had already made considerable progress, we hastened to eat, with excellent appetite, the soup that Samdadchiemba had prepared, and then laid down upon our goat-skins, where we enjoyed a profound sleep till daybreak.

On getting up next morning a glance around the encampment diffused a shudder of terror through all our limbs; for we found ourselves surrounded on every side by deep wells. We had been, indeed, told that we should not find water until we reached the place called Hundred Wells, but we had never imagined, that this denomination, Hundred Wells, was to be taken literally. When we had pitched our tent the night before, it was too dark for us to remark the presence of these numerous precipices, and accordingly we had taken no precautions. When we went out in search of our stray animals we had, without knowing it, made a thousand turnings and windings amongst these deep pits; and that we had thus walked in a dark night, without any accident, could only be attributed to a special protection of Providence. Before our departure, therefore, we planted a small wooden cross on the brink of one of these wells, as a sign of our thankfulness for the goodness of God.

After having made our usual breakfast, we proceeded. Towards noon we perceived before us a great multitude issuing from a narrow defile, formed by two precipitous mountains. We were lost in conjecture as to what this numerous and imposing caravan could be. Innumerable camels, laden with baggage, advanced in single file, one after the other, escorted on either side by a number of horsemen, who, in the distance, appeared to be richly attired. We slackened our pace, to obtain a nearer view of this caravan, which appeared to us a very strange affair.

Encampment at the Hundred Wells.

It was still a considerable distance off, when four horsemen, who formed a sort of vanguard, galloped on towards us. They were all four Mandarins, as we perceived from the blue button which surmounted their cap of ceremony. "Sirs Lamas," they said, "peace be with you! Towards what point of the earth do you direct your steps?" "We are of the West, and it is to the West we are going. And you, brothers of Mongolia, whither do you travel in so large a troop, and in such magnificent apparel?" "We are from the kingdom of Alechan, and our king is making a journey to Peking to prostrate himself at the feet of Him who dwells above the sky." After these few words the four horsemen rose somewhat in their saddles, saluted, and then returned to their position at the head of the caravan.

We had thus encountered on his way the King of Alechan, repairing to Peking with his gorgeous retinue, to be present at the great meeting of the tributary princes, who, on the first day of the first moon, are bound to offer the compliments of the new year to the Emperor. Behind the vanguard came a palanquin carried by two splendid mules, harnessed, the one before, the other behind, to gilt shafts. The palanquin was square, plain, and by no means elegant; its roof was adorned with some silk fringe, and its four panels were decorated with some pictures of dragons, birds, and nosegays. The Tartar monarch was sitting, not upon a seat, but with his legs crossed, in the oriental fashion. He seemed to be about fifty years old; and his full round features gave to his physiognomy a remarkable air of good nature. As he passed us, we cried: "King of the Alechan, peace and happiness be on your way!" "Men of prayer," he answered, "may you also be at peace," and he accompanied these words with a friendly salute. An old white-bearded Lama, mounted upon a magnificent horse, led the fore mule of the palanquin; he was considered the guide of the whole caravan. Generally, the great marches of the Tartars are under the guidance of the most venerable of the Lamas of the district; for these people are persuaded, that they have nothing to fear on their way, so long as they have at their head, a representative of the divinity, or rather the divinity himself incarnate in the person of the Lama.

A great number of horsemen, who surrounded, as a guard of honor, the royal palanquin, made their horses curvet incessantly, and dash up and down, in and out, from one side to the other, without ever stopping in their rapid movements. Immediately behind the carriage of the king, came a white camel of extraordinary beauty and size; a young Tartar, on foot, led it by a silken string. This camel was not laden. From the tip of each hump, which looked like two pyramids, floated pieces of yellow taffeta. There was no doubt, that this magnificent animal was a present destined for the Chinese Emperor. The remainder of the troop consisted of numerous camels, carrying the baggage, the boxes, tents, pots, the thousand and one utensils, that are always wanted in a country where no tavern is to be found.

The caravan had passed on a long time, when meeting with a well, we resolved to pitch our tent beside it. While we were making our tea, three Tartars, one decorated with the red, the other with the blue button, alighted at the entrance of our dwelling. They asked for news of the caravan of the King of the Alechans. We answered that we had met it a long time since, that it must already be at a considerable distance, and that it would doubtless arrive, before night, at the encampment of the Hundred Wells. "As it is so," they said, "we would rather remain here, than arrive by night at the Hundred Wells, at the risk of falling into some hole. To-morrow, by starting a little before day, we shall reach the caravan."

No sooner said than done: the Tartars forthwith unsaddled their horses, sent them off to seek their fortune in the desert, and without ceremony took their seat beside our fire. They were all Taitsi of the kingdom of the Alechan. One of these, he who wore the cap with the red button, was the king's minister; they all three belonged to the great caravan, but the day before, having started to visit a friend, a prince of the Ortous, they had been left behind by the main body.

The minister of the King of Alechan had an open, frank character, and a very acute understanding; he combined Mongol good nature with vivacious and elegant manners, which he had no doubt acquired in his frequent visits to Peking. He asked many questions about the country which the Tartars call the Western Heaven, and informed us, that every three years a great number of our countrymen, from the different western kingdoms, rendered their homage to the Emperor at Peking.

It is needless to observe that, for the most part, the Tartars do not carry very far their geographical studies. The west means with them simply Thibet and some adjacent countries, which they hear mentioned by the Lamas, who have made the pilgrimage to Lha-Ssa. They firmly believe that beyond Thibet there is nothing; there, say they, is the end of the world; beyond, there is merely a shoreless ocean.

When we had satisfied all the inquiries of the red button, we addressed some to him about the country of the Alechan, and the journey to Peking. "Every third year all the sovereigns of the world," said he, "repair to Peking, for the feast of the new year. Princes who live near, are bound to go thither every year; those who live at the extremities of the earth, go every second or third year, according to the distance they have to travel." "What is your purpose in going every year to Peking?" "We ourselves go as the retinue of our king; the king alone enjoys the happiness of prostrating himself in the presence of the Old Buddha (the Emperor)." He entered then into long details about the the ceremony of the first day of the year, and the relations between the Chinese Emperor and the tributary kings.

The foreign sovereigns, under the dominating influence of the China empire, repair to Peking; first, as an act of obeisance and submission; secondly, to pay certain rents to the Emperor, whose vassals they consider themselves. These rents, which are decorated with the fine name of offerings, are, in fact, imposts which no Tartar king would venture to refuse the payment of. They consist in camels, in horses remarkable for their beauty, and which the Emperor sends to augment his immense herds in the Tchakar. Every Tartar prince is, besides, obliged to bring some of the rarer productions of his country; deer, bear and goat venison; aromatic plants, pheasants, mushrooms, fish, etc. As they visit Peking in the depth of winter, all these eatables are frozen; so that they bear, without danger of being spoiled, the trial of a long journey, and even remain good long after they have arrived at their destination.

One of the Banners of the Tchakar is especially charged with sending to Peking, every year, an immense provision of pheasant's eggs. We asked the minister of the King of the Alechan, whether these pheasant's eggs were of a peculiar flavor, that they were so highly appreciated by the court. "They are not destined to be eaten," he answered; "the Old Buddha uses them for another purpose." "As they are not eaten, what are they used for?" The Tartar seemed embarrassed, and blushed somewhat as he replied that these eggs were used to make a sort of varnish, which the women of the imperial harem used for the purpose of smoothing their hair, and which communicates to it, they say, a peculiar luster and brilliancy. Europeans, perhaps, may consider this pomatum of pheasant's eggs, so highly esteemed at the Chinese court, very nasty and disgusting; but beauty and ugliness, the nice and the nasty, are, as everybody knows, altogether relative and conventional matters, upon which the various nations that inhabit this earth have ideas remotest from the uniform.

These annual visits to the Emperor of China are very expensive and extremely troublesome to the Tartars of the plebeian class, who are overwhelmed with enforced labor, at the pleasure of their masters, and are bound to provide a certain number of camels and horses, to carry the baggage of the king and the nobles. As these journeys take place in the depth of winter, the animals find little food, especially when, after leaving the Land of Grass, they enter upon the districts cultivated by the Chinese; and a great number of them, accordingly, die on the road. Hence, when the caravan returns, it is far from being in such good order and condition as when it started; it presents, one might almost say, merely the skeletons of the animals. Those which have still retained a little strength are laden with the baggage necessary on the way; the others are dragged along by the halter, scarcely able to move one leg before the other. It is a very sad, and, at the same time, singular thing, to see the Mongols walking on foot, and leading behind them horses which they dare not mount for fear of breaking them down.

As soon as the tributary kings are arrived at Peking, they repair to the interior of the city, where they inhabit a quarter especially set apart for them. They are generally two hundred in number, each of whom has his palace or inn, which he occupies, with his retinue. A Mandarin, a grand dignitary of the realm, superintends this quarter, and has it in charge to maintain peace and concord amongst these illustrious visitors. The tributes are transferred to the care of a special Mandarin, whom we may consider as steward of the household.

During their stay at Peking, these monarchs have no communication with the Emperor, no solemn audience. Some of them may perchance obtain admittance to the throne; but it is only upon affairs of the highest importance, above the jurisdiction of the ordinary ministers.

On the first day of the year, however, there is a solemn ceremony, at which these two hundred monarchs are admitted to a sort of contact with their suzerain and master, with him who, as they phrase it, sitting beneath the sky, rules the four seas and the ten thousand nations of the world by a single act of his will. According to the ritual which regulates the state proceedings of the Emperor of

China, he is bound to visit every year, on the first day of the first moon, the temple of his ancestors, and to prostrate himself before the tablet of his fathers. There is before the entrance of this temple a long avenue, wherein the tributary princes, who have come to Peking to render homage to the Emperor, assemble. They range themselves right and left of the peristyle, in three lines, each occupying the place appertaining to his dignity. They stand erect, grave, and silent. It is said to be a fine and imposing spectacle, to witness all these remote monarchs, attired in their silk robes, embroidered with gold and silver, and indicating, by the variety of their costumes, the different countries they inhabit, and the degrees of their dignity.

Meantime the Emperor issues in great pomp from his Yellow Town. He traverses the deserted and silent streets of Peking; for, when the Asiatic tyrant appears, every door must be closed, and every inhabitant of the town must, on pain of death, remain silent within his house. As soon as the Emperor has arrived at the temple of the ancestors, the heralds, who precede the procession, cry out, at the moment he places his foot on the first step of the stairs that lead to the gallery of the tributary kings: "Let all prostrate themselves, for here is the Lord of the earth." To this the two hundred tributary kings respond in unison: "Ten thousand congratulations!" And, having thus wished a happy new year to the Emperor, they all fall down with their faces towards the earth. Then passes through their ranks, the son of heaven, who enters the temple of the ancestors, and prostrates himself, in his turn, thrice before the tablet of his fathers. Whilst the Emperor is offering up his adoration to the spirits of his family, the two hundred monarchs remain prostrate on the earth, and they do not rise until the Emperor has again passed through their ranks; after this they re-enter their litters and return to their respective palaces.

And such is the entire and sole fruit of the long patience of these potentates, after leaving their distant countries, and enduring fatigues and dangers of every description, and a long journey through the desert; they have enjoyed the happiness of prostrating themselves in the path of the Emperor! Such a spectacle would with us Europeans be a matter of pity and disgust, for we could not comprehend

Grand Ceremony at the Ancestral Temple.

how there should be so much humility on one side, so much arrogance on the other. Yet it is the simplest thing in the world to Asiatic nations. The Emperor takes his all-mightiness as a grave matter of course; and the Tartar kings think themselves happy and honored in paying homage to it.

The prime minister of the king of the Alechan told us that a sight of the Emperor is not easily obtained. One year, when his master was ill, he was obliged to take his place at Peking, in the ceremony of the temple of the ancestors, and he then hoped to see the Old Buddha, on his way down the peristyle, but he was altogether mistaken in his expectation. As minister, the mere representative of his monarch, he was placed on the third file, so that, when the Emperor passed, he saw absolutely nothing at all. "Those who are in the first line," he said, "if they are cautiously dexterous, may manage to get a glimpse of the yellow robe of the son of heaven; but they must take heed not to lift up their heads, for such an audacity would be considered a great crime, and be punished very severely."

All the Tartar princes are pensioned by the Emperor; the sum allotted to them is a small matter, but it effects a considerable political result. The Tartar princes, in receiving their pay, consider themselves the slaves, or at least, as the servants of him who pays them; and concede, in consequence, to the Emperor the right of requiring their submission and obedience. It is about the first day of the year that the tributary sovereigns receive, at Peking, the allotted pension, which is distributed by some of the great Mandarins, who are said, by slanderous tongues, to speculate in this lucrative employment, and never fail to make enormous profits at the expense of the poor Tartars.

The minister of the king of the Alechan related, for our edification, that in a particular year, all the tributary princes received their pension in ingots of gilt copper. All found it out at once, but were fain to keep silence, afraid to make public an affair that might result in a catastrophe, compromising, not only the highest dignitaries of the empire, but the Tartar kings themselves. As, in fact, the latter were supposed to receive their money from the hands of the Emperor himself, a complaint would, in some sort, have been to charge the Old Buddha, the son of heaven, with being a coiner. They received accordingly their copper ingots with a prostration, and it was not until they returned into their own countries, that they declared, not indeed that they had been cheated, but that the Mandarins, charged with distributing the money, had been the dupes of the Peking bankers. The Tartar Mandarin who related the adventure, gave us completely to understand that neither the Emperor, nor the courtiers, nor the Mandarins, had anything to do with the affair. We took good care not to undeceive him; as to us, who had no great faith in the probity of the government of Peking, we were convinced that the Emperor had regularly swindled the Tartar kings. We were confirmed in this opinion by the fact that the period of this adventure coincided with the British war; when, as we knew, the Emperor was in the last extremity, and knew not where to get the money necessary to keep from starving the handful of soldiers who were charged with the preservation of the integrity of the Chinese territory.

The visit of the three Mandarins of the Alechan was not

only pleasant on account of the narrative they gave us of the relations of the Tartar kings with the Emperor, but it was of essential utility to us. When they understood that we were directing our steps towards the West, they asked us whether we intended passing through the district of the Alechan. On our answering in the affirmative, they dissuaded us from the project; they told us that our animals would perish there, for not a single pasturage was to be met with. We already knew that the Alechan is a tract still more barren than the Ortous. It consists, in fact, of chains of lofty mountains of sand, where you may travel sometimes for whole days together, without seeing a single blade of vegetation. Some narrow valleys, here and there, alone offer to the flocks a few thorny and wretched plants. On this account the Alechan is very thinly inhabited, even in comparison with the other parts of Mongolia.

The Mandarins told us that this year the drought which had been general throughout Tartary had rendered the district of the Alechan almost uninhabitable. They assured us that at least one-third of the flocks had perished of hunger and thirst, and that the remainder were in a wretched state. For their journey to Peking, they had, they said, chosen the best they could find in the country; and we might have observed that the animals of the caravan were very different indeed from those we had seen in Tchakar. The drought, the want of water and pastures, the destruction of the flocks—all this had given birth to an utter state of misery, whence, again, numerous bands of robbers who were ravaging the country, and robbing travelers. They assured us that, being so few in number, it would not be wise for us to enter upon the Alechan mountains, particularly in the absence of the principal authorities.

On receiving this information, we resolved not to retrace our steps, for we were too far advanced, but to diverge a little from our route. The night was far advanced ere we thought of taking rest; we had scarcely slept a few minutes, in fact, when the day broke. The Tartars saddled their steeds, and after having wished us peace and happiness, dashed off at full gallop, to overtake the great caravan which preceded them.

As for us, before setting out, we unrolled the excellent map of the Chinese Empire, published by M. Andriveau-

Goujon, and sought upon it to what point we ought to direct our steps, so as to avoid the wretched district of the Alechan, without, however, deviating too much from our route. After looking at the map, we saw no other way than to recross the Yellow River, to pass the Great Wall of China, and to travel across the Chinese province of Kan-Sou, until we arrived among the Tartars of the Koukou-Noor. Formerly this determination would have made us tremble. Accustomed as we had been to live privately in our Chinese christendom, it would have seemed to us impossible to enter the Chinese empire alone, and without the care of a catechist. At that time it would have seemed to us clear as the day, that our strangulation, and the persecution of all the Chinese missions, would have been the certain result of our rash undertaking. Such would have been our fears formerly, but the time of our fear was gone. Indurated by our two months' journey, we had come to the persuasion that we might travel in China with as much safety as in Tartary. The stay that we had already made in several large commercial towns, compelled as we had been to manage our own affairs, had rendered the Chinese manners and customs more familiar to us. The language presented to us no difficulties; besides being able to speak the Tartar idiom, we were familiar with the colloquial phrases of the Chinese, a very difficult attainment to those who reside in the missions, because the Christians there seek to flatter them by only employing, in the presence of the missionaries, the short vocabulary of words that they have studied in books. Besides these purely moral and intellectual advantages, our long journey had been useful in a physical point of view; the rain, the wind, and the sun, which had during two months raged against our European tint, had in the end embrowned and tanned it so, that we looked quite like wild men of the wood in this respect. The fear of being recognized by the Chinese now no longer troubled us.

We told Samdadchiemba that we should cease, in a few days, to travel in the Land of Grass, and that we should continue our route through the Chinese empire. "Travel among the Chinese!" said the Dchiahour; "very well. There are good inns there. They boil good tea there. When it rains, you can go under shelter. During the night, you are not disturbed by the blowing of the north wind.

But in China, there are ten thousand roads; which shall we take? Do we know which is the best?" We made him look at the map, pointing out all the places which we should have to pass before we reached Koukou-Noor. We even reduced, for his edification, into lis, all the distances from one town to the other. Samdadchiemba looked at our small geographical chart with perfect enthusiasm. "Oh," said he, "how sincerely I regret that I did not study while I was in the Lamasery; if I had listened to my master, if I had paid more attention, I might perhaps now understand the description of the world, that is here drawn on this piece of paper. With this, one can go everywhere, without asking the way. Is it not so?" "Yes, everywhere," answered we; "even to your own family." "How is that? is my country also written down here?" and as he spoke he bent over the chart, so as entirely to cover it with his huge frame. "Stand aside and we will show you your country. Look; do you see this little space beside that green line? That is the country of the Dchiahours, which the Chinese call the Three Valleys (San-Tchouen). Your village must be here; we shall pass not more than two days' journey from your house." "Is it possible?" cried he, striking his forehead; "shall we pass two days' journey from my house? Do you say so? How can that be? Not more than two days' journey! In that case, when we are near it, I will ask my spiritual fathers' permission to go and see once more my country." "What can you have to do now in the Three Valleys?" "I will go and see what is doing there. It is eighteen years since my departure from my house. I will go and see if my old mother is still there; and if she is alive, I will make her enter into the Holy Church. As for my two brothers, who knows whether they will have enough sense not to believe any longer in the transmigrations of Buddha. Ah, yes," added he after a short pause, "I will make a little tea, and we will talk this matter over again."

Samdadchiemba was no longer with us; his thoughts had flown to his native land. We were obliged to remind him of his real position,—"Samdadchiemba, you need not make any tea; and just now, instead of talking, we must fold up our tent, load the camels, and proceed on our way. Look; the sun is already high in the heavens: if we do not get on, we shall never reach the Three Valleys." "True," cried he ; and springing up he set himself busily about making preparations for our departure.

On resuming our route, we abandoned the direction towards the west, which we had strictly followed during our journey, and diverged a little to the south. After having continued our march for half the day, we sat down for a while under a rock to take our repast. As usual, we dined on bread and water ; and what bread and water ! Dough half baked, and brackish water, which we had to draw up with the sweat of our brow, and to carry about with us during our journey.

Towards the conclusion of our repast, while we were trying to scrape together a few grains of tobacco in our snuff phials, by way of dessert, we saw coming towards us a Tartar on a camel ; he seated himself beside us. After having wished each other peace, we let him smell at our empty snuff phial, and then offered him a little loaf baked in the ashes. In an instant he had swallowed the bread, and taken three sniffs of snuff.

We questioned him about the route ; he told us that if we followed the same direction we should arrive in two days at the Yellow River, on crossing which, we should enter the Chinese territory. This information gave us great satisfaction, for it perfectly agreed with our map. We asked him if water was far off. " Yes," answered he, " the wells are distant. If you encamp again to-day, you will find a cistern on the way ; but there is little water, and that is very bad. Formerly it was an excellent well, but it is now abandoned, for a tchutgour (demon) has corrupted its waters."

This information induced us to proceed at once, for we had no time to lose, if we desired to arrive before night. The Mongol mounted his camel, which bounded across the desert, while our little caravan continued slowly its uniform and monotonous march.

Before sunset, we arrived at the indicated cistern, when we pitched our tent, as there was no hope of finding further on better water ; besides, we fancied the cistern might perhaps turn out less diabolical than the Tartar had pretended it to be.

While we were lighting the fire, the Dchiahour went to draw water ; he returned in a few moments, saying that it was unfit to be drunk ; that it was mere poison. He brought a basin full with him, that we might taste it and judge for ourselves.

The stench of this dirty, muddy water was, indeed, intolerable; and on the surface of the nauseous stuff, we saw floating ; a sort of oily drop, which infinitely increased our disgust. We had not the courage to raise it to our lips; we were satisfied with its sight, and, above all, with its smell.

Still we must either drink or die with thirst; we accordingly resolved to make the best we could of this Cistern of the Devil, as it is called by the Tartars. We collected roots, which were growing abundantly around it, half buried in the sand ; a few moments' labor supplied us with an ample provision of them. Then, first of all, we made some charcoal which we broke into small pieces; next we filled our kettle with the muddy, stinking water, placed it upon the fire, and when the water boiled, threw in a quantity of the charcoal.

While we were engaged upon this chemical operation, Samdadchiemba, seated beside the kettle, kept every moment asking us what sort of soup we intended to make with all those detestable ingredients. We gave him, by way of reply, a complete dissertation upon the discoloring and disinfecting properties of charcoal. He listened to our scientific statement with patience, but appeared in no degree convinced by it. His eyes were fixed upon the kettle, and it was easy to see, from the skeptical expression of his features, that he had no sort of expectation or idea that the thick water bubbling in the kettle could at all become a clear and limpid fluid.

By and by, we poured out the liquid thus prepared, and filtered it through an impromptu linen sieve. The water realized was not, indeed, delicious, but it was drinkable, having deposited all its salt and all its ill odor. We had more than once, on our journey, used water in no degree superior.

Samdadchiemba was perfectly intoxicated with enthusiasm. Had he not been a Christian, he would assuredly have taken us for living Buddhas. "The Lamas," said he, "pretend they have all knowledge and all power in their prayer-books; but I am certain they would have died of thirst, or been poisoned, had they only had the water of this cistern to make tea with. They have no more notion than a sheep how to render this bad water good." And then he overwhelmed us with all sorts of odd questions about the natural properties of things. In relation to the purification of water which we had just operated, he asked whether by rubbing his face hard with the charcoal, he could make it as white as ours; but then, when his eyes turned to his hands, still black with the charcoal he had just broken up, he himself laughed immensely at the idea he had propounded.

Night had set in before we had completed the distillation of the water we required. We then made abundance of tea, and the evening was occupied in drinking it. We contented ourselves with infusing a few pinches of oatmeal in the tea, for the ardent thirst which devoured us absorbed all desire to eat. After having deluged our inward man, we sought repose.

We had scarcely, however, stretched ourselves on the turf, when an extraordinary and altogether unexpected noise threw us into a state of stupor. It was a long, lugubrious, deep cry that seemed approaching our tent. We had heard the howl of wolves, the roar of tigers and of bears; but these in no way resembled the sound which now affrighted our ears. It was something like the bellowing of a bull, but crossed with tones so strange and unintelligible, that we were utterly panic-stricken. And we were all the more surprised and confounded, because everybody had assured us that there were no wild beasts of any kind in the whole Ortous country.

Our embarrassment was becoming serious. We were in fear not only for our animals, which were tied round the tent, but also on our own account. As the noise did not cease, but, on the contrary, seemed to approach nearer and nearer, we got up, not indeed, to go forth in search of the villainous beast that was thus disturbing our repose, but in order to try to frighten it. To this intent all three of us set to work, shouting at the pitch of our lungs; then we stopped and so did the beast. After a moment's silence, the roaring was heard once more, but at a considerable distance. We conjectured that in our turn we had frightened the animal, and this somewhat reassured us.

The cries once more approaching, we piled up some brushwood at a few paces from the tent, and made a bonfire. The light, instead of deterring the unknown monster, seemed rather to attract it; and before long, by the flame of the brushwood, we could distinguish the outline of what appeared to be a great quadruped, of reddish hue, the aspect of which, however, as near as we could judge, was by no means so ferocious as its voice. We ventured to advance towards it, but as we advanced, it retreated. Samdadchiemba, whose eyes were very sharp, and accustomed to the desert, assured us that the creature was either a dog or a stray calf.

Our animals were, at the very least, as absorbed with the subject as ourselves. The horse and the mule pointed their ears, and dug up the earth with their hoofs, while the camels, with outstretched necks and glaring eyes, did not for an instant remove their gaze from the spot whence these wild cries issued.

In order to ascertain precisely with what creature we had to do, we diluted a handful of meal in a wooden dish, and placing this at the entrance of the tent, withdrew inside. Soon we saw the animal slowly advance, then stop, then advance again. At last it came to the dish, and with the most remarkable rapidity, lapped up the supper we had prepared for it. We now saw that it was a dog of immense size. After having thoroughly licked and polished the empty dish, it lay down, without ceremony, at the entrance of the tent; and we forthwith followed its example, glad to have found a protector in the apprehended foe.

Next morning, upon awaking, we were able to examine at leisure the dog which, after having so alarmed us, had so unreservedly attached itself to us. Its color was red, its size immense; its excessive meagerness showed that it had been wandering about homeless for some time past. A dislocated leg, which it dragged along the ground, communicated to it a sort of swinging motion, which added to its formidable effect. But it was especially alarming when it sent forth its loud fierce voice. Whenever we heard it, we instinctively looked at the animal whence it proceeded, to see whether it really belonged to the canine race.

We resumed our route, and the new Arsalan accompanied us, its general position being a few paces in advance of the caravan, as though to show us the way, with which it appeared to be tolerably familiar.

After two days' journey we reached the foot of a chain of mountains, the summits of which were lost in the clouds.

We set about ascending them, however, courageously, for we hoped that beyond them we should find the Yellow River. That day's journey was very painful, especially to the camels, for every step was upon sharp, rugged rock; and their feet, accordingly, were very speedily bleeding. We ourselves, were too absorbed with the strange, fantastic aspect of the mountains we were traversing to think of the toil they occasioned us.

In the hollows and chasms of the precipices formed by these lofty mountains, you see nothing but great heaps of mica and laminated stones, broken, bruised, and in some cases absolutely pulverized. This wreck of slate and schist must have been brought into these abysses by some deluge, for it in no way belongs to the mountains themselves, which are of granite. As you approach the summits the mountains assume forms more and more fantastic. You see great heaps of rock piled one upon the other, and apparently cemented together. These rocks are almost entirely encrusted with shells and the remains of a plant resembling seaweed; but that which is most remarkable is that these granitic masses are cut and torn and worn in every direction, presenting a ramification of holes and cavities, meandering in a thousand complicated turns and twists, so that you might imagine all the upper portion of each mountain to have been subjected to the slow and destructive action of immense worms. Sometimes in the granite you find deep impressions, that seem the molds of monsters, whose forms they still closely retain.

As we gazed upon all these phenomena, it seemed to us that we were traveling in the bed of some exhausted ocean. Everything tended to the belief that these mountains had undergone the gradual action of the sea. It is impossible to attribute all you see there to the influence of mere rain, or still less to the inundations of the Yellow River, which, however prodigeous they may be, can never have attained so great an elevation. The geologists who affirm that the deluge took place by sinking, and not by a depolarization of the earth, might probably find in these mountains good argument in favor of their system.

On reaching the crest of these mountains we saw beneath us the Yellow River, rolling its waves majestically from south to north. It was now near noon, and we hoped that same evening to pass the river, and sleep in one of the inns of the little town of Che-Tsui-Dze, which we perceived on the slope of a hill beyond the river.

We occupied the whole afternoon in descending the rugged mountain, selecting as we went, the places right and left that seemed more practicable than the rest. At length we arrived, and before nightfall, on the banks of the Yellow River, our passage across which was most successfully effected. In the first place, the Mongol Tartars who rented the ferry oppressed our purse less direfully than the Chinese ferrymen had done. Next, the animals got into the boat without any difficulty. The only grievance was that we had to leave our lame dog on the bank, for the Mongols would not admit it on any terms, insisting upon the rule that all dogs must swim across the river, the boat being destined solely for men, or for animals that cannot swim. We were fain to submit to the prejudice.

On the other side of the Yellow River we found ourselves in China, and bade adieu for awhile to Tartary, to the desert, and to the nomadic life.

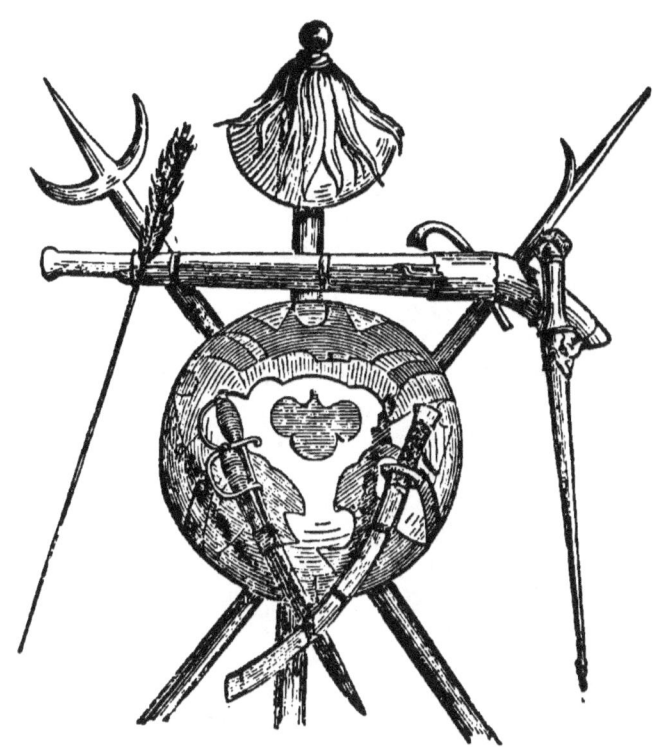

Chinese and Tartar Arms.

CHAPTER XI.

Sketch of the Tartar Nations.

The Tartars, descended from the ancient Scythians, have preserved to this day the dexterity of their ancestors in archery and horsemanship. The early part of their history is veiled in obscurity, enveloped as they are by the wonders and prodigies of the exploits of their first conqueror, Okhous-Han, who seems to be the Madyes of Herodotus. This illustrious leader of the Scythian hordes carried his arms into Syria, and reached even the confines of Egypt.

The Chinese annals frequently mention certain nomad tribes, which they call Hioung-Nou, and which are no other than the Huns. These wandering and warlike tribes gradually extended themselves, and finished by covering the immense deserts of Tartary from east to west. Thenceforward they made continual incursions on their neighbors, and on several occasions made attacks on the frontiers of the empire. It was on such an occasion that Thisin-Chi-Hoang-Ti had the Great Wall built in the year 213 B. C. About 134 B. C. the Huns, under the conduct of Lao-Chan, their emperor, made an attack on the Tartars Youei-Tchi (the Getæ), who dwelt on the confines of the province of Chen-Si. After a series of long and terrible conflicts, Lao-Chan defeated them, slew their chief, and made of his head a drinking cup, which he wore suspended from his girdle. The Getæ did not choose to submit to the victors, and preferred going elsewhere in search of another country. They divided into two principal bands. One advanced towards the northwest, and took possession of the plains situated upon the banks of the river Ili, beyond the glaciers of the Moussour mountains; this is that part of Tartary which is now called the Tourgout. The other division marched southwards, associated with it in its course several other tribes, and reached the regions watered by the Indus. There it laid waste the kingdom founded by the successors of Alexander, strove for some time against the Parthians, and finished by establishing itself in Bactriana. The Greeks call these Tartar tribes Indo-Scythians.

Meanwhile divisions arose among the Huns; and the Chinese, ever politic and cunning, took advantage of this circumstance to enfeeble them. Towards the year 48 of our era, the Tartar empire was divided into northern and southern. Under the dynasty of Han, the Northern Huns were completely defeated by the Chinese armies. They were obliged to abandon the regions wherein they had settled, and proceeded in large numbers towards the west, to the borders of the Caspian Sea; here they spread themselves over the countries watered by the Volga, and round the Palus Mæotis.

They commenced in 376 their formidable irruptions upon the Roman empire. They began by subduing the territory of the Alani, a nomad and pastoral people like themselves; some of these sought refuge in the Circassian mountains, others migrated further west, and finally settled on the shores of the Danube. Later, they drove before them the Suevi, the Goths, the Gepidæ, and the Vandals, and with these advanced to ravage Germany, in the beginning of the fifth century. These large hordes of barbarians resembling waves, one driven on by the other, thus formed, in their destructive course, a fearful torrent, which finally inundated Europe.

The Southern Huns, who had remained in Tartary, were for a long time weakened by the dispersion of their northern countrymen; but they recovered by insensible degrees, and again became terrible to the Chinese: though they did not acquire a political and historical importance till the time of the famous Tchinggiskhan, towards the close of the twelfth century.

The power of the Tartars, long confined within the desert steppes of Mongolia, broke at length its bonds, and innumerable armies might be seen descending from the lofty table-lands of Central Asia, and precipitating themselves with fury on horrified nations. Tchinggiskhan carried pillage and death even to the most remote regions. China, Tartary, India, Persia, Syria, Muscovy, Poland, Hungary, Austria—all these countries successively felt the terrible blows of the victorious Tartar. France, Italy, and the other regions further west, escaped with their fear.

In the year 1260 of our era, Khan-Khoubilai, grandson of Tchinggis, who had commenced the conquest of China, succeeded in subduing that vast empire. It was the first time that it had passed under the yoke of foreigners. Khoubilai died at Peking in the year 1294, aged eighty. His empire was, without dispute, the largest that had ever existed. Chinese geographers state that, under the Mongol dynasty of the Youen, the empire northwards went beyond the In-Chan mountains; westwards it extended beyond the Gobi or sandy desert; to the east, it was terminated by the countries situated on the left of the river Siao; and in the southern direction it reached the shores of the Youé Sea. It is obvious that this description does not include the countries tributary to the empire. Thibet, Turkestan, Muscovy, Siam, Cochin China, Tonking, and Corea, acknowledged the supremacy of the Grand Khan of the Tartars, and faithfully paid him tribute. Even European nations were, from time to time, insolently summoned to acknowledge the Mongol supremacy. Haughty and threatening letters were sent to the Pope, to the King of France, to the Emperor, commanding them to send as tribute the revenues of their states to the depths of Tartary. The descendants of Tchinggiskhan, who reigned in Muscovy, Persia, Bactriana, and Sogdiana, received investiture from the Emperor of Peking, and undertook nothing of importance without first giving him notice. The diplomatic papers which the King of Persia sent, in the thirteenth century, to Philip the Fair, are a proof of this dependence. On these precious monuments, which are preserved to this day in the archives of France, are seals in Chinese characters, which testify the supremacy of the Grand Khan of Peking over the sovereigns of Persia.

The conquests of Tchinggiskhan and of his successors; and, in later times, those of Tamerlan or Timour, which transferred the seat of the Mongol empire to Samarcand, contributed, in as great, and perhaps a greater degree than the Crusades, to renew the intercourse of Europe with the most distant states of the East, and favored the discoveries which have been so useful to the progress of the arts, of the sciences, and of navigation.

On this subject, we will quote in this place, an interesting passage from the Memoirs which M. Abel Rémusat published in 1824, on the political relations of the Christian princes, and particularly of the Kings of France with the Mongol Emperors:—

"The lieutenants of Tchinggiskhan, and of his first successors, on arriving in Western Asia, did not seek at first, to contract any alliance there. The princes, whose domains they entered, silently permitted the impost of a tribute; the rest were required to submit. The Georgians and Armenians were among the first. The Franks of Syria, the Kings of Hungary, the Emperor himself, had to repel their insolent demands. The Pope was not exempted, by the supremacy he enjoyed in relation to the other Christian princes; nor the King of France, by the high renown he enjoyed throughout the East. The terror which the Tartars inspired, precluded a fitting answer to their demands. The course resorted to was conciliation, the seeking their alliance, and the endeavoring to rouse them against the Moslems. The latter attempt would scarcely have been successful, had not the Christians in the East, who, by adhesion as vassals, had obtained credit at the courts of their generals and their princes, zealously employed themselves in the matter. The Mongols were induced at last to undertake war against the Sultan of

Egypt. Such were the relations with this nation during the first period, which lasted from 1224 to 1262.

"In the second period, the Khalifat was destroyed; a Mongol principality was founded in Persia: it bordered on the states of the Sultan of Egypt. A sanguinary rivalry arose between the two countries, which the Eastern Christians did all in their power to irritate. The Mongol empire was divided. Those of Persia had need of auxiliaries, which their Armenian vassals procured for them: these auxiliaries were the Franks. From this time, their power declined more and more; and ere long it was annihilated. Fresh crusades might restore it. The Mongols excited these in the West. They joined their exhortations to those of the Georgians, Armenians, of the wreck of the crusaders, who had taken refuge in Cyprus, and to those of the sovereign pontiffs. The first Tartars had commenced by threats; the last came to offers, and even descended to supplications. Twenty ambassadors were sent by them to Italy, France, and England; and it was no fault of theirs that the fire of the holy wars was not rekindled, and extended over Europe and Asia. These diplomatic attempts, the recital of which forms, so to speak, an epilogue to the transmarine expeditions, scarcely noticed by those who have written their history, and, indeed, unknown to most of them, would deserve perhaps, our fixed attention. We should have to collect facts, resolve difficulties, and place in a clear point of view the political system to which the negotiations with the Tartars belong. Specialties of this class could not be appreciated, whilst they were considered isolately, and without examining them one with another. We might doubt, with Voltaire and De Guignes, that a king of the Tartars had met Saint Louis with offers of service. This fact might seem not tenable, and its recital paradoxical. Yet such skepticism would be unreasonable, after we had seen that the Mongols had acted upon that principle for fifty years; and when we are assured, by reading contemporary writings, and by the inspection of original monuments, that this conduct was natural on their part, that it entered into their views, that it conformed to their interests, and that it is explained by the common rules of reason and policy.

"The series of events which are connected with these negotiations serves to complete the history of the Crusades;

but the part they may have had in the great moral revolution, which soon followed the relations they occasioned between people hitherto unknown to each other, are facts of an importance more general and still more worthy of our particular attention. Two systems of civilization had become established at the two extremities of the ancient continent, as the effect of independent causes, without communication, and consequently without mutual influence. All at once the events of war and political combinations bring into contact these two great bodies, long strangers to each other. The formal interviews of ambassadors are not the only occasions which brought them together. Other occasions more private, but also more efficacious, were established by imperceptible, but innumerable ramifications, by the travels of a host of individuals, attracted to the two extremities of the earth, with commercial views, in the train of ambassadors or armies. The irruption of the Mongols, by throwing everything into agitation, neutralized distance, filled up intervals, and brought the nations together; the events of war transported millions of individuals to an immense distance from the places where they were born. History has recorded the voyages of kings, of ambassadors, of missionaries. Sempad, the Orbelian; Hayton, King of Armenia; the two Davids, Kings of Georgia; and several others were led by political motives to the depths of Asia. Yeroslaf, Grand Duke of Sousdal and vassal of the Mongols, like the other Russian princes, came to Kara-Koroum, where he died of poison, it was said, administered by the Empress herself, the mother of the Emperor Gayouk. Many monks, Italians, French, Flemings, were charged with diplomatic missions to the Grand Khan. Mongols of distinction came to Rome, Barcelona, Valencia, Lyons, Paris, London, Northampton; and a Franciscan of the kingdom of Naples was Archbishop of Peking. His successor was a professor of theology of the Faculty of Paris. But how many others, less celebrated, were led in the train of those men, either as slaves, or impelled by the desire of gain, or by curiosity, to countries hitherto unexplored. Chance has preserved the names of a few. The first envoy who came on the part of the Tartars to the King of Hungary was an Englishman, banished from his country for certain crimes, and who, after having wandered throughout Asia, had finally taken service among the

Mongols. A Flemish Cordelier met in the depth of Tartary a woman of Metz, named Paquette, who had been carried away from Hungary, a Parisian goldsmith whose brother was established in Paris on the Grand Pont, and a young man from the environs of Rouen, who had been present at the capture of Belgrade; he saw there also Russians, Hungarians, and Flemings. A singer, named Robert, after traveling through the whole of Eastern Asia, returned to find a grave in the Cathedral of Chartres. A Tartar was a helmet-maker in the armies of Philip the Fair. Jean de Plan-Carpin met near Gayouk, with a Russian gentleman, whom he calls Temer, who served as interpreter. Several merchants of Breslau, Poland, and Austria, accompanied him in his journey to Tartary; others returned with him through Russia; these were Genoese, Pisans, and two merchants of Venice whom chance had brought to Bokhara. They were induced to go in the suite of a Mongol ambassador, whom Houlagou had sent to Khoubilai. They sojourned several years in China and Tartary, took letters from the Grand Khan to the Pope, and returned to the Grand Khan, bringing with them the son of one of their number, the celebrated Marco-Polo, and quitted once more the Court of Khoubilai to return to Venice. Travels of this kind were not less frequent in the succeeding age. Of this number are those of John de Mandeville, an English physician; of Oderic of Friuli; of Pegoletti; of Guillaume de Boutdeselle, and several others. We may be certain that the journeys which have been recorded are but a small portion of those which were performed, and that there were at that period more people able to make a long journey than to write an account of it. Many of these adventurers must have established themselves and died in the countries they went to visit. Others returned to their country as obscure as when they left it; but with their imaginations full of what they had seen, relating it all to their families and friends, and doubtless with exaggerations; but leaving around them, amidst ridiculous fables, a few useful recollections and traditions productive of advantage. Thus were sown in Germany, in Italy, in France, in the monasteries, among the nobility, and even in the lowest grades of society, precious seeds destined to bud at a later period. All these obscure travelers, carrying the arts of their native country to distant lands, brought back other information about these no less precious, and thus effected, unconsciously, exchanges more productive of good than all those of commerce. By this means not merely the traffic in silks, in porcelains, in commodities from Hindostan, was made more extensive and more practicable, opening new routes to industry and commerce; but, that which was far more valuable, foreign manners and customs of before unknown nations, extraordinary productions, were presented to the European mind, confined, since the fall of the Roman empire, within too narrow a circle. Men began to have an idea that, after all, there was something worthy of notice in the finest, the most populous and the most anciently civilized of the four quarters of the world. People began to think of studying the arts, the religions, the languages of the nations who inhabited it, and there was even a proposition to establish a professorship of the Tartar language in the University of Paris. Romantic narratives, reduced by discussion within reasonable proportions, diffused in all directions juster and more varied information: the world seemed opening towards the East. Geography made immense strides, and ardor of discovery become the new form assumed by the adventurous spirit of Europeans. The idea of another hemisphere ceased, as soon as our own became better known, to present itself to the mind as a paradox destitute of all probability, and it was in going in search of the Zipangri of Marco-Polo that Christopher Columbus discovered the New World.

"I should make too great a digression, were I to investigate what were in the East the effects of the Mongol irruption, the destruction of the Khalifat, the extermination of the Bulgarians, of the Komans, and other northern nations. The decline of the population of Upper Asia, so favorable to the reaction by which the Russians, hitherto the vassals of the Tartars, subdued in their turn all the nomads of the North; the submission of China to a foreign yoke; the definitive establishment of the Indian religion in Thibet and Tartary; all these events deserve to be studied in detail. I will not even pause to inquire what might have been the results, to the nations of Eastern Asia, of the intercourse which they had with the West. The introduction of the Indian numerals into China, a knowledge of the astronomical system of the Moslems, the translation of the New Testament and the Psalms into the Mongol language, executed by the Latin Archbishop of *Khan Balik* (Peking), the foundation of the lamanical hierarchy, framed in imitation of the pontifical court, and produced by the fusion effected between the remnants of the Nestorianism established in Tartary and the dogmas of the Buddhists; such were all the innovations of which there are any traces in Eastern Asia, and therewith the commerce of the Franks has very little to do. The Asiatics are punished for their contempt of the knowledge of Europeans, by the limited results which that very scorn enables them to derive from it. To confine myself to what concerns the people of the West, and to attempt to justify what I said at the commencement of this Memoir, that the effects of the communications with the nations of Upper Asia, in the thirteenth century, had contributed indirectly to the progress of European civilization, I will conclude with a reflection, which I shall offer with the more confidence, that it is not entirely new, while, at the same time, the facts we have just investigated seem calculated to give it a sanction it had not before.

"Before the establishment of the intercourse which, first the Crusades, and then, later, the irruption of the Mongols, caused to spring up between the nations of the East and those of the West, the greater part of those inventions, which distinguished the close of the middle ages, had been known to the Asiatics for centuries. The polarity of the loadstone had been discovered and put into operation in China from the remotest antiquity. Gunpowder had been as long known to the Hindoos and the Chinese, the latter of whom had, in the tenth century, 'thunder carriages,' which seem to have been cannon. It is difficult to account in any other way for the fire-stone throwers, which are so often mentioned in the history of the Mongols. Houlagou, when he set out for Persia, had in his army a body of Chinese artillerymen. Again, the first edition of the classic books engraved on wooden boards is dated in the year 952. The institution of bank-notes, and of banking and exchange offices, took place among the Jou-Tchen in 1154. Banknotes were adopted by the Mongols established in China; they were known to the Persians by the same name as the Chinese give them, and Josaphat Barbaro was informed in 1450 by an intelligent Tartar whom he met at Asof, and who had been on an embassy to China, that this sort of money was printed in China every year *con nuova stampa;* and this expression is remarkable enough, considering the time when Barbaro made this observation. Lastly, playing cards—into the origin of which so many learned antiquarians would not have busied themselves to inquire, were it not that it marked one of the first applications of the art of engraving on wood—were invented in China in the year 1120.

"There are, besides, in the commencement of each of these inventions, particular features which seem calculated to show their origin. I will not speak of the compass, the ancient use of which, in China, Hager seems to me successfully to have demonstrated, and which passed into Europe by means of the Crusades, previous to the irruption of the Mongols, as the famous passage in Jacques de Vitry, and some others, prove. But the oldest playing cards, those used in the *jeu de tarots*, have a marked analogy in their form, their designs, their size, their number, with the cards which the Chinese made use of. Cannons were the first fire-arms made use of in Europe; they are also, it would appear, the only fire-arms with which the Chinese were acquainted at this period. The question as to paper money appears to have been viewed in its true light by M. Langles, and after him by Hager. The first boards made use of to print upon were made of wood and stereotyped, like those of the Chinese; and nothing is more natural than to suppose that some book from China gave the idea. This would not be more surprising than the fragment of the Bible, in Gothic characters, which Father Martini discovered in the house of a Chinese at Tchang-Tcheou-Fou. We have the instance of another usage, which evidently followed the same route—it is that of the Souan-Pan, or arithmetical machine of the Chinese, which was, doubtless, introduced into Europe by the Tartars of the army of Batou, and which has so extensively pervaded Russia and Poland, that women who cannot read use nothing else in the settlement of their household accounts, and their little commercial dealings. The conjecture which gives a Chinese origin to the primitive idea of European typography is so natural, that it was propounded before there was any opportunity for collecting together all the circumstances which make it so probable.

It is the idea of Paulo Jovio, and of Mendoça, who imagine that a Chinese book may have been brought into Europe before the arrival of the Portuguese in the Indies, by the medium of the Scythians and Muscovites. It was developed by an anonymous Englishman; and carefully putting aside from the consideration the impression in movable types, which is, no doubt, an invention peculiar to the Europeans, one cannot conceive any sound objection to an hypothesis which bears so strongly the stamp of probability. But this supposition acquires a still greater degree of probability when we apply it to the totality of the discoveries in question. All were made in Eastern Asia; all were unheard-of in the West. Communication took place: it was continued for a century and a-half, and ere another century had elapsed, all these inventions were known in Europe. Their origin is veiled in obscurity. The region where they manifested themselves, the men who produced them, are equally a subject of doubt. Enlightened countries were not their theater. It was not learned men who were their authors; it was common men, obscure artisans, who lighted up, one after another, these unexpected flames. Nothing can better demonstrate the effects of a communication; nothing can be more in accordance with what we have said above as to those invisible channels, those imperceptible ramifications, whereby the science of the Eastern nations penetrated into Europe. The greater part of these inventions appear at first in the state of infancy in which the Asiatics have left them; and this circumstance alone, almost prevents our having any doubt as to their origin. Some are immediately put in practice; others remain for some time enveloped in obscurity, which conceals from us their progress, and they are taken, on their appearance, for new discoveries; all are soon brought to perfection, and, as it were, fecundated by the genius of Europeans, operating in concert, communicate to human intelligence the greatest impulse known in history. Thus, by this shock of nations, the darkness of the middle age was dispersed. Calamities, which at first aspect seemed merely destined to afflict mankind, served to arouse it from the lethargy in which it had remained for ages; and the subversion of twenty empires was the price at which Providence accorded to Europe the light of modern civilization."

The Mongol dynasty of the Youen occupied the empire

for a century. After having shone with a brilliancy, the reflection of which spread over the most remote regions, it ended with Chun-Ti, a feeble prince, more mindful of frivolous amusements than of the great inheritance which had been left by his ancestors. The Chinese regained their independence; and Tchou-Youen-Tchang, the son of a laborer, and for some time a servant in a convent of bonzes, was the founder of the celebrated dynasty of the Ming. They ascended the imperial throne in 1368, and reigned in the name of Houng-Wou.

The Tartars were massacred in great numbers in the interior of China, and the rest were driven back to their old country. The Emperor Young-Lo pursued them three several times beyond the desert, more than 200 leagues north of the Great Wall, in order to exterminate them. He could not, however, effect this object, and, dying on his return from his third expedition, his successors left the Tartars in peace beyond the desert, whence they diffused themselves right and left. The principal chiefs of the blood of Tchinggiskhan occupied, each with his people, a particular district, and gave birth to various tribes, which all formed so many petty kingdoms.

These fallen princes, ever tormented by the recollection of their ancient power, appeared several times on the frontiers of the empire, and did not cease to disquiet the Chinese princes, without, however, succeeding in their attempts at invasion.

Towards the commencement of the seventeenth century, the Mantchou Tartars having made themselves masters of China, the Mongols gradually submitted to them, and placed themselves under their sovereignty. The Oelets, a Mongol tribe, deriving their name from Oloutai, a celebrated warrior in the fourteenth century, made frequent irruptions into the country of the Khalkhas, and a sanguinary war arose between these two people. The Emperor Khang-Hi, under the pretense of conciliating them, intervened in their quarrel, put an end to the war by subjecting both parties, and extended his domination in Tartary to the frontiers of Russia; the three Khans of the Khalkhas came to make their submission to the Mantchou Emperor, who convoked a grand meeting near Tolon-Noor. Each Khan presented to him eight white horses, and one white camel; from which circumstance this tribute was called, in the Mongol language *Yousoun-Dchayan* (the nine white) ; it was agreed that they should bring every year a similar present.

At the present time the Tartar nations, more or less subject to the sway of the Mantchou emperors, are no longer what they were in the time of Tchinggiskhan and Timour. Since that epoch Tartary has been disorganized by so many revolutions; it has undergone such notable political and geographical changes, that what travelers and writers said about it in former periods no longer applies to it.

During a length of time geographers divided Tartary into three grand parts—1. Russian Tartary, extending from east to west, from the sea of Kamtchatka to the Black Sea, and from north to south, from the regions inhabited by the Tongous and Samoiede tribes, to the lakes Baikal and Aral. 2. Chinese Tartary, bounded east by the sea of Japan, south by the Great Wall of China, west by the Gobi or great sandy desert; and north, by the Baikal Lake. 3. Independent Tartary, extending to the Caspian Sea, and including in its limits the whole of Thibet. Such a division is altogether chimerical, and without any sound basis. All these immense tracts, indeed, once formed part of the great empires of Tchinggiskhan and Timour. The Tartar hordes made encampments there at their will in the course of their warlike wanderings; but now all this is completely changed, and, to form an exact idea of modern Tartary, it is necessary to modify in a great degree the notions that have been transmitted to us by the mediæval authors, and which, in default of better information, have been adopted by all the geographers, down to Malte-Brun, inclusive. To realize a definite idea about Tartary, we think that the clearest, most certain, and consequently the most reasonable rule, is to adopt the opinions of the Tartars themselves, and of the Chinese, far more competent judges of this matter than Europeans, who, having no connection with this part of Asia, are obliged to trust to conjectures which have often little to do with truth. In accordance with a universal usage, the soundness of which we were enabled to confirm in the course of our travels, we will divide the Tartar people into Eastern Tartars (Toung-Ta-Dze), or Mantchous, and Western Tartars (Si-Ta-Dze), or Mongols. The boundaries of Mantchouria are very distinct, as we have already stated. It is bounded on the north by the Kinggan mountains, which separate it from Siberia; on the south by the gulf of Phou-Hai and Corea; on the east by the sea of Japan; and on the west by the Barrier of Stakes and a branch of the Sakhalien-Oula. It would be a difficult matter to define the limits of Mongolia in an equally exact manner; however, without any serious departure from the truth, we may include them between the 75th and the 118th degrees longitude of Paris, and 35th and 50th degrees of north latitude. Great and Little Boukaria, Kalmoukia, Great and Little Thibet—all these denominations seem to us purely imaginary. We shall enter, by and by, into some details on this subject, in the second part of our travels, when we come to speak of Thibet and of the neighboring people.

The people who are comprised in the grand division of Mongolia, that we have just given, are not all to be indiscriminately considered as Mongols. There are some of them to whom this denomination can only be applied in a restricted sense. Towards the northwest, for instance, the Mongols are frequently confounded with the Moslems; and towards the south, with the Si-Fans, or Eastern Thibetians. The best way clearly to distinguish these people, is to pay attention to their language, their manners, their religion, their costume, and particularly to the name by which they designate themselves. The Mongol Khalkhas are the most numerous, the most wealthy, and the most celebrated in history. They occupy the entire north of Mongolia. Their country is of vast extent, including nearly 200 leagues from north to south, and about 500 from east to west. We will not repeat here what we have already said about the Khalkha district; we will merely add that it is divided into four great provinces, subject to four separate sovereigns. These provinces, are sub-divided into eighty-four banners, in Chinese called Ky, in Mongol Bochkhon. Princes of different ranks are at the head of each banner. Notwithstanding the authority of these secular princes, it may safely be said that the Khalkhas are all dependent on the Guison-Tamba, the Grand Lama, the Living Buddha of all the Mongol Khalkhas, who consider it an honor to call themselves Disciples of the Holy One of Kouren (*Kouré bokte ain Chabi*).

The Southern Mongols have no special designation; they

merely bear the name of the principality to which they belong. Thus they say, "Mongol of Souniout, Mongol of Gechekten," etc. Southern Mongolia comprises twenty-five principalities, which, like those of the Khalkhas, are subdivided into several Bochkhon. The principal are the Ortous, the two Toumet, the two Souniout, the Tchakar, Karatsin Oungniot, Gechekten, Barin, Nayman, and the country of the Elents.

The Southern Mongols, near the Great Wall, have little modified their manners by their constant intercourse with the Chinese. You may remark sometimes in their dress a sort of studied elegance, and in their character pretensions to the refined politeness of the Chinese. Laying aside, on the one hand, the frankness, the good-natured openness of the Mongols of the North, they have borrowed from their neighbors somewhat of their cunning and foppery.

Proceeding to the southeast, we encountered the Mongols of the Koukou-Noor or Blue Lake (in Chinese, Tsing-Hai or Blue Sea). This country is far from possessing the extent which is generally assigned to it in geographical charts. The Mongols of the Koukou-Noor only dwell around the lake, from which they derive their name; and, moreover, they are mixed up to a great extent with Si-Fans, who cannot live secure in their own country, because of the hordes of robbers that are constantly ravaging it.

To the west of the Koukou-Noor is the river Tsaidam, on whose banks encamp the numerous tribes, called Tsaidam-Mongols, who must not be confounded with the Mongols of the Koukou-Noor. Farther still, in the very heart of Thibet, we encounter other Mongol tribes. We shall say nothing about them here, as we shall have occasion to speak of them in the course of our narrative. We will revert, therefore, in some detail to the Mongols of the Koukou-Noor and the Tsaidam.

The Torgot-Tartars, who formerly dwelt near Kara-Koroum, the capital of the Mongols in the time of Tchinggis-khan, are now situated to the northwest of Mongolia. In 1672, the whole tribe, having raised their tents and assembled all their flocks, abandoned the district which had served them as a resting-place, migrated to the western part of Asia, and established themselves in the steppes between the Don and the Volga.

The Torgot princes recognized the sovereignty of the Muscovite emperors, and declared themselves their vassals. But these wandering hordes, passionately attached to the independence of their nomad life, could not long accommodate themselves to the new masters they had selected. They soon felt an aversion to the laws and regular institutions which were becoming established in the Russian empire. In 1770, the Torgots again made a general migration. Led by their chief, Aboucha, they suddenly disappeared, passed the Russian frontiers, and halted on the banks of the river Ili. This flight had been concerted with the government of Peking. The Emperor of China, who had been informed beforehand of the period of their departure, took them under his protection, and assigned to them settlements on the banks of the Ili.

The principality of Ili is now the Botany-Bay of China; thither are sent the Chinese criminals, condemned to exile by the laws of the empire. Before their arrival in these distant regions they are obliged to cross frightful deserts, and to climb the Moussour (glacier) mountains. These gigantic summits are entirely formed of icebergs, piled one on the top of the other, so that travelers cannot advance except by hewing steps out of the eternal ice. On the other side of the Moussour mountains the country, they say, is magnificent; the climate temperate enough, and the soil adapted for every kind of cultivation. The exiles have transported thither a great many of the productions of China; but the Mongols continue to follow their nomad life, and merely to pasture herds and flocks.

We had occasion to travel for some time with Lamas of Torgot; some of them arrived with us at Lha-Ssa. We did not remark, either in their costume, in their manners, or in their language, anything to distinguish them from the Mongols. They spoke a good deal about the *Oros* (Russians), but in a way to make us understand that they were by no means desirous of again becoming subject to their sway. The Torgot camels are remarkably fine, and generally much larger and stronger than those in the other parts of Mongolia.

It would be a very desirable thing to send missionaries to Ili. We believe that there would be found already formed there a numerous and fervent body of Christians. It is well known that for many years past, it is hither that the Christians who have refused to apostatize, have been exiled from all the provinces of China. The missionary who should obtain permission to exercise his zeal in the Torgot, would doubtless have to undergo great privations during his journey thither; but he would be amply compensated, by the thought of carrying the succor of religion to all those generous confessors of the faith, whom the tyranny of the Chinese government has sent to die in these distant regions.

To the southwest of Torgot is the province of Khachghar. At the present day, this district cannot at all be considered a part of Mongolia. Its inhabitants have neither the language, nor the physiognomy, nor the costume, nor the religion, nor the manners of the Mongols; they are Moslems. The Chinese, as well as the Tartars, call them Hoei-Hoei, a name by which they designate the Mussulmen who dwell in the interior of the Chinese empire. This description of Khachghar, is also applicable to the people to the south of the Celestial Mountains, in the Chinese tongue called Tien, Chan, and in Mongol, Bokte-oola (holy mountains).

Not long since the Chinese government had to sustain a terrible war against Khachghar. We are indebted for the following details to some military Mandarins who accompanied this famous and distant expedition.

The Court of Peking kept in Khachghar two grand Mandarins, with the title of Delegates Extraordinary (*Kintchai*), who were charged to guard the frontiers, and to keep an eye on the movements of the neighboring people. These Chinese officers, instead of merely watching, exercised their power with such horrible and revolting tyranny, that they wore out the patience of the people of Khachghar, who, at length, rose in a body, and massacred all the Chinese residents in the country. The news reaching Peking, the Emperor, who knew nothing of the misconduct of his officers, assembled his troops, and marched them against the Moslems. The contest was long and bloody. The Chinese government had several times to send reinforcements. The Hoei-Hoei were commanded by a hero called Tchankoeul; his stature, they say, was prodigious, and he had no weapon but an enormous club. He frequently defeated the Chinese army, and destroyed several grand military Mandarins. At length, the Emperor sent the famous Yang, who put an end to the war. The conqueror of Khachghar is a military Mandarin of the province of Chang-Tong, remarkable for his lofty stature, and above all for the prodigious length of his beard. According to the account we heard of him, his manner of fighting was singular enough. As soon as the action commenced, he tied up his beard in two great knots, in order that it might not get in his way, and then he placed himself behind his troops. There, armed with a long saber, he drove his soldiers on to combat, and massacred, without pity, those who were cowards enough to draw back. This method of commanding an army will seem somewhat peculiar; but those who have lived among the Chinese will see that the military genius of Yang was founded on a thorough knowledge of the soldiers he had to deal with.

The Moslems were defeated, and Tchankoeul was, by means of treachery, made a prisoner. He was conveyed to Peking, where he had to undergo the most barbarous and humiliating treatment, even the being exposed to the people, shut up in an iron cage, like a wild beast. The Emperor Tao-Kouang wished to see this warrior, of whom fame spoke so much, and ordered him to be brought to him. The Mandarins immediately took alarm; they were afraid lest the prisoner should reveal to the Emperor the causes which had brought about the revolt of Khachghar, and the horrible massacres which had followed it. The great dignitaries saw that these revelations would be dangerous for them, and would make them seem guilty of negligence in the eyes of the Emperor, for not having duly observed the conduct of the Mandarins who were placed in charge of distant provinces. To obviate this danger, they made the unfortunate Tchankoeul swallow a draught which took away his speech, and threw him into a disgusting state of stupor. When he appeared in the presence of the Emperor, his mouth, they say, foamed, and his visage was horrible; he could not answer any of the questions which were addressed to him. Tchankouel was condemned to be cut into pieces, and to be served up as food for the dogs.

The Mandarin Yang was loaded with favors by the Emperor, for having so happily terminated the war of Khachghar. He obtained the dignity of Batourou, a Tartar word signifying valorous. This title is the most honorable that a military Mandarin can obtain.

The Batourou Yang was sent against the English, in their last war with the Chinese; but there it would appear his tactics did not avail. During our travels in China we inquired of several Mandarins, how it was that the Batourou Yang had not exterminated the English: the answer everywhere was, that he had had compassion on them.

The numerous principalities of which Mongolia is composed, are all more or less dependent on the Mantchou Emperor, in proportion as they show more or less weakness in their relations with the Court of Peking. They may be considered as so many feudal kingdoms, giving no obedience to their sovereign beyond the extent of their fear or their interest; and indeed, what the Mantchou dynasty fears above all things, is the vicinity of these Tartar tribes. The Emperors are fully aware that, headed by an enterprising and bold chief, these tribes might successfully renew the terrible wars of other times, and once more obtain possession of the empire. For this reason, they use every means in their power to preserve the friendship of the Mongol princes, and to enfeeble the strength of these terrible nomads. It is with this view, as we have already remarked, that they patronize Lamaism, by richly endowing the Lamaseries, and by granting numerous privileges to the Lamas. So long as they can maintain their influence over the sacerdotal tribe, they are assured that neither the people nor the princes will stir from their repose.

Alliances are another means by which the reigning dynasty seeks to consolidate its power in Mongolia. The daughters and nearest relations of the Emperor, intermarrying with the royal families of Tartary, contribute to maintain between the two peoples pacific and friendly relations. Yet these princesses continue to have a great predilection for the pomp and grandeur of the imperial court. The mournful, monotonous life of the desert soon fatigues them, and they sigh for the brilliant fêtes of Peking. To obviate the inconvenience that might attend their frequent journeys to the capital, a very severe regulation has been made to moderate the wandering humor of these princesses. First, for the first ten years after their marriage, they are forbidden to come to Peking, under penalty of having the annual pension the Emperor allows to their husbands suspended. This period having elapsed, they are allowed to go to Peking but never at their own mere fancy. A tribunal is appointed to examine their reasons for temporarily quitting their family. If these are considered valid, they allow them a certain number of days, on the expiration of which they are enjoined to return to Tartary. During their stay at Peking, they are supported at the expense of the Emperor, suitably to their dignity.

Chinese Princess.

The most elevated personages in the hierarchy of the Mongol princes, are the Thsin-Wang and the Kiun-Wang. Their title is equivalent to that of king. After them come the Peile, the Beisse, the Koung of the first and second class, and the Dchassak. These may be compared to our ancient dukes, barons, etc. We have already mentioned that the Mongol princes are bound to pay certain rents to the Emperor; but the amount of these is so small, that the Mantchou dynasty can only levy it on account of the moral effect that may result. As simple matter-of-fact, it would be nearer the truth to say that the Mantchous are the tributaries of the Mongols; for, in return for the few beasts they receive from them, they give them annually large sums of money, silken stuffs, clothes, and various articles of luxury and ornament, such as buttons, sables, peacocks' feathers, etc. Each Wang of the first degree receives annually 2,500 ounces of silver (about £800), and forty pieces of silk stuff. All the other princes are paid according to the rank they derive from the Emperor. A Dchassak, for example, receives yearly one hundred ounces of silver, and four pieces of silk.

There exist certain Lamaseries, termed Imperial, where each Lama, on obtaining the degree of Kalon, is obliged to offer to the Emperor an ingot of silver of the value of fifty ounces; his name is then inscribed on the register of the imperial clergy at Peking, and he is entitled to the pension given yearly to the Lamas of the Emperor. It is obvious that all these measures, so calculated to flatter the self-love and avarice of the Tartars, do not a little contribute to maintain their feelings of respect and submission towards a government which takes such pains to court their friendship.

The Mongols, however, of the district of the Khalkhas do not seem to be much affected by these demonstrations. They only see in the Mantchous a rival race, in possession of a prey which they themselves have never ceased to desire. We have frequently heard the Mongol Khalkhas use the most unceremonious and seditious language in speaking of the Mantchou Emperor. "They are subject," say they, "to the Guison-Tamba alone, to the *Most Holy*, and not to the black-man (layman), who sits on the throne of Peking." These redoubtable children of Tchinggiskhan still seem to be cherishing in their inmost heart schemes of conquest and invasion. They only await, they say, the command of their Grand Lama to march direct upon Peking, and to regain an empire which they believe to be theirs, for the sole reason that it was formerly theirs. The Mongol princes exact from their subjects or slaves certain tributes, which consist in sheep, and here is the absurd and unjust regulation, in accordance with which this tribute must be paid:

The owner of five or more oxen must contribute one sheep: the owner of twenty sheep must contribute one of them; if he owns forty he gives two; but they need give no more, however numerous their flocks. As may be seen, this tribute really weighs upon the poor only; the wealthy may possess a great number of cattle without being obliged to contribute more than two sheep.

Besides these regular tributes, there are others which the princes are accustomed to levy on their slaves, on some extraordinary occasions; for instance, marriages, burials, and distant voyages. On these occasions, each collection of ten tents is obliged to furnish a horse and a camel. Every Mongol who owns three cows must pay a pail of milk; if he possesses five, a pot of koumis or wine, made of fermented milk. The owner of a flock of 100 sheep furnishes a felt carpet or a tent covering; he who owns three camels must give a bundle of long cords to fasten the baggage. However, in a country where everything is subject to the arbitrary will of the chief, these regulations, as may be supposed, are not strictly observed. Sometimes the subjects are altogether exempted from their operation, and sometimes also there is exacted from them much more than the law decrees.

Robbery and murder are very severely punished among the Mongols; but the injured individuals, or their parents, are themselves obliged to prosecute the prisoner before the tribunals: the worst outrage remains unpunished if no one appears to prosecute. In the ideas of a semi-barbarous people, the man who attempts to take the property or life of any one is deemed to have committed merely a private offense, reparation for which ought to be demanded, not by the public, but by the injured party or his family. These rude notions of justice are common to China and to Thibet; and for that matter, we know that Rome herself had no other until the establishment of Christianity, which caused the right of the community to prevail over the right of the individual.

Mongolia, generally speaking, wears a gloomy and savage aspect; the eye is nowhere recreated by the charm and variety of landscape scenery. The monotony of the steppes is only interrupted by ravines, by vast rents of the earth, or by stony and barren hills. Towards the north, in the district of Khalkhas, nature is more animated; tall forests decorate the summits of the mountains, and numerous rivers water the rich pastures of the plains; but in the long winter season the earth remains buried under a thick bed of snow. Towards the Great Wall, Chinese industry glides like a serpent into the desert. Towns arise on all sides. The Land of Grass is crowned with harvests, and the Mongol shepherds find themselves driven back northwards, little by little, by the encroachments of agriculture.

Sandy plains occupy, perhaps, the greater part of Mongolia; you do not see a single tree there; some short, brittle grass, which seems to have much difficulty in issuing from this unfruitful soil, creeping briers, a few scanty tufts of heath, such is the sole vegetation and pasturage of Gobi. Water is very rarely seen; at long intervals you meet with a few deep wells, dug for the convenience of the caravans that are obliged to cross this dismal tract.

In Mongolia there are only two seasons in the year,— nine months for winter and three for summer. Sometimes the heat is stifling, particularly on the sandy steppes, but it only lasts a few days. The nights, however, are almost invariably cold. In the Mongol countries, cultivated by the Chinese, outside the Great Wall, all agricultural labor must be comprehended within three months. As soon as the earth is sufficiently thawed, they hastily set to work, or rather they do nothing but touch the surface of the ground lightly with the plow; they then immediately sow the seed; the corn grows with astonishing rapidity. Whilst they are waiting for it to come to maturity, the men are incessantly occupied in pulling up the weeds that overrun the plain. Scarcely have they gathered in the harvest when the winter comes with its terrible cold; during this season they thresh the corn. As the cold makes vast crevices in the earth, they throw water over the surface of the threshing-floor, which freezes forthwith, and creates for the laborers a place always smooth and admirably clean.

The excessive cold which prevails in Mongolia may be attributed to three causes:—to the great elevation of the country, to the nitrous substances with which it is strongly impregnated, and to the almost entire absence of cultivation. In the places which the Chinese have cultivated the temperature has risen in a remarkable degree; the heat goes on increasing, so to speak, from year to year, as cultivation advances; so that particular grain crops, which at first would not grow at all, because of the cold, now ripen with wonderful success.

Mongolia, on account of its immense solitudes, has become the haunt of a large number of wild animals. You see at every step hares, pheasants, eagles, yellow goats, gray squirrels, foxes and wolves. It is remarkable that the wolves of Mongolia attack men rather than animals. They may be seen, sometimes, passing at full gallop through a flock of sheep, in order to attack the shepherd. About the Great Wall they frequently visit the Tartaro-Chinese villages, enter the farms, and disdaining the domestic animals they find in the yard, proceed to the inside of the house, and there select their human victims, whom they almost invariably seize by the throat and strangle. There is scarcely a village in Tartary where, every year, misfortunes of this kind do not occur. It would seem as though the wolves of this country were resolved to avenge on men the sanguinary war which the Tartars make upon their brethren.

The stag, the wild goat, the mule, the wild camel, the yak, the brown and black bear, the lynx, the ounce and the tiger, frequent the deserts of Mongolia. The Tartars never proceed on a journey, unless armed with bows, fusils and lances.

When we consider the horrible climate of Tartary, that climate ever so gloomy and frozen, we should be led to think that the inhabitants of these wild countries must be of an extremely fierce and rugged temperament: their physiognomy, their deportment, the costume they wear, all would seem to confirm this opinion. The Mongol has a flat face, with prominent cheek bones, the chin short and retiring, the forehead sunken, the eyes small and oblique, of a yellow tint, as though full of bile, the hair black and rugged, the beard scanty, the skin of a deep brown, and extremely coarse. The Mongol is of middle height, but his great leathern boots and large sheep-skin robe, seem to take away from his height, and make him appear diminutive and stumpy. To complete this portrait, we must add a heavy and ponderous gait, and a harsh, shrill, discordant language, full of frightful aspirates. Notwithstanding this rough and unprepossessing exterior, the disposition of the Mongol is full of gentleness and good nature; he passes suddenly from the most rollicking and extravagant gaiety to a state of melancholy, which is by no means disagreeable. Timid to excess in his ordinary habits; when fanaticism or the desire of vengeance arouses him, he displays in his courage an impetuosity which nothing can stay; he is candid and credulous as an infant, and he passionately loves to hear marvelous anecdotes and narratives. The meeting with a traveling Lama is always for him a source of happiness.

Aversion to toil and a sedentary life, the love of pillage and rapine, cruelty, unnatural debaucheries, are the vices which have been generally attributed to the Mongol Tartars. We are apt to believe that the portrait which the old writers have drawn of them was not exaggerated, for we always find these terrible hordes, at the period of their gigantic conquests, bringing in their train, murder, pillage, conflagration, and every description of scourge. But are the Mongols the same now that they were formerly? We believe we can affirm the contrary, at least to a great extent.

Wherever we have seen them, we have found them to be generous, frank and hospitable ; inclined, it is true, like ill-educated children, to pilfer little things which excite their curiosity, but by no means in the habit of practising what is called pillage and robbery. As to their aversion for toil and a sedentary life, they are just the same as heretofore. It must also be admitted that their manners are very free, but their conduct has more in it of recklessness than of absolute corruption. We seldom find among them those unbridled and brutal debaucheries to which the Chinese are so much given.

The Mongols are strangers to every kind of industry. Some felt carpets, some rudely tanned hides, a little needlework and embroidery, are exceptions not deserving of mention. On the other hand, they possess to perfection the qualities of a pastoral and nomad people. They have the senses of sight, hearing, and scent prodigiously developed. The Mongol is able to hear at a very long distance the trot of a horse, to distinguish the form of objects, and to detect the distant scent of flocks, and the smoke of an encampment.

Many attempts have already been made to propagate Christianity among the Tartars, and we may say that they have not been altogether fruitless. Towards the end of the eighth century and in the commencement of the ninth, Timothy, patriarch of the Nestorians, sent some monks to preach the Gospel to the Hioung-Nou Tartars, who had taken refuge on the shores of the Caspian Sea. At a later period they penetrated into Central Asia, and into China. In the time of Tchinggiskhan and his successors, Franciscan and Dominican missionaries were despatched to Tartary. The conversions were numerous; even princes, it is said, and emperors were baptized. But we must not entirely credit the statements of the Tartar ambassadors, who, the more easily to draw the Christian princes of Europe into a league against the Moslems, never failed to state that their masters had been baptized, and had made profession of Christianity. It is certain, however, that at the commencement of the fourteenth century, Pope Clement V. erected at Peking an archbishopric, in favor of Jean de Montcorvin, a Franciscan missionary who preached the Gospel to the Tartars for forty-two years; he translated into the Mongol language the New Testament and the Psalms of David, and left at his death a very flourishing Christendom. We find on this subject some curious details in "Le livre de l'Estat du Grant Caan"[1] (The book of the State of the Grand Khan), extracted from a manuscript of the National Library, and published in the " Nouveau Journal Asiatique" (vol. vi.), by M. Jacquet, a learned orientalist. We conceive that it may be acceptable to quote a few passages from this production.

OF THE MINORITES WHO DWELL IN THIS COUNTRY OF CATHAY (CHINA).

" In the said city of Cambalech was an archbishop, who was called Brother John of Mount Curvin, of the order of Minorites, and he was legate there for Pope Clement V. This archbishop erected in that city aforesaid, three houses of Minorites, and they are two leagues distant from one another. He likewise instituted two others in the city of Racon, which is a long distance from Cambalech, being a journey of three months, and it is on the sea coast; and in these two places were put two Minorites as bishops. The one was named Brother Andrew of Paris, and the other, Brother Peter of Florence. These brothers, and John the Archbishop, converted many persons to the faith of Jesus

[1] This compilation was made in the fourteenth century by order of Pope John XXII.

Christ. He is a man of irreproachable life, agreeable to God and the world, and very much in the Emperor's favor. The Emperor provided him and all his people with all things necessary, and he was much beloved by both Christians and Pagans; and he certainly would have converted all that country to the Christian and Catholic faith, if the false and misbelieving Nestorian Christians had not prevented it. The archbishop had great trouble in restoring these Nestorians to the obedience of our Holy Mother the Roman Church; without which obedience, he said, they could not be saved; and on this account these Nestorian schismatics disliked him greatly. This archbishop had just departed, as it pleased God, from this life. A great multitude of Christians and Pagans attended his funeral; and the Pagans tore their funeral robes, as is their custom. And these Christians and infidels took, with great reverence, the robes of the archbishop, and held them in great respect, and as relics. He was buried there honorably, in the fashion of the faithful. They still visit his tomb with great devotion."

OF CERTAIN NESTORIAN CHRISTIAN SCHISMATICS WHO DWELL THERE.

"In the said city of Cambalech there is a sort of Christian schismatics whom they call Nestorians. They observe the customs and manners of the Greek Church, and are not obedient to the Holy Church of Rome; but they are of another sect, and are at great enmity with all the Catholic Christians who are loyal to the Holy Church of Rome aforesaid. And when the archbishop, of whom we spoke just now, built those abbeys of Minorites aforesaid, the Nestorians destroyed them in the night, and did them all the mischief in their power; for they dared not injure the said archbishop, or his brethren, or the other faithful Christians publicly and openly, because the Emperor loved them and showed them his favor. These Nestorians dwelling in the said empire of Cathay, number more than 30,000, and are very rich; but many of them fear the Christians. They have very beautiful and very holy churches, with crosses and images in honor of God and of the saints. They receive from the said Emperor several offices, and he grants them many privileges, and it is thought that if they would consent to unite and agree with these Minorites and with other good Christians who reside in this country, they might convert the whole of this country and the Emperor to the true faith."

OF THE EXTRAORDINARY FAVOR WHICH THE GRAND KHAN SHOWS TO THE SAID CHRISTIANS.

"The Grand Khan protects the Christians who in this said kingdom are obedient to the Holy Church of Rome, and makes provision for all their wants, for he shows them very great favor and love; and whenever they require anything for their churches, their crosses, or their sanctuaries, in honor of Jesus Christ, he awards it with great willingness. But they must pray to God for him and his health particularly in their sermons. And he is very anxious that they should all pray for him; and he readily allows the brethren to preach the faith of God in the churches of the infidels, which they call *vritanes*, and he also permits the infidels to hear the brethren preach; so that the infidels go there very willingly, and often with great devotion, and give the brethren much alms; and, likewise, the Emperor lends and sends his servants to aid and assist the Christians when they require their services, and so solicit the Emperor."

While the Tartars remained masters of China, Christianity made great progress in the empire. At the present day (we say it with sorrow), there is not to be found in Mongolia the least vestige of what was done in ages gone by, in favor of these nomad people. We trust, however, that the light of the Gospel will ere long shine once more in their eyes. The zeal of Europeans for the propagation of the faith will hasten the accomplishment of Noah's prophecy. Missionaries, the children of Japheth, will display their courage and devotion; they will fly to the aid of the children of Shem, and will esteem themselves happy to pass their days under the Mongol tents: " God shall enlarge Japheth, and he shall dwell in the tents of Shem."—Genes. cap. ix. v. 27.

Irrigation of the Fields.

CHAPTER XII.

Hotel of Justice and Mercy—Province of Kan-Sou—Agriculture—Great Works for the Irrigation of the Fields—Manner of Living in Inns—Great Confusion in a Town caused by our Camels—Chinese Life-guard—Mandarin Inspector of the Public Works—Ning-Hia—Historical and Topographical Details—Inn of the Five Felicities—Contest with a Mandarin, Tchong-Wei—Immense Mountains of Sand—Road to Ili—Unfavorable aspect of Kao-Tan-Dze—Glance at the Great Wall—Inquiry after the Passports—Tartars traveling in China—Dreadful Hurricane—Origin and Manners of the Inhabitants of Kan-Sou—The Dchiahours—Interview with a Living Buddha—Hotel of the Temperate Climates—Family of Samdadchiemba—Mountain of Ping-Keou—Fight between an Innkeeper and his Wife—Water-mills—Knitting—Si-Ning-Fou—House of Rest—Arrival at Tang-Keou-Eul.

Two months had elapsed since our departure from the Valley of Black Waters. During that period, we had undergone in the desert continual fatigue and privations of every kind. Our health, it is true, was not as yet materially impaired, but we felt that our strength was leaving us, and we appreciated the necessity of modifying, for a few days, our late rough manner of living. In this point of view a country occupied by Chinese could not be otherwise than agreeable, and, in comparison with Tartary, would place within our reach all sorts of comforts.

As soon as we had passed the Hoang-Ho, we entered the small frontier town called Ché-'Tsui-Dze, which is only separated from the river by a sandy beach. We proceeded to take up our lodging at the Hotel of Justice and Mercy (*Jeuy-Ting*). The house was large and recently built. With the exception of a solid floor of gray tiles, the whole construction was of wood. The host received us with that courtesy and attention which are always displayed when people desire to give a character to a new establishment; and besides, the man having a most unprepossessing aspect, was anxious, probably, by his amiability of manners, to redeem his ugliness of feature; his eyes, which squinted horribly, were always turned away from the person whom he was addressing. However, if the organ of sight was defective, the organ of speech had marvelous elasticity. In his quality of an old soldier, he had seen much, heard much, and what is more, he remembered much; he was acquainted with all countries, and had had to do with all sorts of men. His loquacity was far from being troublesome to us: he gave us details of every kind, as to the places, great and small, which we had to visit before our arrival at Koukou-Noor. That part of Tartary was well known to him; for, in the military part of his career, he had served against the Si-Fan. The day after our arrival he brought us, early in the morning, a large scroll, on which were written, in order, the names of the towns, villages, hamlets, and places that we had to pass in the province of Kan-Sou; and then he proceeded to give us a description of the localities with so much enthusiasm, so much gesticulation, and in such a loud key, that he made our heads turn.

The time which was not absorbed in long interviews, partly compulsory, partly voluntary, with our host, was occupied in visiting the town. Ché-Tsui-Dze is built in the corner of an angle, formed on one side by the Alechan mountains, and on the other by the Yellow River. On its eastern bank the Hoang-Ho is bordered by dark hills, wherein are abundant coal mines, which the inhabitants work with great activity, and whence they derive their chief wealth. The suburbs of the town are occupied by great potteries, where you observe colossal urns used in families as reservoirs of water, and large stoves of admirable construction, and a large collection of vases of all shapes and sizes. There is in the province of Kan-Sou a large trade in this pottery.

At Ché-Tsui-Dze, provisions are abundant, varied, and of astonishingly moderate price. Nowhere, perhaps, can a person live so economically. At every hour of the day and night, itinerant restaurateurs bring to your house whatever provisions you need: soups, ragouts of mutton and beef, vegetables, pastry, rice, vermicelli, etc. There are dinners for every appetite, and for every purse—from the complicated banquet of the rich, to the simple and clear broth of the beggar. These restaurateurs are coming and going to and fro almost without interval. They are generally Moslems—a blue cap distinguishing them from the Chinese.

After two days repose in the Inn of Justice and Mercy, we proceeded on our way. The environs of Ché-Tsui-Dze are uncultivated. On all sides nothing is to be seen but sand and gravel, drifted by the annual inundation of the Yellow River. However, as you advance, the soil, becoming imperceptibly higher, improves. An hour's distance from the town, we crossed the Great Wall, or rather passed over some miserable ruins that still mark the ancient site of the celebrated rampart of China. The country soon becomes magnificent, and we could not but admire the agricultural genius of the Chinese people. The part of Kan-Sou which we were traversing is especially remarkable by its ingenious and extensive works for facilitating the irrigation of the fields.

By means of creeks cut in the banks of the Yellow River, the waters are conveyed into broad artificial canals; these again supply others of a larger size, which, in their turn, fill the ditches with which all the fields are surrounded. Sluices, great and small, admirable in their simplicity, serve to raise the water and to carry it over all the inequalities of the land. The distribution of the water is perfectly arranged; each landowner waters his fields in his turn, and no one is allowed to open his flood-gate before his regularly appointed time.

Few villages are met with; but you observe, in all directions, farms of various sizes separated from one another by meadows. The eye does not rest upon either groves or pleasure-gardens. Except a few large trees round the dwellings, all the land is devoted to the cultivation of corn;

they do not even reserve a space for stacking the harvest, but pile it up on the tops of the houses, which are always flat-roofed. On the days of the general irrigation, the country gives you a perfect idea of those famous inundations of the Nile, the descriptions of which have become so classic. The inhabitants traverse their fields in small skiffs, or in light carts with enormous wheels, and generally drawn by buffaloes.

These irrigations, so conducive to the fertility of the land, are a great pest to travelers. The roads are generally covered with water and mud, so that you cannot use them, but must labor along the mounds which form the boundaries of the fields. When you have to guide camels over such roads, it is the height of misery. We did not advance a single step without the fear of seeing our baggage fall into the mud; and more than once such an accident did occur, throwing us into infinite embarrassment. In fact, that the misfortune did not oftener befall us, was solely attributable to the skill in mud-walking which our camels had acquired in their apprenticeship amongst the marshes of the Ortous.

In the evening of our first day's march, we arrived at a small village called Wang-Ho-Po; we had expected to find here the same facility in obtaining provisions as at Ché-Tsui-Dze, but we were soon undeceived. The customs were not the same; those amiable restaurateurs, with their baskets of ready-dressed viands, were no longer visible. Forage-dealers were the only persons who came to offer their goods. We therefore commenced by giving the animals their rations, and afterwards went into the village to see if we could find any provisions for our own supper. On our return to the inn, we were obliged to cook our own supper; the host merely furnished us with water, coal, and a meal-kettle. Whilst we were peaceably occupied in appreciating the result of our culinary labors, a great tumult arose in the courtyard of the inn. It was occasioned by a caravan of camels, conducted by Chinese merchants, who were going to the town of Ning-Hia. Destined for the same route as themselves, we soon entered into conversation. They told us that the direct road to Ning-Hia was so bad as to be impracticable, even for the best camels; but they added, they were acquainted with a cross road shorter and less dangerous, and they invited us to go with them. As they were to depart in the night, we called the host in order to settle our account. After the Chinese fashion, when sapeks are in question, on one side they ask much, on the other they offer too little; then there is a long squabble, and after mutual concessions you come to an agreement. As they thought us Tartars, it was quite a matter of course with them to ask us nearly triple the just amount: the result was, that the dispute was twice as long as it ordinarily is. We had to discuss the matter vigorously; first, for ourselves, then for our beasts, for the room, the stabling, the watering, the kettle, the coal, the lamp, for every single item, until at length we got the innkeeper down to the tariff of civilized people. The unfortunate Tartar exterior, which, for other reasons, we had assumed, had been the occasion of our acquiring a certain degree of dexterity in discussions of this kind; for not a day passed, during our journey through the province of Kan-Sou, in which we had not to quarrel, in this manner, with innkeepers. Such quarrels, however, involve no disagreeable results; you dispute, and dispute, and then you come to an agreement, and the matter is over, and you are as good friends as ever with your antagonist.

It was scarcely past midnight when the Chinese cameldrivers were on foot, making with great tumult, their preparations for departure. We rose, but it was to no purpose that we expedited the saddling of our animals; our fellow-travelers were ready before us and went on, promising to proceed slowly till we came up with them. The instant that our camels were ready, we departed. The night was dark; it was impossible to discover our guides. With the aid of a small lamp we sought traces of them, but we were not successful. Our only course, therefore, was to proceed, at chance, across these marshy plains, which were altogether unknown to us. We soon found ourselves so involved in the inundated soil, that we dared advance no farther, and halted at a bank, and there awaited daybreak.

As soon as the day dawned, we directed our steps, by a thousand ins and outs, towards a large walled town that we perceived in the distance; it was Ping-Lou-Hien, a town of the third class. Our arrival in this town occasioned lamentable disorder. The country is remarkable for the number and beauty of its mules; and at this juncture, there was one of these standing, fastened by a halter, before each of the houses of the long street, which we were traversing from north to south. As we proceeded, all these animals, seized with fright at the sight of our camels, reared on their hind legs and dashed with violence against the shops; some broke the halters which confined them, tore off at a gallop, and overthrew, in their flight, the stalls of the street merchants. The people gathered together, sent forth shouts, anathematized the stinking Tartars, cursed the camels, and increased the disorder instead of lessening it. We were grieved to find that our presence had such unfortunate results; but what could we do? We could not render the mules less timid, nor prevent the camels from having a frightful appearance. One of us, at last, determined to run on before the caravan, and inform the people of the approach of the camels. This precaution diminished the evil, which did not, however, entirely cease until we were outside the gates of the town.

We had intended to breakfast at Ping-Lou-Hien; but, not having conciliated the good-will of its inhabitants, we dared not stop there. We had only the courage to purchase some provisions, for which we paid an exorbitant price, the occasion not being favorable for bargaining. At some distance from the town, we came to a guard-house, where we stopped to rest awhile, and to take our morning repast. These guard-houses are very numerous in China, the rule being that there shall be one of them at every half-league, on all the great roads. Of a singular and entirely Chinese construction, these barracks consist of a little edifice either of wood or earth, but always whitewashed. In the center, is a kind of shed entirely without furniture, and with one large opening in front. This is reserved for unfortunate travelers, who, during the night, being overtaken by bad weather, cannot take refuge in an inn. On each side is a little room with doors and windows, and sometimes with a wooden bench painted red, by way of furniture. The exterior of the barrack is decorated with rude pictures, representing the gods of war, cavalry, and fabulous animals; on the walls of the shed are drawn all the weapons used in China, matchlocks, bows, and arrows, lances, bucklers, and sabers of every description. At a little distance from the barrack, you see on the right a square tower, and on the left five small posts standing in a line. These denote the five lis which are the distance from one guard-house to another; frequently a large board, on two poles, informs the traveler of the names of the nearest towns in that quarter. The directions on the board now before us were these:—

> From Ping-Lou-Hien to Ning-Hia, fifty lis.
> Northwards to Ping-Lou-Hien, five lis.
> Southwards to Ning-Hia, forty-five lis.

In time of war, the square tower serves during the night for giving signals by means of fireworks, combined in particular ways. The Chinese relate that the Emperor Yeou-Wang, the thirteenth emperor of the Tcheou dynasty, 780 B. C., yielding to the absurd solicitations of his wife, ordered one night the signals of alarm to be made. The Empress wanted at once to amuse herself at the expense of the soldiers, and to ascertain, at the same time, whether these fireworks would really bring the troops to succor the capital. As the signals passed on to the provinces, the governors despatched the military Mandarins and their forces to Peking. When the soldiers learned, on their arrival, that they had been called together for the capricious amusement of a woman, they returned home full of indignation. Shortly afterwards, the Tartars made an irruption into the empire, and advanced with rapidity to the very walls of the capital. This time the Emperor gave the alarm in grave earnest, but throughout the provinces not a man stirred, thinking the Empress was again amusing herself; the consequence was, that the Tartars entered Peking, and the imperial family was massacred.

The profound peace which China has enjoyed so long has much diminished the importance of these guard-houses. When they decay they are seldom repaired; in most cases their doors and windows have been carried off, and no one lives in them at all. On some of the more frequented roads, they keep in repair the direction-boards and the posts.

The barrack where we halted was deserted. After having tied our beasts to a thick post, we entered a room, and took in peace a wholesome refreshment. Travelers looked at us as they passed, and seemed a little surprised to find the place turned into a dining-room. The finer people especially, smiled at these three uncivilized Mongols, as they deemed us. Our halt was brief. The direction-board officially announced that we had yet forty-five lis' march before we reached Ning-Hia, so that, considering the difficulty of the road, and the slowness of our camels, we had no time to lose. We proceeded along the banks of a magnificent canal, supplied by the waters of the Yellow River, and destined for the irrigation of the fields. Whilst the small caravan was slowly marching over a muddy and slippery ground, we saw advancing towards us a numerous party of horsemen. As the retinue came up, the innumerable laborers who were repairing the banks of the canal, prostrated themselves on the earth, and exclaimed, " Peace and happiness to our father and mother ! " We at once understood that the person so addressed was a superior Mandarin. In accordance with the strict rules of Chinese etiquette, we ought to have dismounted, and have prostrated ourselves, as the others did ; but we considered that, in our quality of priests of the Western Heaven, we might dispense with this troublesome and disagreeable ceremony. We remained, therefore, gravely seated on our steeds, and advanced quietly. At sight of our camels, the other horsemen prudently removed to a respectful distance ; but the Mandarin, to show his bravery, spurred his horse, and compelled it to come towards us. He saluted us politely, and made inquiries in Mongol as to our health and our journey. As his horse grew more and more afraid of our camels, he was constrained to cut short the conversation, and to rejoin his retinue, but he went away, triumphant at the reflection that he had found an opportunity of speaking Mongol, and of thus giving the horsemen of his suite a high notion of his knowledge. This Mandarin appeared to us to be a Tartar-Mantchou; he was making an official inspection of the irrigating canals.

We proceeded still some way along the banks of the same canal, meeting nothing on our road but some carriages on large wheels, drawn by buffaloes, and a few travelers mounted on asses of lofty stature. At length, we discerned the lofty ramparts of Ning-Hia, and the numerous kiosks of the pagodas, which looked in the distance like tall cedars. The brick-walls of Ning-Hia are ancient, but well preserved. The antiquity, which has almost entirely covered them with moss and lichen, gives them a grand and imposing aspect. On every side they are surrounded by marshes, where canes, reeds, and water-lilies grow in abundance. The interior of the town is poor and miserable; the streets are dirty, narrow and tortuous; the houses smoke-dried and tottering; you see at once that Ning-Hia is a town of very great antiquity. Although situated near the frontiers of Tartary, the commerce there is considerable.

After having gone nearly half up the central street, as we found we had still a league to go before we reached the other extremity, we resolved to make a halt. We entered a large inn, where we were soon followed by three individuals who impudently demanded our passports. We saw at once that we had to defend our purses against three swindlers. "Who are you that dare to demand our passports?" "We are employed by the great tribunal: it is not lawful for strangers to pass through the town of Ning-Hia without a passport." Instead of replying we called the innkeeper and desired him to write upon a small piece of paper, his name and that of his inn. Our demand greatly surprised him. "What is the good of this writing? what are you going to do with it?" "We shall soon have need of it. We are going to the great tribunal, to inform the Mandarin that three thieves have sought to rob us in your inn." At these words the three collectors of passports took to their heels; the landlord loaded them with imprecations, and the mob, who were already assembled in great numbers, laughed heartily. This little adventure caused us to be treated with especial respect. Next morning, ere day had dawned, we were awakened by a terrible noise, which arose all at once in the courtyard of the inn. Amid the confusion of numerous voices that seemed in violent dispute, we distinguished the words, "Stinking Tartar—camel—tribunal." We hastily dressed ourselves, and proceeded to investigate the nature of this sudden uproar, with which it struck us we had something to do, and so it turned out; our camels had devoured, in the course of the night, two cart-loads of osiers which were in the yard. The remnants still lay scattered about. The owners, strangers at the inn like ourselves, required to be paid the price of their goods, and their demand we considered perfectly just, only, we thought that the landlord alone was bound to repair the damage. Before going to rest, we had warned him of the danger in which the osiers lay. We had told him that he had better place them elsewhere, for that the camels would certainly break their halters in order to get at them. The owners of the carts had joined with us in advising their removal, but the landlord had laughed at our fears, and asserted that camels did not like osiers. When we had sufficiently explained the matter, the mob, the standing jury among the Chinese, decided that the whole loss should be made good by the landlord; however, we had the generosity not to demand the price of the halters of our camels.

Immediately after this impartial judgment had been pronounced, we departed on our way. The southern part of the town seemed to us in even a worse condition than that which we had passed through on the preceding evening. Several portions were altogether pulled down and deserted; the only living things to be seen were a few swine, raking up the rubbish. The inhabitants of this large city were in a state of utter misery. The greater number of them were covered with dirty rags. Their pale visages, haggard and thin, showed that they were often without the necessaries of life. Yet Ning-Hia was once a royal town, and, doubtless, opulent and flourishing.

In the tenth century, a prince of Tartar race, a native of Tou-Pa, at present under the dominion of the Si-Fan, having induced a few hordes to follow him, came, and formed, despite the Chinese, a small state not far from the banks of the Yellow River. He chose for his capital, Hia-Tcheou, which afterwards came to be called Ning-Hia. It was from this town, that this new kingdom was called Hia. It was in a very flourishing state for more than two centuries; but in 1227, it was involved in the common ruin, by the victories of Tchinggiskhan, the founder of the Mongol dynasty. At present, Ning-Hai is one of the towns of the first class in the province of Kan-Sou.

On quitting Ning-Hai, you enter upon a magnificent road, almost throughout bordered by willows and jujube trees. At intervals, you find small inns, where the traveler can rest and refresh himself at small expense. He can buy there tea, hard eggs, beans fried in oil, cakes, and fruit preserved in sugar or salt.

This day's journey was one of absolute recreation. Our camels, which had never traveled except in the deserts of Tartary, seemed thoroughly sensible to the charms of civilization; they turned their heads majestically right and left, observing, with manifest interest, all that presented itself on the way, men and things. They were not, however, so wholly absorbed in the investigations of the industry and manners of China, as to withdraw their attention altogether from its natural productions. The willows, especially, attracted their interest; and when at all within their reach, they did not fail to pluck the tender branches, which they masticated with entire satisfaction. Sometimes, also, expanding their long necks, they would smell the various delicacies displayed over the inn doors, a circumstance which, of course, elicited vehement protests from the innkeepers and other persons concerned. The Chinese were not less struck with our camels, than our camels were with China. The people collected from all directions to see the caravan pass, and ranged themselves on each side of the road; taking care, however, not to approach too near the animals which excited their surprise, and whose strength they instinctively dreaded.

Towards the close of this day's march we arrived at Hia-Ho-Po, a large village without ramparts. We proceeded to dismount at the Hotel of the Five Felicities (*Ou-Fou-Tien*). We were occupied in giving forage to our beasts, when a horseman, bearing a white button on his cap, appeared in the court of the inn. Without dismounting, or making the accustomed salutation, he proceeded to bawl for the landlord. "The great Mandarin is on his way here," cried he, in curt and haughty tones; "let everything be clean and well swept. Let these Tartars go and lodge elsewhere; the great Mandarin will not have camels in the inn." Coming from the courier of a Mandarin, these insolent words did not surprise but they irritated us. We pretended not to hear them, and quietly pursued our occupation. The innkeeper, seeing that we paid no attention to the order that had been made, advanced towards us, and laid before us, with politeness mingled with embarrassment, the state of the case. "Go," we said to him firmly; "go tell this white button that you have received us into your inn, that we will remain there, and that Mandarins have no right to come and take the places of travelers, who are already lawfully established anywhere." The innkeeper was spared the trouble of reporting our words to white button, for they had been pronounced in such a manner that he could hear them himself. He dismounted forthwith; and addressing us directly, said, "The grand Mandarin will soon arrive; he has a large retinue, and the inn is small; besides, how would the horses venture to remain in this yard in presence of your camels?" "A man in the suite of a Mandarin, and, moreover, adorned like you with a white button, should know how to express himself—first, politely, and next, justly. We have a right to remain here, and no one shall expel us; and our camels shall remain tied to the door of our room." "The grand Mandarin has ordered me to come and prepare apartments for him at the Hotel of the Five Felicities." "Very well; prepare them, but don't meddle with our things. If you cannot accommodate yourselves here, reason suggests that you go and seek a lodging elsewhere." "And the great Mandarin?" "Tell your Mandarin that there are three Lamas of the Western Heaven in this place, who are ready to return to Ning-Hia to discuss the matter with him: or before the tribunal, if it be necessary, at Peking; they know their way thither." White button mounted and disappeared. The host came to us immediately, and begged us to be resolute. "If you remain here," said he to us, "I am sure to profit a little by you; but if the Mandarin takes your place, his people will turn my inn upside down, will make us work all night, and then go away in the morning without paying a farthing. And besides that, if I were forced to send you away would not the Hotel of the Five Felicities lose its reputation? Who would afterwards enter an inn where they receive travelers only for the purpose of turning them out again?" Whilst the host was exhorting us to courage, the courier of the Mandarin reappeared; he dismounted and made us a profound bow, which we returned with the best grace possible. "Sirs Lamas," said he, "I have ridden through Hia-Po-Ho; there is no other convenient inn. Who says you are bound to cede to us your place? To speak so were to talk inconsistently with reason! Now, observe, Sirs Lamas; we are all travelers: we are all men far distant from our families; cannot we consult together in a friendly manner and arrange the matter like brothers?" "No doubt," said we, "men ought always to deal together like brothers; that is the true principle. When we travel, we should live like travelers. When each gives way a little, all are, in the end, accommodated." "Excellent saying! excellent saying!" cried the courier; and thereupon the most profound bows recommenced on both sides.

After this brief introduction, which had perfectly reconciled both parties, we deliberated amicably how we should best arrange our common residence in the Hotel of the Five Felicities. It was agreed that we should keep the room in which we were already installed, and that we should tie up our camels in a corner of the court, so that they might not terrify the horses of the Mandarin. The courier was to dispose of the rest of the place as he pleased. We hastened to remove our camels from the door of our room and to place them as had been settled. Just after sunset we heard the Mandarin's party approaching. The two folding doors of the great gate were solemnly opened, and a carriage drawn by three mules advanced into the middle of the court of the inn, escorted by a numerous body of horsemen. In the carriage was seated a man about sixty years old, with gray mustaches and beard, and having his head covered with a red hood. This was the great Mandarin. On entering, he scanned, with a quick and searching glance, the interior of the inn. Perceiving us, and remarking, above all, three camels at the end of the court, the muscles of his lean face were suddenly contracted. When all the horsemen had dismounted they invited him to descend from his vehicle. "What!" cried he in a dry, angry voice; "who are those Tartars? what are those camels? let the landlord be brought to me." On this unexpected summons the host took to his heels, and white button remained for an instant like one petrified: his face turned pale, then red, then olive-color. However, he made an effort, advanced to the carriage, put one knee to the ground, then rose, and approaching the ear of his master, spoke to him for some time, in an undertone. The dialogue ended, the great Mandarin consented to dismount, and after having saluted us with his hand in a protecting manner, he retired like a simple mortal to the small room which had been prepared for him.

The triumph we had thus obtained in a country, admission even to which was prohibited to us under pain of death,[1] gave us prodigious courage. These terrible Mandarins, who had formerly occasioned us such alarm, ceased to be terrible to us the instant that we dared to approach them, and to look at them closely. We saw men puffed up with pride and insolence, pitiless tyrants towards the weak, but dastardly in the extreme before men of energy. From this moment we found ourselves as much at our ease in China as anywhere else, and able to travel without fear, and with our heads erect in the open face of day.

After two days' journey, we arrived at Tchong-Wei, on the banks of the Yellow River, a walled town of moderate size. Its cleanliness, its good condition, its air of comfort, contrasted singularly with the wretchedness and ugliness of Ning-Hia; and judging merely from its innumerable shops, all well stocked, and from the large population crowding its streets, we should pronounce Tchong-Wei to be a place of much commercial importance; yet the Chinese of this district have no notion of navigation, and not a boat is to be seen on the Yellow River in this quarter—a circumstance remarkable in itself, and confirmatory of the opinion that the inhabitants of this part of Kan-Sou are of Thibetian and Tartar origin; for it is well known that the Chinese are everywhere passionately addicted to navigating streams and rivers.

On quitting Tchong-Wei we passed the Great Wall, which is wholly composed of uncemented stones, placed one on top of the other; and we reentered Tartary, for a few days, in the kingdom of the Alechan. More than once the Mongol Lamas had depicted in frightful colors the horrors of the Alechan mountains. We were now in a position to see with our own eyes that the reality exceeds all description of this frightful district. The Alechans are a long chain of mountains, wholly composed of moving sand, so fine, that when you touch it, it seems to flow through your fingers like a liquid. It were superfluous to add that, amid these gigantic accumulations of sand, you do not find anywhere the least trace of vegetation. The monotonous aspect of

---

[1] At this period there was no French embassy in China, and no treaty in favor of Europeans. All missionaries, therefore, who penetrated into the interior were, *ipso facto*, liable to be put to death.

these immense sands is only relieved by the vestiges of a small insect, that, in its capricious and fantastical sports, describes a thousand arabesques on the moving mass, which is so smooth and fine, that you can trace upon it the meanderings of an ant. In crossing these mountains, we experienced inexpressible labor and difficulty. At each step our camels sank up to the knees; and it was only by leaps that they could advance. The horses underwent still greater difficulties, their hoofs having less purchase on the sand than the large feet of the camels. As for ourselves, forced to walk, we had to keep constant watch that we did not fall from the top of these mountains, which seemed to disappear under our feet, into the Yellow River, whose waters flowed beneath us. Fortunately, the weather was calm. If the wind had blown, we should certainly have been swallowed up and buried alive in avalanches of sand. The Alechan mountains themselves appear to have been formed by the sand which the north wind incessantly sweeps before it from the Chamo, or Great Desert of Gobi. The Yellow River arrests these sandy inundations, and thus preserves the province of Kan-Sou from their destructive assaults. It is to the great quantity of sand that falls into it from the Alechan mountains that this river owes the yellow color which has given to it its name *Hoang-Ho* (Yellow River). Above the Alechan mountains its waters are clear and limpid.

By degrees, hills succeeded to mountains, the sand heaps imperceptibly diminished, and towards the close of the day we arrived at the village of Ever-Flowing Waters (*Tchang-Lieou-Chouy*). Here we found, amidst those sand hills, an oasis of surpassing beauty. A hundred rills disporting through the streets, trees, little houses built of stone, and painted white or red, communicated to the spot an aspect highly picturesque. Weary as we were, we halted at Ever-Flowing Waters with inexpressible delight; but the poetry of the thing vanished when we came to settle with our host. Not only provisions but forage came from Tchong-Wei, and the transport being very difficult, they were dear to a degree that altogether disconcerted our economical arrangements. For ourselves and our animals, we were obliged to disburse 1,600 sapeks, a matter of nearly seven shillings. Only for this circumstance we should perhaps have quitted with regret the charming village of Tchang-Lieou-Chouy; but there is always something which intervenes to aid man in detaching himself from the things of this world.

On quitting Tchang-Lieou-Chouy, we took the road followed by the Chinese exiles on their way to Ili. The country is somewhat less dreadful than that which we had traveled through on the preceding day, but it is still very dismal. Gravel had taken the place of sand, and with the exception that it produced a few tufts of grass, hard and prickly, the soil was arid and barren. We reached, in due course, Kao-Tan-Dze, a village repulsive and hideous beyond all expression. It consists of a few miserable habitations, rudely constructed of black earth, and all of them inns. Provisions are even more scarce there than at Ever-Flowing Waters, and correspondingly dearer. Everything has to be brought from Tchong-Wei, for the district produces nothing, not even water. Wells have been sunk to a very great depth, but nothing has been found except hard, rocky, moistureless earth. The inhabitants of Kao-Tan-Dze have to fetch their water a distance of more than twelve miles, and they accordingly charge travelers a monstrous price for every drop. A single bucket costs sixty sapeks. Had we attempted to water our camels, we should have had to lay out fifty fifties of sapeks; we were therefore forced to be content with drinking ourselves, and giving a draught to our horses. As to the camels, they had to await better days and a less inhospitable soil.

Kao-Tan-Dze, miserable and hideous as it is, has not even the advantage of that tranquillity and security which its poverty and its solitude might reasonably be supposed to give it. It is constantly ravaged by brigands, so that there is not a house in it which does not bear the marks of fire and devastation. At the first inn where we presented ourselves, we were asked whether we desired to have our animals defended against robbers. This question threw us into utter amazement, and we requested further explanation of a point which struck us as so very singular. We were informed that at Kao-Tan-Dze there are two sorts of inns: inns where they fight, and inns where they do not fight; and that the prices at the former sort are four times greater than those at the latter. This explanation gave us a general notion of the matter: but still we requested some details. "How!" said the people. "Don't you know that Kao-

Tan-Dze is constantly attacked by brigands?" "Yes, we know that." "If you lodge in an inn where they don't fight, any brigands that come will drive off your animals, for no one has undertaken to protect them. If, on the contrary, you lodge in an inn where they fight, you have a good chance of preserving your property, unless the brigands are the more numerous party, which sometimes happens." All this seemed to us very singular, and very disagreeable. However, it was necessary to make up our minds on the subject. After grave reflection, we decided upon lodging in an inn where they fought. It occurred to us that the worthy innkeepers of Kao-Tan-Dze had an understanding with the brigands, having for its result the spoliation of travelers, one way or the other, and that therefore it was better, upon the whole, to pay the larger sum, by way of blackmail, than to lose our animals, whose loss would involve our own destruction.

Upon entering the fighting inn, to which we had been directed, we found everything about it on a war footing. The walls were regularly covered with lances, arrows, bows, and matchlocks. The presence of these weapons, however, by no means rendered us perfectly satisfied as to our safety, and we resolved not to lie down at all, but to keep watch throughout the night.

Kao-Tan-Dze, with its robber assailants and its pauper population, was to us an inexplicable place. We could not conceive how men should make up their minds to inhabit a detestably ugly country like this, sterile, waterless, remote from any other inhabited place, and desolated by the constant inroad of brigands. What could be their object? What possible advantage could be their inducement? We turned the matter over in all ways; we framed all sorts of suppositions; but we could achieve no likely solution of the problem. During the first watch of the night, we conversed with the innkeeper, who seemed a frank, open sort of man enough. He related to us infinite anecdotes of brigands, full of battle, murder, and fire. "But," said we, "why don't you leave this detestable country?" "Oh," replied he, "we are not free men; the inhabitants of Kao-Tan-Dze are all exiles, who are only excused from going to Ili on the condition that we remain here for the purpose of supplying with water the Mandarins and soldiers who pass through the place, escorting exiles. We are bound to furnish water gratuitously to all the government officers who come to the village." When we found that we were among exiles, we were somewhat reassured, and began to think that, after all, these people were not in collusion with the brigands; for we learned that a petty Mandarin lived in the village to superintend the population. We conceived a hope that we might find some Christians at Kao-Tan-Dze, but the innkeeper informed us that there were none, for that all exiles on account of the religion of the Lord of Heaven, went on to Ili.

After what the innkeeper had told us, we conceived that we might, without risk, take a brief repose; we accordingly threw ourselves on our goat-skins, and slept soundly till daybreak, the favor of God preserving us from any visit on the part of the brigands.

During the greater part of the day, we proceeded along the road to Ili, traversing with respect, with a degree of religious veneration, that path of exile so often sanctified by the footsteps of the confessors of the faith, and conversing, as we went, about those courageous Christians, those strong souls, who, rather than renounce their religion, had abandoned their families and their country, and gone to end their days in unknown lands. Let us fervently pray that Providence may send missionaries, full of devotion, to bear the consolations of the faith amongst these our exiled brethren.

The road to Ili brought us to the Great Wall, which we passed over without dismounting. This work of the Chinese nation, of which so much is said and so little known, merits brief mention here. It is known that the idea of raising walls as a fortification against the incursions of enemies, was not peculiar, in old times, to China: antiquity presents us with several examples of these labors elsewhere. Besides the works of this kind executed in Syria, Egypt, Media, and on the continent of Europe, there was, by order of the Emperor Septimus Severus, a great wall constructed in the northern part of Britain. No other nation, however, ever effected anything of the sort on so grand a scale as the Great Wall, commenced by Tsin-Chi-Hoang-Ti, A. D. 214. The Chinese call it *Wan-li-Tchang-Tching* (the Great Wall of ten thousand lis). A prodigious number of laborers was employed upon it, and the works of this gigantic enterprise continued for ten years. The Great Wall extends from the westernmost point of Kan-Sou to the Eastern Sea. The importance of this enormous construction has been variously estimated by those who have written upon China, some of whom preposterously exaggerate its importance, while others laboriously seek to ridicule it; the probability being, that this diversity of opinion arises from each writer having judged the whole work by the particular specimen to which he had access. Mr. Barrow, who, in 1793, accompanied Lord Macartney to China, as historiographer to the British embassy, made this calculation: he supposed that there were in England and Scotland 1,800,000 houses, and estimating the masonry work of each to be 2,000 cubic feet, he prepounded that the aggregate did not contain as much material as the Great Wall of China, which, in his opinion, was enough for the construction of a wall to go twice around the world. It is evident that Mr. Barrow adopted, as the basis of his calculation, the Great Wall such as he saw it north of Peking, where the construction is really grand and imposing; but it is not to be supposed that this barrier, raised against the irruptions of the barbarians, is, throughout its extent, equally high, wide, and solid. We have crossed it at fifteen different points, and on several occasions have traveled for whole days parallel with it, and never once losing sight of it; and often, instead of the great double turreted rampart that exists towards Peking, we have found a mere low wall of brickwork, or even earthwork. In some places, indeed, we have found this famous barrier reduced to its simplest expression, and composed merely of flint-stones roughly piled up. As to the foundation wall, described by Mr. Barrow, as consisting of large masses of free-stones cemented with mortar, we can only say that we have never discovered the slightest trace of any such work. It is indeed obvious that Tsin-Chi-Hoang-Ti, in the execution of this great undertaking, would fortify with especial care the vicinity of the capital, as being the point to which the Tartar hordes would first direct their aggressive steps. It is natural, farther, to conceive, that the Mandarins charged with the execution of the Emperor's plan, would, with especial conscientiousness, perfect the works which were more immediately under the Emperor's eye, and content themselves with erecting a more or less nominal wall at remote points of the empire, particularly those where the Tartars were little to be feared, as, for example, the position of the Ortous and the Alechan mountains.

The barrier of San-Yen-Tsin, which stands a few paces beyond the wall, is noted for its great strictness towards the Tartars who seek to enter within the intramural empire. The village possesses only one inn, which is kept by the chief of the frontier guards. Upon entering the courtyard we found several groups of camels assembled there belonging to a great Tartar caravan that had arrived on the preceding evening. There was, however, plenty of room for us, the establishment being on a large scale. We had scarcely taken possession of our chamber than the passport question was started. The chief of the guards himself made an official demand for them. " We have none," replied we. At this answer his features beamed with satisfaction, and he declared that we could not proceed unless we paid a considerable sum. " How ! a passport or money? Know that we have traveled China from one end to the other, that we have been to Peking, and that we have journeyed through Tartary, without anything in the shape of a passport, and without having paid a single sapek in lieu of a passport. You, who are a chief of guards, must know that Lamas are privileged to travel wherever they please without passports." " What words are these? Here is a caravan at this very moment in the house, and the two Lamas who are with it have both given me their passports like the rest of the party." " If what you say be true, the only conclusion is, that there are some Lamas who take passports with them and others who do not. We are in the number of those who do not." Finding at last that the dispute was becoming tedious, we employed a decisive course. " Well, come," said we, " we will give you the money you ask, but you shall give us in return a paper signed by yourself, in which you shall acknowledge that, before you would permit us to pass, you exacted from us a sum of money instead of passports. We shall then address ourselves to the first Mandarin we meet, and ask him whether what you have done is consistent with the laws of the empire." The man at once gave up the point. " Oh," said he, " since you have been to Peking, no doubt the Emperor has given you special privileges," and then he added, in a whisper, and smilingly, "Don't tell the Tartars here that I have let you pass *gratis*."

It is really pitiable to observe these poor Mongols traveling in China; everybody thinks himself entitled to fleece them, and everybody succeeds in doing so to a marvelous extent. In all directions they are encountered by impromptu custom-house officers, by persons who exact money from them on all sorts of pretenses, for repairing roads, building bridges, constructing pagodas, etc., etc. First, the despoilers proffer to render them great services, call them brothers and friends, and give them wholesale warnings against ill-designing persons who want to rob them. Should this method not effect an unloosening of the purse-strings, the rascals have recourse to intimidation, frighten them horribly with visions of Mandarins, laws, tribunals, prisons, punishments, threaten to take them up, and treat them, in short, just like mere children. The Mongols themselves materially aid the imposition by their total ignorance of the manners and customs of China. At an inn, instead of using the room offered to them, and putting their animals in the stables, they pitch their tent in the middle of the courtyard, plant stakes about it, and fasten their camels to these. Very frequently they are not permitted to indulge this fancy, and in this case they certainly enter the room allotted to them, and which they regard in the light of a prison; but they proceed there in a manner truly ridiculous. They set up their trivet with their kettle upon it, in the middle of the room, and make a fire beneath with argols, of which they take care to have a store with them. It is to no purpose they are told that there is in the inn a large kitchen where they can cook their meals far more comfortably to themselves; nothing will dissuade them from their own kettle and their own aboriginal fire in the middle of the room. When night comes they unroll their hide-carpets round the fire, and there lay down. They would not listen for a moment to the proposition of sleeping upon the beds or upon the kang they find in the room ready for their use. The Tartars of the caravan we found in the inn at San-Yen-Tsin were allowed to carry on their domestic matters in the open air. The simplicity of these poor children of the desert was so great that they seriously asked us whether the innkeeper would make them pay anything for the accommodation he afforded them.

We continued on our way through the province of Kan-Sou, proceeding to the southwest. The country, intersected with streams and hills, is generally fine, and the people apparently well off. The great variety of its productions is owing partly to a temperate climate and a soil naturally fertile, but above all, to the activity and skill of the agriculturists. The chief product of the district is wheat, of which the people make excellent loaves, like those of Europe. They sow scarcely any rice, procuring almost all the little they consume from the adjacent provinces. Their goats and sheep are of fine breed, and constitute, with bread, the principal food of the population. Numerous and inexhaustible mines of coal place fuel within every one's reach. It appeared to us that in Kan-Sou any one might live very comfortably at extremely small cost.

At two days' distance from the barrier of San-Yen-Tsin we were assailed by a hurricane which exposed us to very serious danger. It was about ten o'clock in the morning. We had just crossed a hill, and were entering upon a plain of vast extent, when, all of a sudden, a profound calm pervaded the atmosphere. There was not the slightest motion in the air, and yet the cold was intense. Insensibly, the sky assumed a dead-white color; but there was not a cloud to be seen. Soon, the wind began to blow from the west; in a very short time it became so violent that our animals could scarcely proceed. All nature seemed to be in a state of dissolution. The sky, still cloudless, was covered with a red tint. The fury of the wind increased; it raised in the air enormous columns of dust, sand, and decayed vegetable matter, which it then dashed right and left, here, there, and everywhere. At length the wind blew so tremendously, and the atmosphere became so utterly disorganized, that, at midday, we could not distinguish the very animals upon which we were riding. We dismounted, for it was impossible to advance a single step, and after enveloping our faces in handkerchiefs in order that we might not be blinded with the dust, we sat down beside our animals. We had no notion where we were; our only idea was that the frame of the world was unloosening, and that the end of all things was close at hand. This lasted for more than an hour. When the wind had somewhat mitigated, and we could see around us, we found that we were all separated from one another, and at considerable distances, for amid that frightful tempest, bawl as loud as we might, we could not hear each other's voices. So soon as we could at all walk we proceeded towards a farm at no great distance, but which we had not before perceived. The hurricane having thrown down the great gate of the court we found no difficulty in entering, and the house itself was open to us with almost equal facility; for Providence had guided us in our distress to a family truly remarkable for its hospitality.

Immediately upon our arrival, our hosts heated some water for us to wash with. We were in a frightful state; from head to foot we were covered with dust which had saturated, so to speak, our clothes and almost our skins. Had such a storm encountered us on the Alechan mountains, we should have been buried alive in the sand, and all trace of us lost forever.

When we found that the worst of the storm was over, and that the wind had subsided to occasional gusts, we proposed to proceed, but our kind hosts would not hear of this; they said they would lodge us for the night, and that our animals should have plenty of food and water. Their invitation was so sincere and so cordial, and we so greatly needed rest, that we readily availed ourselves of their offer.

A very slight observation of the inhabitants of Kan-Sou, will satisfy one that they are not of purely Chinese origin. The Tartaro-Thibetian element is manifestly predominant amongst them; and it displays itself with especial emphasis in the character, manners, and language of the country people. You do not find amongst them the exaggerated politeness which distinguishes the Chinese; but, on the other hand, they are remarkable for their open-heartedness and hospitality. In their particular form of Chinese you hear an infinitude of expressions which belong to the Tartar and Thibetian tongues. The construction of their phrases, instead of following the Chinese arrangement, always exhibits the inversions in use among the Mongols. Thus, for example, they don't say, with the Chinese, open the door, shut the window; but, the door open, the window shut. Another peculiarity is that milk, butter, curds, all insupportably odious to a Chinese, are especially favorite food with the inhabitants of Kan-Sou. But it is, above all, their religious turn of mind which distinguishes them from the Chinese, a people almost universally skeptical and indifferent as to religious matters. In Kan-Sou there are numerous and flourishing Lamaseries in which reformed Buddhism is followed. The Chinese, indeed, have plenty of pagodas and idols of all sorts and sizes in their houses; but with them religion is limited to this external representation, whereas in Kan-Sou every one prays often and long and fervently. Now prayer, as every one knows, is that which distinguishes the religious from the irreligious man.

Besides differing materially from the other peoples of China, the inhabitants of Kan-Sou differ materially amongst themselves, the Dchiahours marking that subdivision, perhaps, more distinctly than any of the other tribes. They occupy the country commonly called *San-Tchouan* (Three Valleys), the birthplace of our cameleer Samdadchiemba. The Dchiahours possess all the knavery and cunning of the Chinese without any of their courtesy, and without their polished form of language, and they are accordingly feared and disliked by all their neighbors. When they consider themselves in any way injured or insulted, they have immediate recourse to the dagger, by way of remedy. With them the man most to be honored is he who has committed the greatest number of murders. They have a language of their own, a medley of Mongol, Chinese, and Eastern Thibetian. According to their own account, they are of Tartar origin. If it be so, they may fairly claim to have preserved, in all its integrity, the ferocious and independent character of their ancestors, whereas the present occupiers of Mongolia have greatly modified and softened their manners.

Though subject to the Emperor of China, the Dchiahours are immediately governed by a sort of hereditary sovereign belonging to their tribe, and who bears the title of Tou-Sse. There are in Kan-Sou, and on the frontiers of the province of Sse-Tchouan, several other tribes, having their own special rulers and their own especial laws. All these tribes are called Tou-Sse, to which each adds, by way of distinction, the family name of its chief or sovereign. Samdadchiemba, for example, belonged to the Ki-Tou-Sse tribe of Dchiahours. Yang-Tou-Sse is the most celebrated and the most redoubtable of all these tribes, and for a long time exercised great influence at Lha-Ssa, the capital of Thibet, but this influence was destroyed in 1845, in consequence of an event which we shall relate by and by.

After thoroughly resting from our fatigue, we departed early next morning. Everywhere, on our way, we saw traces of the tempest, in trees uprooted and torn, houses unroofed, fields devastated and almost entirely deprived of their surface soil. Before the end of the day, we arrived at Tchoang-Long, more commonly called Ping-Fang, an ordinary town, with a tolerable amount of trade, but in no way noticeable, whether for its beauty or for its deformity. We went to lodge at the Hotel of the Three Social Relations (*San-Kan-Tien*), whose landlord was one of the best humored and most amusing persons we had hitherto met with. He was a thorough Chinese: to give us a proof of his sagacity, he asked us, point blank, whether we were not English; and that we might thoroughly understand his question, he added that he understood by Ing-Kie-Li, the sea-devils (*Yang-Kouei-Dze*) who were making war at Canton. "No, we are not English! nor are we devils of any sort, whether of sea or land." An idler who was standing by, interposed to prevent the ill effect of this awkward question. "You," said he to the innkeeper, "you know nothing of physiognomy. How could you suppose that these people are Yang-Kouei-Dze? Don't you know that they have all blue eyes and red hair?" "You're right," returned the host, "I had not thought of that." "No," said we, "clearly you had not thought at all. Do you suppose that sea-monsters could live as we do, on land, and ride on horses?" "You're right, quite so; the Ing-Kie-Li, they say, never venture to quit the sea, for when they're on land they tremble and die like fish out of water." We were favored with a good deal more information of the same class, respecting the manners and characters of the sea-devils, the upshot of which, so far as we were concerned, was the full admission that we did not belong to the same race.

A little before night, an immense bustle pervaded the inn. A Living Buddha had arrived, with a numerous train, on his return from a journey into Thibet, his native country, to the grand Lamasery, of which for many years he had been the superior, and which was situated in the country of the Khalkhas, towards the Russian frontier. As he entered the inn, a multitude of zealous Buddhists, who had been awaiting him in the great courtyard, prostrated themselves before him, their faces to the ground. The Grand Lama proceeded to the apartment which had been prepared for him, and night coming, the crowd withdrew. When the inn had become tolerably clear, this strange personage gave full play to his curiosity; he poked about all over the inn, going into every room, and asking everybody all sorts of questions, without sitting down or staying anywhere. As we expected, he favored us also with a visit. When he entered our chamber, we were gravely seated on the kang; we studiously abstained from rising at his entrance, and contented ourselves with welcoming him by a motion of our hands. He seemed rather surprised at this unceremonious reception, but not at all disconcerted. Standing in the middle of the room, he stared at each of us intently, one after the other. We, like himself, preserving entire silence all the while, exercised the privilege of which he had set us the example, and examined him closely. He seemed about fifty years old; he was enveloped in a great robe of yellow taffeta, and he wore red velvet Thibetian boots, with remarkably thick soles. He was of the middle height, and comfortably stout; his dark brown face denoted extreme good nature, but there was in his eyes, when you attentively examined them, a strange, wild, haggard expression, that was very alarming. At length he addressed us in the Mongol tongue, which he spoke with great facility. In the first instance, the conversation was nothing more than the ordinary phrases exchanged between travelers, about one another's health, destination, horses, the weather, and so on. When we found him prolonging his visit, we invited him to sit down beside us on the kang; he hesitated for a moment, conceiving, no doubt, that in his quality as Living Buddha, it did not become him to place himself on a level with mere mortals like ourselves. However, as he had a great desire for a chat, he at last made up his mind to sit down, and in fact he could not, without compromising his dignity, remain any longer standing while we sat.

A Breviary that lay on a small table beside us, immediately attracted his attention, and he asked permission to examine it. Upon our assenting, he took it up with both hands, admired the binding and the gilt edges, opened it and turned over the leaves, and then closing it again, raised it reverentially to his forehead, saying, "It is your Book of Prayer; we should always honor and respect prayer." By-and by he added, "Your religion and ours are like this," and so saying he put the knuckles of his two forefingers together. "Yes," said we, "you are right; your creed and ours are in a state of hostility, and we do not conceal from you that the object of our journey and of our labors is to substitute our prayers for those which are used in your Lamaseries." "I know that," he replied, smilingly; "I knew that long ago." He then took up the Breviary again, and asked us explanations of the engravings. He evinced no surprise at what we told him, only, when we had related to him the subject of the plate representing the crucifixion, he shook his head compassionately, and raised his joined hands to his head. After he had examined all the prints, he took the Breviary once more in both hands, and raised it respectfully to his forehead. He then rose, and having saluted us with great affability, withdrew, we escorting him to the door.

Upon being left alone, we felt for a moment stupefied as it were at this singular visit. We tried to conceive what thoughts could have filled the mind of the Living Buddha as he sat there beside us, and what impression he had derived from the sketch we gave him of our holy religion. Now, it seemed to us that strange feelings must have arisen in his heart; and then again, we imagined that after all he had felt nothing whatever, but that, a mere ordinary person, he had mechanically availed himself of his position, without reflection, and without himself attaching any real importance to his pretended divinity. We became so interested in the point, that we determined to see this personage once more before we departed. As that departure was fixed for an early hour next morning, we went, accordingly, to return his visit before we slept. We found him in his apartment, seated on thick large cushions, covered with magnificent tiger-skins; before him stood, on a small lacquer table, a silver tea-pot, and a steatite cup in a richly-worked gold saucer. He was evidently in the last stage of ennui, and was correspondingly delighted to see us. For fear he should take it into his head to let us remain standing, we proceeded, upon entering the room, to seat ourselves beside him. His suite, who were assembled in a contiguous room, which opened into their principal's, were extremely shocked at this familiarity, and gave utterance to a murmur of disapprobation. The Buddha himself, however, who passed over the circumstance with a half-angry smile, rang a silver bell, and desired a young Lama, who obeyed the summons, to bring us some tea with milk. "I have often seen your countrymen," said he; "my Lamasery stands at no great distance from your native land; the *Oros* (Russians) often pass the frontier, but I have never known any of them before to advance so far as you." "We are not Russians," said we; "our country is a long way from Russia." This answer seemed to surprise the Buddha; he looked at us closely for some time, and then said, "From what country come you, then?" "We are from the Western Heaven." "Oh! you are Péling,[1] of *Dchou-Ganga* (Eastern Ganges), and your city is Galgata (Calcutta)." The notions of the Living Buddha, it is observable, though not exactly correct, were not altogether destitute of meaning; he could of course only class us among the peoples who were known to him, and in supposing us first Russians and then English, he manifested an acquaintance with geographical terms, by no means contemptible under the circumstances. He would not be persuaded, however, that we were not either Oros or Péling of Galgata. "But after all," said he, "what matters it from what country we come, since we are all brothers? Only let me advise you, while you are in China, to be cautious not to tell everybody who you are. The Chinese are a suspicious and ill-conditioned race, and they might do you a mischief." He then talked to us about Thibet, and the dreadful road thither that we should have to traverse. Judging from our appearance, he said, he doubted very much whether we were strong enough for the undertaking. The words and the manner of the Grand Lama were perfectly affable and kind, but there was a look in his eyes to which we could not reconcile ourselves. We seemed to read there something infernal, fiend-like. But for this circumstance, which perhaps after all was mere fancy on our part, we should have esteemed our Grand Lama friend a most amiable personage.

[1] The Thibetians call the English in Hindostan, Péling, a word signifying stranger, and equivalent to the Chinese y-jin, which the Europeans translate, barbarian, probably with the notion of flattering their self-love by the implied contrast.

From Tchoang-Long, or Ping-Fang, we proceeded to Ho-Kiao-Y, or, as it is named on the maps, Tai-Toung-Fou. The latter is the ancient denomination of the place, and is no longer in popular use. The road was, throughout, covered with oxen, asses, and small carts, all with loads of coal. We resolved to sojourn for a few days at Ho-Kiao-Y, for the purpose of giving rest to our animals, whose strength had become almost exhausted; the horse and the mule, in particular, had tumors on their sides, occasioned by the constant rubbing of the saddle, and it was essential to have these cured before we proceeded further. Having formed this project, our next business was to inspect all the inns in the place, for the purpose of selecting as our abode that which presented the most favorable indications, and the Hotel of the Temperate Climates was ultimately honored with our choice.

Ever since our entry into the province of Kan-Sou, not a day had passed in which Samdadchiemba had not enlarged upon the subject of the Three Valleys and the Dchiahours. Though there was no very immense amount of sentiment about him, he had a great desire to revisit his native place, and to see once more any members of his family who might happen to be surviving there. We could not do otherwise than aid so laudable a purpose; accordingly, when we were established in the Hotel of the Temperate Climates, we granted to our cameleer eight days' leave of absence, wherein to revisit his so long abandoned home. Eight days appeared to him fully sufficient for the purpose: two to go in, two to come back in, and four to be spent in the bosom of his family, relating to them all the marvels he had witnessed abroad. We allowed him the use of a camel, that he might appear among his friends with the greater distinction; and five ounces of silver which we placed in his purse completed his recommendations to a favorable reception.

While awaiting the return of our Dchiahour, we were exclusively occupied in taking care of our animals, and of ourselves. Every day we had to go into the town to buy our provisions, then to cook them, and, morning and evening, to water our cattle at some distance from the inn. The master of the house was one of those good-natured persons who, in their very eagerness to oblige, become troublesome; and whose amiability of intention scarcely induces one to pardon their importunity of attention. The worthy man was incessantly thrusting himself into our room, to give us advice how we ought to do this, that, and the other. After altering the position of everything in the chamber according to his fancy for the moment, he would go up to the furnace, take off the lid of the saucepan, dip his finger into the ragout, and licking it to see how the mess was going on, add salt or ginger, or other condiment, to the infinite annoyance of M. Huc, who was officially charged with the cooking department. At other times he would loudly protest that we knew nothing about making up a fire, that the coals ought to be laid so, and the wood so, and that a draught of air ought to be kept up in this or that direction; and thereupon he would take up the tongs and overturn our fire, to the immense discomfiture of M. Gabet, who presided over that department. At night he appeared to consider himself especially indispensable, and would skip in every quarter of an hour to see that the lamp was burning properly, and that the wick was long enough, or short enough, and what not. At times he had really the air of asking us how it was possible that we had contrived to live without him, the one of us up to thirty-two years of age, the other up to thirty-seven. However, among the exuberance of attentions with which he bored us, there was one which we readily accepted; it was in the matter of warming our beds, the process of which was so singular, so peculiar, that we had never had the opportunity elsewhere of observing it.

The kang, a species of furnace on which you lie, is not in Kan-Sou constructed altogether of brickwork, as is the case in Northern China, but the upper flooring consists of movable planks, placed closely beside one another. When they want to heat the kang for sleeping purposes, they remove the planks, and strew the interior of the kang with horse-dung, quite dry and pulverized. Over this combustible they throw some lighted cinders, and then replace the planks; the fire immediately communicates itself to the dung, which, once lighted, continues to smolder; the heat and the smoke, having no exit, soon warm the planks, and this produces a tepid temperature which, in consequence of the slow combustion of the material, prevails throughout the night. The talent of the kang-heater consists in putting neither too much nor too little dung, in strewing it properly, and in so arranging the cinders that combustion shall commence at different points in the same moment of time, in order that all the planks may equally benefit by the warmth. Ashamed to have our bed warmed for us like children, we one night essayed to perform this service for ourselves, but the result was by no means happy, for while one of us was nearly broiled to death, the other trembled with cold all night long; the fact being, that owing to our want of skill, the fire had actually caught the planks on one side of the kang, while on the other the fuel had not lighted at all. The host of the Hotel of the Temperate Climates was naturally disgusted at the mischance, and in order to prevent its recurrence, he locked the closing plank of the furnace, and himself came every time to light it.

Our various domestic occupations, and the recitation of our Breviary, passed away the time very smoothly at Ho-Kiao-Y. On the eighth day, as had been agreed, Samdadchiemba returned, but not alone; he was accompanied by a lad, whose features bespoke him a brother of our cameleer, and as such Samdadchiemba presented him to us. Our first interview was very brief, for the two Dchiahours had scarcely presented themselves before they disappeared. We imagined, at first, that they were gone to pay their respects to the host, but it was not so, for they almost immediately reappeared with somewhat more solemnity of manner than before. Samdadchiemba marched in first: "Babdcho," said he to his brother, "prostrate thyself before our masters, and present to them the offerings of our poor family." The younger Dchiahour made us three salutations in the Oriental fashion, and then laid before us two great dishes, one of them full of fine nuts, the other laden with three large loaves, in form resembling those made in France. To afford Samdadchiemba the most practical proof in our power that we were sensible to his attention, we forthwith applied ourselves to one of the loaves, which, with some of the nuts, constituted quite a delicious repast, for never since our departure from France had we tasted such excellent bread.

While engaged upon our banquet, we observed that the costume of Samdadchiemba was reduced to its simplest expression; that whereas he had gone decently attired, he had come back half-covered with a few rags. We asked for an explanation of this change, whereupon he gave us an account of the miserable condition in which he had found his family. The father had been dead for some time; his aged mother had become blind, so that she had not enjoyed the happiness of seeing him. He had two brothers, the one a mere child, the other the young man whom he had brought with him, and who, the sole support of the family, devoted his time to the cultivation of a small field which still belonged to them, and to the tending the flocks of other people for hire. This narrative at once explained what Samdadchiemba had done with his clothes; he had given them all to his poor old mother, without even excepting his traveling cloak. We thought it our duty to propose that he should remain, and devote himself to the assistance of his wretched family; but he did not at all adopt the suggestion. "What," said he, "could I have the cruelty to do such a thing as that! Could I ever think of going to devour the little substance that remains to them? They can scarcely subsist themselves: how could they possibly support me; for I myself have no means of making a livelihood there—I cannot labor at the soil, and there is no other way in which I could help them." We considered this resolution neither good nor great; but knowing, as we did, the character of Samdadchiemba, it in no degree surprised us. We did not insist upon his remaining, for we were even better convinced than he himself was, that he could be of no sort of service to his family. We did all we could ourselves to aid these poor people, by giving Samdadchiemba's brother as large an alms as we could spare; and we then proceeded to the preparations for our departure.

During these eight days of repose, the condition of our animals had so improved as to enable us to venture upon the difficult road we had to traverse. The next day after quitting Ho-Kiao-Y, we began the ascent of the high mountain called Ping-Keou, the terribly rugged paths of which interposed almost insurmountable difficulties in the way of our camels. On the ascent, we were obliged to be constantly calling out, at the pitch of our voices, in order to warn any muleteers who might be coming down the road, which was so narrow and dangerous that two animals could not pass each other abreast. Our cries were to enable any persons coming the other way to lead their mules aside, so that they might not take alarm at the sight of our camels, and dash over the precipice. We began the ascent of this mountain before daybreak, and yet it was noon before we reached its summit. There we found a little inn, where, under the denomination of tea, they sold a decoction of burned beans. We stopped at this place for a brief period to take a repast, which hunger rendered very succulent and savory, of some nuts and a slice of the famous bread which the Dchiahour had brought us, and which we expended with the utmost parsimony. A draught of cold water should have been, according to our previous plan, the complement of our feast; but the only water attainable on this mountain was affected with an insupportable stench. We were fain, therefore, to have recourse to the decoction of baked beans, a dreadfully insipid fluid, but for which, notwithstanding, we were charged extortionately.

The cold was by no means so severe as we had expected from the season of the year and the great elevation of the mountain. In the afternoon, indeed, the weather was quite mild; by and by, the sky was overcast, and snow fell. As we were obliged to descend the mountain on foot, we soon got absolutely hot, in the perpetual struggle, of a very laborious kind, to keep from rolling down the slippery path. One of our camels fell twice, but happily in each instance he was stayed by a rock from tumbling over the mountain's side.

Having placed behind us the formidable Ping-Keou, we took up our lodging in the village of the Old Duck (*Lao-Ya-Pou*). Here we found a system of heating in operation different from that of Ho-Kiao-Y. The kangs here are warmed, not with dried horse-dung, but with coal-dust, reduced to paste, and then formed into bricks; turf is also used for the purpose. We had hitherto imagined that knitting was unknown in China; the village of the Old Duck removed this misconception from our minds, and enabled us, indeed, to remove it from the minds of the Chinese themselves in other parts of the empire. We found here in every street men, not women, occupied in this species of industry. Their productions are wholly without taste or delicacy of execution; they merely knit coarse cotton into shapeless stockings, like sacks, or sometimes gloves, without any separation for the fingers, and merely a place for the thumb, the knitting needles being small canes of bamboo. It was for us a singular spectacle to see parties of mustached men sitting before the door of their houses in the sun, knitting, sewing, and chattering like so many female gossips; it looked quite like a burlesque upon the manners of Europe.

From Lao-Ya-Pou to Si-Ning-Fou was five days' march: on the second day we passed through Ning-Pey-Hien, a town of the third order. Outside the western gate, we stopped at an inn to take our morning meal; a great many travelers were already assembled in the large kitchen, occupying the tables which were ranged along the walls; in the center of the room were several furnaces, where the innkeeper, his wife, several children, and some servants were actively preparing the dishes required by the guests. While everybody seemed occupied, either in the preparation or in the consumption of victuals, a loud cry was heard. It was the hostess, thus expressing the pain occasioned by a knock on her head, which the husband had administered with a shovel. At the cry all the travelers looked in the direction whence it proceeded; the woman retreated, with vehement vociferations, to a corner of the kitchen; the innkeeper explained to the company that he had been compelled to correct his wife for insolence, insubordination, and an indifference to the interests of the establishment, which eminently compromised its prosperity. Before he had finished his version of the story, the wife, from her retreat in the corner, commenced hers; she informed the company that her husband was an idle vagabond, who passed his time in drinking and smoking, expending the result of her labors for a whole month in a few days of brandy and tobacco. During this extempore performance, the audience remained imperturbably calm, giving not the smallest indication of approbation or disapprobation. At length the wife issued from her retreat, and advanced with a sort of challenging air to the husband: "Since I am a wicked woman," cried she, "you must kill me. Come, kill me!" and so saying, she drew herself up with a gesture of vast dramatic dignity immediately in front of the husband. The latter did not adopt the suggestion to kill her, but he gave her a formidable box on the ear, which sent her back, screaming at the pitch of her voice, into her previous corner. Hereupon, the audience burst into loud laughter; but the affair, which seemed to them so diverting, soon took a very serious turn. After the most terrible abuse on the one hand, and the most awful threats on the other, the innkeeper at length drew his girdle tight about his waist, and twisted his tress of hair about his head, in token of some decided proceeding. "Since you will have me kill you," cried he, "I will kill you!" and so saying, he took from the furnace a pair of long iron tongs, and rushed furiously upon his wife. Everybody at once rose and shouted; the neighbors ran in, and all present endeavored to separate the combatants, but they did not effect the object until the woman's face was covered with blood, and her hair was all down about her shoulders. Then a man of ripe years, who seemed to exercise some authority in the house, gravely pronounced these words by way of epilogue: "How! what!" said he, "husband and wife fighting thus! and in presence of their children, in presence of a crowd of travelers!" These words, repeated three or four times, in a tone which expressed at once indignation and authority, had a marvelous effect. Almost immediately afterwards the guests resumed their dinner, the hostess fried cakes in nut-oil, and the host silently smoked his pipe.

When we were about to depart, the innkeeper, in summing up our account, coolly inserted fifty sapeks for the animals which we had tied up in the courtyard during our meal. He had evidently an idea of making us pay *en Tartare*. Samdadchiemba was indignant. "Do you think," asked he, "that we Dchiahours don't know the rules of inns? Where did you ever hear of making people pay for fastening their animals to a peg in the wall? Tell me, master publican, how many sapeks are you going to charge us for the comedy we've just witnessed of the innkeeper and his wife?" The burst of laughter on the part of the bystanders which hailed this sarcasm carried the day triumphantly for Samdadchiemba, and we departed without paying anything beyond our personal expenses.

The road thence to Si-Ning-Fou, generally well made and well kept, meanders through a fertile and well cultivated country, picturesquely diversified by trees, hills, and numerous streams. Tobacco is the staple of the district. We saw on our way several water-mills, remarkable for their simplicity, as is the case with all Chinese works. In these mills, the upper story is stationary, while the lower is turned by means of a single wheel, kept in motion by the current. To work these mills, though they are frequently of large proportions, a very small stream suffices, as the stream plays upon the wheel in the form of a cascade, ·at least twenty feet high.

On the day before arriving at Si-Ning-Fou, we passed over a road extremely laborious, and so dangerously rugged that it suggested frequent recommendations of ourselves to the protection of the Divine Providence. Our course was amid enormous rocks, beside a deep, fierce current, the tumultuous waves of which roared beneath us. There was the gulf perpetually yawning to swallow us up, should we make but one false step; we trembled, above all, for our camels, awkward and lumbering as they were, whenever they had to pass over an uneven road. At length, thanks to the goodness of God, we arrived without accident at Si-Ning. The town is of very large extent, but its population is limited, and itself, in several parts, is falling into absolute decay. The history of the matter is, that its commerce has been in great measure intercepted by Tang-Keou-Eul, a small town on the banks of the Keou-Ho, on the frontier which separates Kan-Sou from Koukou-Noor.

It is the custom, we may say the rule, at Si-Ning-Fou, not to receive strangers, such as the Tartars, Thibetians, and others, into the inns, but to relegate them to establishments called Houses of Repose (*Sie-Kia*), into which no other travelers are admitted. We proceeded accordingly to one of these Houses of Repose, where we were exceedingly well entertained. The Sie-Kia differ from other inns in this important particular, that the guests are boarded, lodged, and served there gratuitously. Commerce being the leading object of travelers hither, the chiefs of the Sie-Kia indemnify themselves for their outlay by a recognized percentage upon all the goods which their guests buy or sell. The persons who keep these Houses of Repose have first to procure a license from the authorities of the town, for which they pay a certain sum, greater or less, according to the character of the commercial men who are expected to frequent the house. In outward show, the guests are well-treated, but still they are quite at the mercy of the landlords, who, having an understanding with the traders of the town, manage to make money of both parties.

When we, indeed, departed from Si-Ning-Fou, the Sie-Kia with whom we had lodged had made nothing by us in the ordinary way, for we had neither bought nor sold anything. However, as it would have been preposterous and unjust on our part to have lived thus at the expense of our neighbors, we paid the host of the House of Repose for what we had had, at the ordinary tavern rate.

After crossing several torrents, ascending many rocky hills, and twice passing the Great Wall, we arrived at Tang-Keou-Eul. It was now January, and nearly four months had elapsed since our departure from the Valley of Dark Waters. Tang-Keou-Eul is a small town, but very populous, very animated, and very full of business. It is a regular tower of Babel, wherein you find collected Eastern Thibetians, *Houng-Mao-Eul* (Long-haired Folk), Elents, Kolos, Chinese, Tartars from the Blue Sea, and Mussulmans, descended from the ancient migrations from Turkestan. Everything in the town bears the impress of violence. Nobody walks the streets without a great saber at his side, and without affecting, at least, a fierce determination to use it on the shortest notice. Not an hour passes without some street combat.

The Jin Seng, a Medicinal Root of China.

www.ingramcontent.com/pod-product-compliance
Lightning Source LLC
Chambersburg PA
CBHW021159230426
43667CB00006B/471